No Appointments Necessary

Missionary Adventures From A Road Less Traveled

Charlynne M. Boddie

Published by NEWW Publishing LLC
2401 South Downing Street, Denver, CO 80210

ISBN-13: 978-1-7328783-0-3

SECOND EDITION

DEDICATION

To my Dad, Charles Edgar Boddie, who enjoys the thrill of travel as much as I do, and to my Mother, Sandra Ruth Boddie, who taught me that the only travel essential I need wherever I go is Jesus Christ. To all the other travelers in the world who are seeking the leading of the King of Kings down every highway and byway of life.

"Go into all the world...knowing signs and wonders follow all who believe."
Mark 16:16-17

CONTENTS

INTRODUCTION

If you're someone who's read my first book, *True Grid: Discovering God's Custom-designed Blueprint for You*, then you may be wondering what this book is about. Let me shed some light.

First of all, I must confess that coming off the success of the first book and seminar that *True Grid* is based on made it difficult to decide what the next book would focus on. There are so many great testimonies of what God can do with a life given to His ways and purposes that I've witnessed. Which stories would I share? There are just so many!

At the same time that I was pondering those thoughts, I kept experiencing some amazing acts and exploits of the Lord while on the road. Wild and wonderful things continually follow me wherever I go. Supernatural occurrences happen whether I'm alone or traveling with my teammates. These 'suddenlies', as I like to call them, happen as much on the road as off of it. I knew that Jesus, King of Kings and Lord of Lords, was indeed traveling with me. He is always leading me into adventures that are full of His favor and grace.

Okay –so I've established that this book is going to be a sort of travelogue. "What does the main title mean?" you say. I'll explain.

About 20 years ago, my sister Shaunya and I were befriended by a performance artist by the name of Katherine the Grape. One day, Katherine told me that she saw two distinct types of people in the world. One type came from what she described as 'The Land of Weights and Measures.' These folks see things through the eyes of man only and have natural or limited spiritual sight. Hence the label of 'weights and measures'. The other type of people in the world live in 'The Land of No-Appointments-Necessary.' These people live in God's supernatural world of favor and what the Italians call *abundanza* or abundance. They are not limited by what they can see with their natural eyes, but see life through the eyes of God and choose to live by the protocols of the unseen realm (2 Corinthians 4:18). Where man says you can't 'get in' without an appointment, people living in this second category don't need any appointments to enter a place or accomplish something. They live by the protocols of Heaven and trust in God's Word, promises, and all that those encompasses. They can hear God's still, small voice and they choose to OBEY His voice when they hear it. This gives the hearer an all-access pass to the supernatural realm. Katherine said that I live in that supernatural place, or what she dubbed, The Land of No-Appointments-Necessary.

As I ponder the workings of Jesus and my travels with Him over almost 30 years of my life, to places near and far, I can see what Katherine meant. We all have choices and we can choose which realm we'd like to live in. The Lord loved us enough to give us this freedom of choice.

What you are about to read are personal accounts of various experiences I've had in numerous places in the globe, with Jesus by my side. I've separated these adventures by country. It is my supernatural travelogue. I have found that any time I step out of my home and onto a plane, train, bus, or boat, something miraculous is just around the corner. Stuff even happens when I am just walking down the street. Some of what I will share may put a smile on your face, while other events will cause you to ponder the greatness of the God we serve.

My overall desire is to encourage you in your faith and your own travels with the King, wherever He may lead you. We serve a mighty and supernatural God and I want to make Him more famous through the testimonies I share with you in this book, for we are all on the same journey. How you get there is up to you. Will you choose to follow the leading of the King's still, small voice during your journey? Or will you choose to heed an entirely different voice altogether? The choice is yours.

On the other side of our obedience to His still, small voice, there are myriads of adventures waiting for each one of us. If we'll just listen, the magnificent Holy Spirit will share with us God's heavenly protocols that allow us to be carriers of His Presence and experience the supernatural right here on earth! This is part of our inheritance and walking through it is so much fun. In this book, I'm giving you a sneak peek into some of my most memorable travels with the King...where NO APPOINTMENTS HAVE BEEN NECESSARY. He is always with us and will never leave us. When you know Jesus, you are a carrier of His all-consuming Presence. So sit back and enjoy the ride!

Charlynne Boddie
February 2015

ACKNOWLEDGMENTS

None of these trips would have been possible without the help, support, prayers, and laughter of the following individuals:

Antonio Mendrinos, Stephine, and Shaunya, for the roles you three played in my big, fat, Greek missions trip. Thank you!

Carrie, for the host you were and for all you did to help me prepare for my first time in Israel.

Heidi and Andy , Beate and Michael, and Martin and Angela, for all you did to make ministering trips to Germany such a treat.

Cynthia Lang, for being the best traveling companion ever...anywhere we've gone in Europe. Eight countries down and so many more to explore together. Lynne and Lang Tours forever!!

Lesley and John, Caroline, and all of the PITS UK Team who've ever gone out on the road with me in the UK or America. You all rock! It's been a joy and a privilege to go the distances we've traveled together. I couldn't do what I do without your consistent faithfulness. Thank you all!

Now a word of thanks to my unsung heroes:

Simon and Samantha, for all the British Airways tickets you've sown to make so many of these amazing adventures possible and many years of fantastic British hospitality. I have witnessed so many supernatural events at 35,000 feet up in the air! All that you have done is a sweet aroma to The Lord! May The Lord continue to bless you and your family.

My two sets of spiritual parents: Jackie and Stan, for the honor of living with you in the mountains and for teaching me so much about how to sing and dance in the rain. I can hear that precious, still, small voice because of the love and mentoring you have consistently given to me throughout my life. Words seem so inadequate. And to Morris and Carol, for all the timely wisdom, prayer, and inspiration you've sown into my various trips and adventures. Your prophetic gifts and books are eternal treasures to me!

Keith, for always being an excellent cheerleader for all of the gifts and talents God's given me. You unknowingly said something to me that broke the writer's block I had regarding this book. Hallelujah! I praise God for your friendship and encouragement when the going gets tough.

Sally and Lesley Anne for choosing to pray, support, and oftentimes sow into these trips mentioned here. Your words to me in due season spur me on and help keep me focused on the King's promises to me as I go along this road less traveled.

A very special thank you to all of the waitressing women: Lucy, Gemma, Jamie, Kate, Jade, Sam, Grace, and Abby at The Riviera diner in Selsey, West Sussex, England. You make the best cuppa cappuccino and gave me lots of comic relief as I sat writing in my special booth. Jamie, I thank you for helping to keep me on target!

The entire group of intercessors all over the globe who faithfully pray over my comings and goings. No ministry can operate successfully without folks like you! God bless you all and please know that I carry you and your prayers with me on each journey!!

And finally, all glory, praise and honor be given to My Lord and King forever--Jesus Christ. In You I live and move and have my being. None of what is written here has been possible without Your Holy Spirit, My Great Teacher. I dare not go anywhere without You. I thank you for the most amazing ride thus far! Your will, not mine, be done for all future travels.

1

ADVENTURES IN AMERICA

"Kindness is more important than wisdom, and the recognition of this is the beginning of wisdom."
Theodore Isaac Rubin

"Vision without action is a daydream. Action without vision is a nightmare."
Japanese Proverb

"There is no try. There is do or do not."
Yoda-Jedi Master

"There is a time for departure even when there's no certain place to go."
Tennessee Williams

Your Money's No Good Here

One thing I have learned on this tour of life with God is that His favor operating in your life is worth more than money in the bank. I have also learned that if we'll obey Him when we hear Him speaking to us, He will reveal some amazing surprises for us.

I left my high-flying US government job in public affairs before I moved to the UK. I needed to heal from a series of car accidents I'd been in, and also wanted to pursue my dream job in Hollywood before going into full-time ministry in the UK. During the time away from government, I began to create a production company with my sister and in so doing, took on several different part-time jobs. One of these jobs was hostessing for a downtown Denver, Colorado restaurant for a trio of restaurant owners. One of the owners said he wanted to hire me for my smile. I decided to take him up on his offer.

So I began to work at one of his three restaurants. It was my job to show folks, especially 'important' community leaders, to their tables and remember where they liked to sit. I also took care of bakery and most to-go orders on the days and nights that I worked.

I come from a family of professional chefs and I had started my own catering company too, so I knew that food service was an often thankless job. I also knew that consistent, quality service and credibility could make or break any catering operation.

In taking care of the folks who asked for to-go orders, I often took orders from the men and women who stopped in Denver on America's train service, Amtrak. Our service to them needed to be efficient and swift because they didn't have long before the train would be pulling out of Denver. Our restaurant was located right across the street from Union Station so I saw Amtrak personnel all the time, and I got to know the regulars and what they would usually order.

During the summer when I had that job, my family decided to hold a sort of mini-reunion with my Mom's siblings and their kids in Nevada. It was going to be a birthday party trip by train to celebrate my Aunt's birthday with my relatives. The only way to travel by train across country in America is by Amtrak, so that's what we did. It's a great way to see the American West!

Everyone was either meeting us in Denver or was already on the same train but coming from some other part of America. We were all very excited.

Once the train left Denver, we started searching for each other by train car and made plans to meet in the scenic observation car for snacks and laughs. This coach has giant, glass observation windows and really allows you to take in the glorious Rocky Mountains in all of their splendor. We sat back in comfy swivel seats and enjoyed the ride and each other. Our laughter was very contagious and soon everyone wanted to sit with our group. We made lots of friends that day.

Soon it was time for us to make some reservations for dinner in the dining car. We chose what sitting we'd like and met again in the dining car. No sooner had all of my family sat down to eat, when I heard my nickname being called: "Charlie!" said one of the porters. I looked up and standing before me was one of my regular Amtrak customers who got to-go orders from the restaurant where I worked!

The porter told us that he was going to pick up the tab for my *entire* family for that dinner!! There were 15 of us sitting there! My aunts, uncles, and cousins were astounded. The Amtrak employee told my family that in all the months since I had started working in the restaurant, I'd never messed up customers' orders or forgotten anything they especially asked for. He said that I was always so kind to them, no matter what time of day or night they came into the restaurant. For this reason, he decided that he would pay for everyone's dinner that night.

God's Word in Psalm 23:6 says that 'goodness and mercy will follow us'. That day I witnessed a literal example of it and I sat in amazement at the extravagant goodness of God. I saw that my actions not only affect my life but also the lives of those around me. Not everyone in my family was a believer, and for them, this event was a real testimony of the love of God.

In another instance, I remember going to meet with some clients of mine, twin boys, and their mother. We met in their neighborhood for dinner at a restaurant. Our meeting was full of joy and laughter. There is nothing like fellowshipping with God's people!

The boys decided to go to the restroom along with their mother. I decided to pay for all of us while they were gone. When I went to the cashier to pay our bill, I was told that the entire bill had been paid for by an anonymous stranger who had just walked out of the door! I looked over my shoulder and the door was swinging gently. The waitress said it had been a man sitting alone in a booth about 20 feet away from us. I asked her if I could pay for the tip at least. She said that the tall stranger had paid her a handsome tip too!

By the time the twins and their mother came back to the cashier, I told them what the waitress had said. The boys were *so* excited and couldn't wait to tell their father what had obviously been a miracle. They each wondered whether we'd been served by an angel of The Lord or not. Their mother and I believe that we were. None of us could stop grinning with joy! The Lord had clearly blown our minds again! Could the tall stranger have been an angel sent by God Himself to bless us because we were singing His praises during our meal? I believe so. It was a thrill beyond words. Again, I was shown that God's favor really is worth more than money in the bank..

May I Pray For You?

On the same trip that my family's dinner was paid for by the kindly porter, I witnessed the miraculous again on the return journey home to Denver. In those days, my mother was experiencing pain in her legs and needed to sit on the lower level of the train coach. Three of us sat with her on the lower level of the train coming back.

As the train sped past the desert landscapes of the American West from where we'd been in Nevada, I marveled at the beauty of God's handiwork in desolate places. I soon discovered that it is often in the most desolate of places where we hear the voice of The Lord wooing us to Himself (Hosea 2:14).

In the wee hours of the morning, The Lord began to woo me to wake up and pray with Him. As I tuned my spiritual ears to His voice, my sister and mother went into the restroom at the end of the car. While they were gone from their seats, I distinctly heard The Lord ask me if I would go and pray for someone in need. He said, 'Do you hear the woman moaning in her sleep at the end of the coach? She's the one.'

This was something that I'd never been asked to do on a train before. I wanted to do it for The Lord but knew that I'd need some backup prayer. So I hurried down the coach, past the woman and into the restroom to find my sister and mom. Once I got there, they asked if everything was all right and I gave them my request for prayer. Both of them agreed to pray for me as I returned to my seat. Man oh man! I needed prayer.

The next thing I heard The Lord say to me was that the man who sat across the aisle from the woman in pain was her husband. He then told me to ask the husband's permission to pray for his ailing wife. My heart was pounding at this point, and yet I knew that I absolutely had to take this assignment. I could hear the Holy Spirit so clearly. My mom and sister were now in their seats, praying in tongues for me and wondering what The Lord was about to do.

I said one more breath prayer to The Lord and thanked Him for the opportunity to be used for His glory. Then I got up from my seat and began a slow walk down to the end of the car where the husband was awake and looking out the window. I bent down to him and told him that I

was a minister who had been praying and that while I was praying, The Lord asked me to pray for his wife.

The husband looked me up and down and finally said, 'You might as well, she's going home to die.' And with that response, he turned back toward the window and continued to gaze out in a very dejected way. He clearly was not anticipating a miracle or anything else at that moment.

I thanked him for his permission to pray for his wife and turned to the two seats across the aisle from him. His wife sat in the window seat, groaning and obviously in a lot of pain, while hooked up to an oxygen tank. Next to her sat her daughter, a woman I later found out was called Mitzi. The mother's eyes were closed and her breathing was raspy. I knelt down to whisper into Mitzi's ear that I had received permission from her father to pray for her mother. Mitzi's immediate response was "Ma'am, we don't go to church or nothin'."

I told her that didn't matter to The Lord and asked what was wrong with her mother. Mitzi told me that her mom had an inoperable brain tumor the size of a peach and that they'd been to Nevada to visit family one last time before her mom died. The doctors had said that she had only a few more days left to live and the family was hoping they might get her home before she died.

In my head, I thought: "No way, Lord!! No pressure here!" I had to take those stinkin' thinkin' thoughts I was getting in my flesh and subdue them with my spirit man's mind of Christ thinking (2 Corinthians 10: 4-5; 1 Corinthians 2:16). Once I got back into my spirit man, I asked Mitzi's mom if it would be okay for me to lightly touch the top of her head where the tumor was. The mother said, "Yes," in the quietest whisper ever. By this time, her husband had left his seat and was standing next to me. 'Help me, Lord Jesus!' I thought.

I reached out my right hand and lightly touched the mother's head and asked The Great Physician, *Jesus*, to come and take away that peach-sized brain tumor and bring total healing to her body. The mother whispered back to me, 'Thank you,' and closed her eyes again.

The next thing I heard The Lord say to me was that I must sing over this family out loud. Now my mom and sister were standing in the aisle as well. I leaned over to them and told them what God had said to me. And I began to sing Amazing Grace out loud on a full train coach, just before the sun came up. My mom and sister joined in with me and I saw Mitzi's father weeping like a baby next to me. Mitzi cried with him. Neither of them said a word as we sang. In fact, no one in the full coach said anything. The silence was deafening!

Once our song was over, The Lord told me to hug and kiss the mother, Mitzi, and her father. He would have done just that had He been there in the flesh. Mitzi and her father held onto me and my family for a long while. I felt led to give them my card so they could contact me with any new developments in the mom's health. They were going all the way to Connecticut, on the east coast of America, and we were getting off in Denver.

After one more hug and a promise to call me about any change in the mom's condition, the conductor called out that we were arriving in Denver. And we got off the coach.

My mom and my sister were with me when I received a collect phone call three days later from someone in Connecticut named Mitzi. I told the operator that I'd pay for the call and then I heard lots of commotion and yelling in the background. I asked Mitzi where she was and she told me that they were in the hospital where her mother had just gotten the latest CAT scan results. I asked what the results were. She said that the brain tumor was gone and the loud shouts I was hearing were the jubilant cries of her family who were all there in her mother's room!

It was my family's turn to holler and scream with joy! We high-fived each other and praised God all at once. It was incredible.

I asked Mitzi what they were all planning to do now that the crisis was over. She said, 'Charlynne, we're *all* gonna go meet this Jesus of yours in church this coming Sunday!' I giggled with joy over that news. And I told Mitzi that if we never met again in this life, I'd see her again in the next life in glory with King Jesus. She said I most definitely would!

The joy I felt after I hung up the phone was indescribable. God had chosen to use my hands, mouth, and imperfect voice to usher in

His miracle-working power on a moving train in the wee hours of the morning, for a family that had never felt His extravagant love before. They admitted they didn't even know Him and yet He moved on their behalf!

When I had boarded the train in Denver to go to Nevada with my family for our little family reunion, I had no idea what lay ahead of me on the return trip back to Denver! How very, very sneaky of God to save the best for last! Isn't that His nature though? When we least expect Him, He shows up in the wildest and most amazing of ways. There is still no God like Him and there never will be. There is only One Jesus.

He Knows Your Name

I said in my introduction that I have learned that whenever I leave my home, any and every thing supernatural is possible with The Lord. Let me share what happened one day when I was running errands, with The Lord speaking to me throughout the day about various things.

It was summer and very warm in Denver, so I didn't feel like a heavy, hot meal, just something cold and refreshing. I thought about how wonderful a cool smoothie would feel . My favorite smoothie place on the planet is Jamba Juice and I knew there was one in a shopping center nearby.

Before I even got out of my car, I heard The Lord say to me, 'Wanna have some fun?' This is what I hear Him say when He wants to do something supernatural with me in tow. There was a flutter of excitement inside of me as I wondered what He was going to do next. I told Him I was up for it and got out of the car. I had parked right in front of the smoothie shop.

As I opened the door to Jamba Juice, I could see a long line of thirsty customers like me. Directly in front of me was a female soldier in fatigues and combat boots, with her back to me. I couldn't see her face or name tag on the front of her jacket and she couldn't see me.

The Lord then told me to call her by name. I told The Lord that would be great *if* I knew her, but I didn't. The Lord then said to me, 'Yes, this is true but *I do*!' I asked Him how I was supposed to call her by name if I didn't know her. The Lord told me that He would whisper her name to me.

Instantly, He told me her name, but my flesh started to second guess what God had told me. Again, I had to take those thoughts captive and focus on what The Lord had told me. He said her name was 'Yvette'. There. I heard it loud and clear and all I had to do was say it out loud. Easier said than done, I told myself. The Lord encouraged me again to call her by name, out loud.

Finally, I said, 'Yvette?' And as soon as I said the name out loud, the soldier in front of me turned around and got out of line. I got out of line too and waited to hear what she would say. She looked at me with the biggest grin on her face and said, 'You're a Christian, aren't you?' And I answered her back with a grin on my face, saying, 'Absolutely!' She said, 'We've never met before, have we?' I told her 'no' but that The Lord specifically asked me to call her out. I then asked her where she was traveling next and she said she was going to Iraq later that week. I asked her if I could pray with her and she said, 'Please do!' So we prayed together in the middle of the smoothie shop. She thanked and hugged me and I told her that if I didn't see her again, I'd see her in glory. She saluted me and said that was a sure thing.

After she turned the corner, The Lord said to me, 'Now wasn't that fun?' Yes, Lord! I was walking on sunshine all day long because of that fun caper with The Lord.

Calling a stranger by name by the leading of the Holy Spirit is prophetically known as a word of knowledge. A word of knowledge is a truth that is told about a person's past or present and must be factual to truly be from the Holy Spirit. When told by a stranger to a stranger, it brings encouragement to the person receiving it because it proves that Jesus sees them and really knows them by name (Isaiah 45:3). It reminded me that I really do hear God's voice.

This testimony begs the question: 'Why do we hear His still, small voice and question what He tells us?!' The reason is that our flesh is always going to be warring against our flesh until the day of Christ's return. It is our job to take every thought captive that tries to raise itself up against the knowledge of Jesus Christ. If we want to flow in His supernatural power as a lifestyle, we must! The choice is ours.

"We demolish arguments and every pretension that sets itself up against the knowledge of God, and we take captive every thought to make it obedient to Christ."

2 Corinthians 10:4

Doctor, Doctor Give Me The News

On a recent road trip with an old gal pal of mine, we went to visit the delightful town of Glenwood Springs, Colorado. We had no set plan for anything in particular. We were just looking at the possibility of my friend moving to that area in the future. Relaxation and some sightseeing were on our minds. But God had another plan.

Colorado has lots of natural thermal springs in the state and so Glenwood's springs are a favorite spot for Colorado locals and tourists alike. As soon as we checked into the hotel next to the springs, we asked about getting a pass to try the waters. I hadn't been there since I was a child and could hardly wait to get into the soothing, hot water. We decided that we'd go that night after dinner.

After dinner, we checked our things into the pool lockers and went out to the spring. It was dark by the time we arrived and most of the children were in their beds. It was really wonderful. I have always loved swimming at night, under the stars. There is something special and magical about doing that.

My friend is a good photographer and always seeks to 'capture the moment' with her camera. I watched her and chatted with her from time to time but didn't want to hinder her photo snapping moments. That is when it's good to be an extrovert. No one is ever a stranger to an extrovert. While she snapped her shots of people, I was happily chatting to people who had come from far and wide to enjoy the springs.

At some point, my friend got out of the hotter pool and decided to go to the pool that wasn't as hot. I stayed where I was and drank in the sight of the evening stars. I soon spotted a woman who was pushing a baby stroller with a sleeping baby inside of it. She was dressed for the pool but busy watching the baby. I saw a wedding ring on her finger. That was when I heard the stirring of the still, small voice asking me if I'd like to get out of the pool and approach her. I did. God always has ideas that are more fun than anything we can ever dream of.

I walked over to her quietly and asked how old her baby was. She told me and we exchanged a few pleasantries. Soon her husband, Jared, came and joined us. He told me he was a doctor and she, Andrea, was a nurse. They had one child and another on the way. It was clear to me that both of them loved The Lord.

After the husband told me about their occupations, The Lord gave me a word for both of them about their identity in Him in their workplace. It specifically spoke to a situation that I sensed was going on with the husband.

With joy on their faces, the doctor said that I must be a prophet because there was no way that I, a stranger, could know what was happening to him at the hospital. I told him that I *didn't know* but that Jesus knows everything and sees everything that is happening to us from every angle. I just shared what The Lord showed me about his life. Jared thanked me for sharing and then told me that the only reason they had left Denver to drive up to the mountains that weekend was that they had asked The Lord for a prophetic word about what to do in their situation!

I told Jared and Andrea to give all the glory and praise to The Lord as they drove back home to Denver. They had been obedient to The Lord by going away to get some quiet time and He had answered their prayers by giving me a word of knowledge that spoke directly into their situation. Hallelujah!

God is so gracious to His children! When we obey Him, He will absolutely bless us and give us what we request. It pleases Him to see us obey and follow His commands. I was blessed that I could be a blessing to a brother and sister in The Lord without any foreknowledge that God was about to use me in that way.

Spontaneity and God go hand in hand. God loves what I call *suddenlies*. By catching us by surprise, He can have total control in the situation because we have no earthly idea what is going to happen next. Every time you see the word *suddenly*, you can be sure that The Lord is preparing you for a supernatural occurrence in the Bible. Here are a couple of examples from the Book of Acts;

"As he neared Damascus on his journey, **suddenly** *a light from heaven flashed around him. He fell to the ground and heard a voice say to him, "Saul, Saul, why do you persecute me?"*

Acts 9:3-4

"When the day of Pentecost came, they were all together in one place. **Suddenly** *a sound like the blowing of a violent wind came from heaven and filled the whole house where they were sitting. They saw what seemed to be tongues of fire that separated and came to rest on each of them. All of them were filled with the Holy Spirit and began to speak in other tongues as the Spirit enabled them."*

Acts 2:1-4

Rabbi On My Doorstep

Have you noticed how very spontaneous The Lord can be? Scripture tells us that His mind is always on us (Psalm 121). It boggles our mind doesn't it? There are over seven billion people on our planet and yet He has all the time in the world for each of us. He has plenty of adventures for you and me to enjoy with Him until the day of His return.

One day as I sat in my ministry office in England doing administrative stuff, I heard The Lord asking me to slow down and listen to Him. So I put down what I was working on at the time and just sat there, waiting. This is a very important thing to do if we want to have supernatural adventures with Jesus. To know where to be and go and what to do, we must be very *still* (Psalm 46: 10).

I sat and tuned my spiritual ear to His rhythms and I heard Him ask me to come away with Him. Just like the Lover said in the Bible's Song of Songs (Song of Songs 2:10). Immediately, I asked The Lord if it was for a day or a weekend. He told me 30 days! I thought I misunderstood Him and that couldn't be right. So I waited again for His voice. Sure enough, I heard the same amount of time again. I could hardly believe my spiritual ears! I began to wonder why God wanted that much time with me! 30 days was a very long time for He and I to be alone with each other.

He asked me why I was hesitating. I told Him that 30 days would cause me to miss a course I was supposed to be teaching in London, I also had no idea where He wanted me to go, I didn't have any extra 'dosh' (cash) to go somewhere for that long, let alone airfare to go somewhere. He asked me if I'd go nevertheless. I said that I'd be happy to go *if* He fixed all three of my hesitations for the course, the destination, and the funds needed to be gone for 30 days. I was, in effect, putting out three fleeces for confirmation before The Lord. A guy by the name of Gideon had done this thousands of years before me and The Lord had confirmed everything for him. Gideon came out of his situation super victorious and I wanted the same thing (See Judges 6:36-40).

When I called my assistant Lesley and told her what had just happened in my office, she couldn't believe it because it seemed such a wild thing for me to do just before the beginning of a course that a church had been waiting so long to take. She asked me about the three fleeces and I told her I had no idea about any of them but that I knew in my spirit that The Lord had spoken to me. I prayed and asked The Lord what He'd have me to do first.

He told me to call the pastor in London of the church I was supposed to be teaching at in January 2008. He told me to explain the situation to the pastor and wait for his response. When I called the pastor, he joyfully said that my time away with The Lord sounded great and that they were happy to begin the course at a later date once I returned! I heard a bell ring: Ding! That was fleece number one all sorted out. The course would start late with the host pastor's blessing.

Then The Lord asked me to do some Godly reasoning with Him about my destination for the time away. So I made a list of possible places for me to go to. There were 10 in all. The Lord said to pray over them. The one that seemed the craziest to me was Miami, Florida. I had not been there since 1989 for a family reunion cruise to the Bahamas. As I waited on The Lord, that was *the* place that He wanted me to go away with Him to visit. I was blown away! It is not a cheap destination by any means. But I just said,' Yes, Lord, *Your will not mine be done*. And what is my next step, Lord?'

The Lord told me to email my godson's father and humbly ask for a plane ticket from his vat of air miles for an assignment from The Lord. I knew this busy man may not respond to me right away because I knew he was in China on business. I emailed him and gave him my request and got a prompt response that he would check and see what was available for flights to Miami. At that point, I knew he might find a flight but was praying I could get a return flight in 30 days. In a matter of hours, he responded and said that the *only* flight he could get on his air miles was for a 30-day stay in Miami!!! Ding, Ding! The second fleece was taken care of.

Now I just needed to know where God wanted me to stay and how I was going to sort out the funding for this amazing adventure that was unfolding. At this point, I knew that I was bound for Florida. There was such a tingling in my spirit and I just prayed about that last fleece and sat waiting in my office. So much had already happened in those few short hours since I had chatted with my faithful assistant, Lesley!

Next thing I knew, my phone was ringing and my dear friend Cynthia who lived in Florida was on the phone. It was early in the work day for her but she was obviously chomping at the bit to call me with some news. What happened next put me on the floor! She phoned to say that her friends in Florida had a lovely beach house, with a private beach, north of Miami that they wanted to offer to me! I could hardly believe my ears. These friends of hers were very successful business leaders who *did not know me and they just offered their spacious home to me, sight unseen and no questions asked!* Apparently, they wanted to go ski in Utah and were tired of the beach and sun in Florida!! They wanted to know if I could stay for—you guessed it— *30 days!!* Ding, ding, ding!! In one day, The Lord had moved some serious mountains for this adventure to take place and all I could think was, 'What is going to happen on the other side of the pond?!' The third fleece was all sorted out.

Let me just say that when God wants something done, it gets done!! Are you starting to understand the title of this book., *No Appointments Necessary?* What a thrill to know with mind-blowing confirmation that I was hearing His still, small voice *and* I was in the center of His will for me at that moment in time. Now God had made His voice very clear to me and His will along with that and so I knew it was just as important for me to obey His wishes for what I'd do with my time once I got to America.

The Lord knew I had relatives in Florida who would love to see me. It had been years since I'd seen anyone down there! Yet The Lord told me to not tell anyone in my family anything about the trip until after the third week I was there, if at all. That meant I had to check in with Him at all times once I was there and really listen to what He wanted and said. I packed my bags and told no one in my family what was going on or where I'd be staying on my first-ever missionary sabbatical. Where most sabbaticals are voluntary, this one

The Lord was sending me on was most definitely *involuntary*. I sensed right away that this was going to be an assignment of some sort.

I said 'yes' to any and everything The Lord might have in mind for this trip to a place I had not been to in over 20 years. I was both excited and full of questions for The Lord about what I could expect. As my old friend and mentor, Jackie Jacobsen, always said, expect the unexpected. Always. Well, that is exactly what I was doing. And yet, who can know the mind of God (1 Corinthians 2:16)? I was sure that He'd bring something incredible to me during this time away.

Cynthia picked me up at the airport in Fort Lauderdale on December 16, 2007, and drove me to see her condo and then on to her friends' beach house. My eyes could hardly believe what they were seeing. The house was very modern and tastefully appointed with every convenience. I was reminded of places my friends owned in Beverly Hills, only I was on the other coast of America. I especially loved how the outdoors seemed to extend inside because of the great use of glass everywhere you looked. The ocean's colors and changing tides were all around you in that home. The kitchen was *huge* and had the most amazing marble countertops. I knew I'd have fun creating meals in it during my stay. The owner told me to enjoy the new home theatre he had just had put in but had never used. I am a professional movie critic and this feature just made me giggle because there was real stadium seating in the theatre room, and the carpet was laced with a zany popcorn and film reel design. The owner also said to enjoy his home but that I mustn't touch one thing. That one thing was the Lamborghini sports car in the garage! Well, I knew that wouldn't even be tempting to me since the pedals on cars like that are usually so small and my feet were an elongated American size 11! Hah! Dream on, Char. God has a great sense of humor!

God had *really* blown my mind and set me up for some sort of magical mystery tour with Him. Let it be said that our God never does anything halfway! His lovingkindness is so extravagant!

Once I put my luggage in the downstairs guest bedroom which, by the way, had a gorgeous sunken Jacuzzi tub in the floor. I unpacked a few things and said goodbye to my hosts and my friend Cynthia. I was all alone except for Father God, Jesus, and The Holy Spirit. The air in that house was pregnant with something supernatural waiting to happen.

I walked outside to breathe in all the sights, sounds, and smells around me. The beach was indeed private and besides the handful of landowners on that stretch of coastline, only the police who patrolled it and the tractor that erased the footprints in the sand each morning were allowed to be there. And then there was me. God had arranged it so that I had access to a very heavenly place on earth. I sat on the sand and pondered in my heart the nature of God.

When I went back inside, I looked at the clock and it said that I'd been alone for about an hour. It was at that moment that the supernatural began to unfold. No sooner had I locked the patio sliding door when the doorbell rang. The owners had told me that their kids might come by to meet me and so I assumed it was them. My boss in the news business, for reasons I won't repeat here, said: Never assume!

I opened the door to find the most unbelievable visitors on the doorstep of that grand house. There in front of me stood not one, but two Orthodox Jewish rabbis. I had heard that Florida has a large population of Jewish people residing there. So I was not shocked by seeing them. It was their reason for being there that surprised me!

As it turned out, both rabbis were French and only one of them could speak English. He introduced himself and his friend to me. He told me he was Rabbi Shalom. By his last name, I knew that he could be a direct descendant of Aaron, Moses' brother. I was astounded to hear that God had told him that he must come to that address! He asked me if he was at the correct place. I assured him he was and he then asked if I was the owner. I chuckled over that question and said no, but I was a visiting guest and minister on sabbatical. The rabbi then clapped his hands and said with excitement that this was proof of a divine appointment set up by God Himself! I then felt led to invite the rabbi into the foyer of the house.

Rabbi Shalom and his friend came in and asked me if I knew what day it was. I thought I had better put my Jewish thinking cap on. Help me, Lord Jeshua! I told rabbi Shalom I thought it was the second day of Hanukkah. He grinned and said, 'Yes! That is correct!' All the while, he was interpreting what we were saying for the other rabbi. I kept thinking, 'Thank you, Lord.' I didn't want to offend these precious gentlemen in any way.

Next, Rabbi Shalom told me he had a gift for me. I asked if I could make a donation to his synagogue. He told me that was not necessary and that he felt God wanted me to receive what he had for me. Out of his long, black overcoat came a box with a Hanukkah menorah in it with candles! I was so blessed by this kind gesture. Then he pulled a blue, Israeli spinning top out of his coat pocket. He then asked me if I knew what that was. I told him it was a dreidel. Once again, he grinned with joy that I knew so many Jewish truths. At that point, he had one more question for me: Did I really know God? I told him that I *did* know God and that God had spared my life at least five times that I could remember. To that, Rabbi Shalom replied, 'God has saved *my* life 10 times!' No way was this Jewish rabbi going to be outdone by a Gentile woman. Both of us laughed. With that, he said it was time for him and his fellow rabbi to leave. He gave me his cell phone number and told me that he had something of grave importance to discuss with me. Rabbi Shalom then made me promise that I would call him before the end of Hanukkah. I promised to call. He shook my hand and both rabbis left.

As I closed the door, I felt a tingling in the air. I knew that I knew that I knew that something miraculous had just happened. For two Orthodox Jewish rabbis to have a lengthy discussion with a *non-Jewish woman* is extremely unbelievable in my experience. I grew up in an Orthodox Jewish neighborhood and also bought my first house in a Jewish neighborhood. Due to customs of religious modesty, I had never known an Orthodox Jewish man to go out of his way to speak with a woman who was not his wife, especially a Gentile woman! Let alone two Orthodox Jewish men who happen to be rabbis! I was beyond bewildered. At that precise moment, anyone could have knocked me over with a feather.

I couldn't stop smiling to myself. I'd only been in the house for just over an hour and already the Holy Spirit was moving! My friends had all left for their respective Christmas holidays and there I was getting ready for a wild escapade with The Lord. It would be hard to close my eyes that night. I was raised to love and honor the Jewish people and their nation—the center of God's universe. I was looking forward to my next encounter with Rabbi Shalom.

What happened after that first night was very precious to me. Each morning, I heard the still, small voice of God calling me out of sleep and calling me to the beach with Him. It was always just as the sun was beginning to rise that He'd call to me. I saw the most amazing 'brushstrokes' of God's handiwork in the heavens each morning, while sitting alone on that private beach. Just me, Father God, Jesus, and The Holy Spirit. Every day, The Lord spoke to me through nature, and I captured it in my journal.

On one of the mornings as I woke up with The Lord, He encouraged me to call Rabbi Shalom. There are 8 days for the festival and so I had to try to contact him before it ended. We met on the second day of Hanukkah, and in keeping with his request, I made the call. He decided to come back to the beach house and meet me on the last day of Hanukkah, before sundown.

When the rabbi arrived, he seemed very serious. Something was definitely on his mind. He asked for a drink and then, as is customary, asked me where he could wash his hands. I took him to the downstairs powder room and waited for him in the formal dining area that looks out toward the sea. Rabbi Shalom asked if we could pray together! Again, I was shocked by this, but was happy to say 'yes'. We faced the east and he prayed in Hebrew and I prayed in tongues When does something like that ever happen?! In that moment, I could feel the thick, weightiness of the shekinah or Presence of God's glory. It was so tangible!

We moved toward the long dining table and he took a seat across from me. I asked him what was on his mind. He told me that he was distressed about a serious decision he wanted to make. I asked if he cared to share it with me and he said he felt that God had given him the vision of the address of this house because I was the one that God wanted him to speak to about his decision. That was mind-blowing for me to ponder later, but I chose to focus on what was obviously troubling the man of God.

Rabbi Shalom began to share with me his concerns about the rising anti- Semitism across the planet and especially in Europe, where he was from. I told him that I was a missionary to the UK and that I was well aware of the serious things he was speaking about, and that I too was grieved about it all. As he shared from his heart, he finally told me that he had come to a decision to leave his calling and stop being a rabbi. I was astounded but could understand the grieving of his heart. Yet, I knew The Lord was going to prompt me to say something from His heart to the rabbi. Once again, no pressure, right? I felt very inadequate at that moment. How in the world was a Gentile going to share words of wisdom with a rabbi who knew

God's first words to man better than she?! Jesus interrupted my thoughts and reminded me that in my weakness, He is stronger (2 Corinthians 12:9). Hallelujah! I became silent in my thoughts and waited on Him for what to say to this precious rabbi.

God began to give me a sort of Scriptural prescription for Rabbi Shalom. The Lord told me that I'd better use nothing but Old Testament verses to bring the truths to the rabbi's troubled spirit. So I wrote out several verses for the rabbi and his wife to read later and then I opened my mouth to ask him a question that I knew he knew better than me. I asked him what is better to God: obedience or sacrifice. He said obedience. I nodded my head yes in agreement and he sat in silence across from me with folded hands on the table. I told him that both of us had several things in common, two of them being that we served the same God and both of us were called by God to serve Him in key roles for the building up of His church. Now the rabbi nodded his head in agreement with me. Jesus beckoned me onward in my chat and so I went out on a limb and told the rabbi that it wasn't any better for me to walk away from my calling than it was for him to do the same. Again, I asked him what was better to God: obedience or sacrifice? Again, the rabbi told me, 'obedience'.

Now the irony in this whole sequence of events is that I was putting some hard questions to The Lord at that time in my life and was very discouraged in *my* calling. I felt just like the rabbi but for different reasons! And there I was telling the rabbi, on God's behalf, that if I couldn't leave my post, neither could he. Man oh man, did I feel inadequate. I desperately needed Jesus to speak to me!

I asked the rabbi what he would do for work if he was not working at the synagogue, he shrugged and said quite simply, 'I'd work in my family's diamond business.' In my experience, that was a very Jewish response and I smiled at him.

The rabbi then said he must be home before sundown and that he was very grateful for my time and listening ear, and that he'd be sure to share the verses with his wife. I walked him to the door and as he turned to leave, he came back to me and asked if we could speak again before my 30 days were up. I assured him that I'd like to do that.

In fact, the next day, Rabbi Shalom called me to say that his wife said I was a very wise woman and that he absolutely should pray with me again before I left Florida! As a result of our chat, Rabbi Shalom changed his mind and decided not to go into the diamond business. What a humbling moment!

I had come to Florida because God had asked me to come away with Him. He and I needed to sort out my thoughts and feelings about where I was in my ministry and my deep discouragements. On the way to my big discussion with Him on my own troubled heart issues, He sent me on an errand to help someone else with their troubled heart! God wastes no time in His universe. None. After that little 'errand', I realized that God is higher than my pain.

Entertaining Angels

I would be remiss if I didn't share what happened after that blessed week of Hanukkah in 2007. In our Led By The Spirit School of Prophecy, we teach our students that angels often appear to human beings in faith-or life-threatening situations. Scripture says that we sometimes entertain angels in our midst without even knowing it.

"Do not forget to entertain strangers, for by so doing some people have entertained angels without knowing it."

Hebrews 13:2

The week after my two first encounters with the rabbi, I heard The Lord wake me up by calling out my name, 'Charlynne!' in a head-turning voice. I shot out of bed as if a human-being had called out to me. It was so clear. I said, 'Yes, Lord. What do you want me to do?' He told me to quickly brush my teeth, get dressed, and bring my Bible and notebook out to the beach. Once again, it was very early and the tractor that erases footprints had already come and gone. I was the first person out for a walk that morning. No other tracks could be seen.

Soon, a cop on an ATV drove up to me; he wore shorts, sunglasses, and a baseball cap. It was already a scorching hot day. The officer asked me if I was okay and if I needed his assistance in any way. I told him I was fine and to be safe in all of his activities. He promised he would be and sped away down the sands. I was alone with The Lord again. It was very still, and so as not to be distracted by the gulls or the jumping fish, I closed my eyes in prayer and reverence, just waiting on The Lord.

When I opened my eyes, it was even hotter and I thought I saw four legs with feet attached in front of me! It startled me because I hadn't heard a soul walk up to me. Maybe it was the heat, I thought. So I closed my eyes and opened them again. No, there were definitely four legs right in front of me with feet attached to them.

I looked up from where I was sitting down in the sand and asked if the two men in front me were lifeguards. They just smiled down at me and said, 'No.' They seemed intent on telling me something and I felt the hairs on the back of my neck standing up. They had no intention of leaving and seemed to have all the time in the world. I had a sneaky suspicion that they were not of this world!

Then I heard The Lord tell me to open my journal and write down what they said. Now I knew these guys were *not* of this earth! I was shaking inside and berating myself for suggesting that they were mere lifeguards. Of course they weren't lifeguards! In my humanness, I guess I hoped they were. Something supernatural was happening right then and I needed to sit up and take notice.

As I took a closer look at my heavenly messengers, the thing that stood out most to me was the gold lettering I saw embedded into their necks. It looked Hebrew and I wanted so much to ask them what the emblems meant but dared not. I didn't want my own flesh to get in the way of the Lord's purposes at that moment in time. So I sat, watching and listening.

Then it happened; the angel closest to me reached out and touched me on my shoulder saying, 'Charlynne, do you know a Great War is coming?' I quickly scribbled down what he said and then I nodded my head yes. The other angel was smiling down at me and was silent. If I doubted they were angels before, I surely couldn't now because *they had just called me by name!*

My heart was racing and I was feeling sort of faint. It was really, *really* hot by now. I asked if it would be all right if I went inside and got us three bottled waters. 'Would angels drink something with me?' I asked myself. Instantly, I heard The Lord reminding me of the three heavenly visitors that Abraham and Sarah hosted with food and drink on a hot day back in Genesis, before the destruction of Sodom and Gomorrah (Genesis 18: 1-7). So I ran into the house and pulled out three bottles of water and ran back out to the beach. The Lord told me there was no need to run, but I didn't want them to leave yet!

Sure enough, my visitors were still there, smiling intently and looking through me. I handed them their water bottles and together we drank from them and they kept on encouraging me to basically 'get back on my horse and ride' for The Lord. They told me that God had assignments for me that were yet to be revealed (my paraphrase). They drank the last of their water and handed their empty bottles to me. They asked me if I fully understood what they'd said to me. I told them I understood. They turned to go and walked off to my left.

I asked them to wait. As they turned back around to face me, I asked them what their names were. The angel who had spoken to me said, 'We are Gabriel and Daniel.' Shock of all shocks! I jotted that down and when I looked up, they were gone!! I stood where their tracks ended and mine had stopped. They literally disappeared into the thin air!

I turned around and went back to my place in the sand, shaking and crying all at once. On that day, I'd totally forgotten that my friend Cynthia would be back from her Christmas break and would be coming to see how I was doing at the beach house. The minute I sat down in the sand, crying and shaking, was the same moment that she came around the side of the house. She'd rung the doorbell, and when I didn't answer, she came to the beach. She ran over to me and could see that I was upset. She put her arm around me and led me into the house. Then I told her what had just happened to me.

Cynthia said, 'Charlynne, God has clearly placed you under an open heaven ever since you came to this house.' I told her about Rabbi Shalom as well. Together, we rejoiced in The Lord and praised His holy name. Nothing like that had ever happened at that house in all the years that the owners had lived there. There had never been any Jewish people in their home and there certainly had never been any visible angels! When they came home, they rejoiced too over my news and were sad that they had missed out!

God was showing me the serious importance of obedience over sacrifice. Scripture talks about it several times, yet do we really understand what God meant when He originally spoke that truth through Samuel to Saul? It is such a serious offense to The Lord when we hear Him and do not obey.

"But Samuel replied: Does The Lord delight in burnt offerings and sacrifices as much as in obeying the voice of The Lord? To obey is better than sacrifice, and to heed is better than the fat of rams. For rebellion is like the sin of divination, and arrogance like the evil of idolatry. Because you have rejected the word of The Lord, He has rejected you as king."

1 Samuel 15: 22-23

The wonderful thing about our obedience to His voice is that we can never fully know what is waiting for us on the other side of our obedience. It is always a *good* thing. When our flesh rules us, we miss out. But when the Spirit of The Lord rules us, the possibilities for the miraculous in our lives are endless.

Steak and Angel

When challenging times hit God's people, we often question where He is in our circumstances. In 1996, I survived a head-on collision with a drunk driver. It was definitely one of the scariest experiences I had ever been through. The entire series of events before and after this accident proved to be very supernatural.

Two weeks before my crash, I had been having lunch with some colleagues of mine in the film industry in my favorite restaurant. During the meal, a crazed woman approached our table and she pointed her finger at me, hurling a verbal curse at me. Payback was coming for something I'd done that the enemy didn't like, she'd said. I knew in my spirit, as soon as it happened, that she was a witch and I instantly rebuked what she'd spoken in the restaurant. She turned on her heels and walked out of the building, and I carried on with my business meeting.

Two weeks later, I was hit by a car as I was returning home from seeing one of my favorite plays, 'A Christmas Carol'. I was alone in the car and remember screaming out the name of Jesus before the impact. When I woke up, my car was smoking and the police and firemen were telling me they were going to get me out. They had to cut me out of the car because all of the electrical systems in my car were out. I walked away from that accident and everyone was shocked by that. It was clearly a miracle. Unbeknownst to me and my doctors, I had some internal injuries that I would suffer from for many years after that.

My faith had been jolted by all of the fallout from this, being the third car accident I'd had in just 10 months. I wondered where The Lord was and what He was saying to me in all of this. I couldn't stop wondering why I'd been singled out to have so many attacks. I was just a normal girl in Colorado, trying to serve God, right? What was all the commotion about? From a prophetic point of view, I had been warned by three different prophetic voices that a long season of attacks was coming to me. But I had no idea what was going to happen and how those words were going to pan out.

When we get words like this, we are advised to weigh and test them with trusted believers (1 Corinthians 14:29). I had hoped that those prophecies were figurative and not literal. I'd also been taught to pray bold prayers of restraint against the enemy's plans for me in instances like this. Clearly, the words had a literal meaning for me. I only found out that night the seriousness of what was happening to me.

After I got released from the emergency room, I went home and began to chat with God about all that had just happened. One supernatural thing after another happened. The doctors had said that they didn't want me to be alone because I had a closed head injury, so my sister stayed with me for a bit. That first night, I woke up screaming the Word of God in my sleep. When I opened my eyes, I saw demons, for the first time, dancing around my bed. Instantly, I commanded them to leave in the name of Jesus Christ!

My sister could hear all the commotion down the hall, and she got up and asked, 'What's going on in there?!' My bedroom door was shut and she said it sounded like wild horses were storming through my house. That was exactly what it sounded like.

I opened my bedroom door smiling and told her that demons had come and left! She heard the rumbling noise they made as they exited my house. I went back to bed with peace, and so did she. In my heart and spirit, I began to ponder what had made the enemy so mad and then I knew: I had just led a prominent, gay cover model to The Lord. Yes, that would make the enemy angry. The model had left the gay lifestyle and was dating women, totally healed from his troubled past.

The week after the demonic experience, I got a phone call from an actress from the theatre world in New York City. She was in Denver to do a play and wondered if I would meet with her. I was bruised and still sore after the accident, but never passed up an opportunity to share The Lord with people in the entertainment business. I was also nervous to attempt winter driving since the car crash. The head-on collision was my third hit in ten months! I was very skittish about driving anywhere, to say the least. But I said yes to meeting the actress in downtown Denver.

Ironically, the actress chose the same restaurant where the curse had been spoken over me, before the accident. The weather was awful that night. There was a blizzard warning, but I knew she was staying near the restaurant and I only lived 15 minutes away, so I decided to risk going out in my little rental car (my car had been destroyed in the wreck.).

I got to the restaurant first. She had said that if the weather got worse, we'd have to re-schedule. Still, I went in. No one was there except a lone stranger sitting in a booth with his back to me. He was eating dinner. I knew the manager and he told me they might close early because of the nasty weather, but that they'd be happy to feed me something before they made that decision.

So I sat down in a booth that faced the lone stranger. I looked at him and he nodded his head as he continued to eat what looked like a big steak dinner. They quickly took my order and I found out from the manager that my actress friend had called to say she wasn't coming out.

It was then that the lone stranger picked up his plate and asked if he could join me. That had never happened to me before, and since we were clearly the only people eating there on such a stormy night, I said he could join me.

He was tall with clear blue eyes, and had a dark beard. He sat down across from me, in my booth, and continued to eat his big steak. As I watched him, he opened his mouth, in between bites, and asked, 'What has The Lord done for you lately?' What a provocative thing for a stranger to ask me! The hairs on the back of my neck began to stand up on end with that question.

My order hadn't come out yet, and it was easy for me to answer that in light of what had just happened to me in the accident the two weeks prior. The EMT guys and everyone in the emergency room had told me how very lucky I was to be alive. In their experience, not many people survived a head-on collision.

I told the stranger that Jesus had saved my life once again. He nodded his head and kept eating, but soon he asked me for the specifics of the accident. So I told him. He asked me how I was feeling, and I told him that I was still a little bit shaken. I was experiencing some memory loss and nerve damage where the air bags hit me, and could definitely see the bruising and feel the pain of the impact in my neck and back.

When my food came out, he had finished his steak and began to share some amazing insights with me about heaven that I cannot remember the details of. All I can tell you is that with each thing the stranger spoke to me, the more the hairs on the back of my neck stood up. I knew that this was at least a very divine appointment, if not something even more special.

Once I had finished my meal, the manager came over to us and said that the snow had really picked up and that the restaurant was going to close early that night. The stranger told me that he would take care of our bill. I was even more blown away by that! Then he came back to the table and helped me into my long overcoat. He gave me his arm to lean on, saying that the last thing I needed was to spin out on the ice in the parking lot. The manager told us that he and the staff were going to lock the front door behind us and leave through the kitchen.

As the stranger and I made our way down the sidewalk to the parking lot where my rental car was, he asked if I had an ice scraper for the windshield. I told him I wasn't sure, but if I had one, it was probably in the trunk of the car. He led me to the driver's side of the car and told me to turn on the engine and the defrost while he looked for the scraper. Thankfully, he found it and began to scrape the hoary frost off of all the car windows, while I sat in the warming car.

As I sat inside, listening to the constant scraping of the blade against the glass, I was pondering all that we'd discussed over that dinner in the restaurant, just the two of us. It was so unusual and I felt, very supernatural. This was not a chance meeting! Who was this tall, bearded stranger?! Was God trying to relay a message to me by bringing him across my path? Little did I know, but the answers to those questions, and many other things, were about to be revealed to my wondering mind.

Once the windows of the car were all clear, the stranger knocked on the passenger side window and asked me if he could come inside.

In my flesh, I wondered if I should say yes. We were the only people in the parking lot and the restaurant staff had left through the back door. No one was there to help me if this man was not a safe person. I was either crazy for being alone with a stranger in a parking lot, or was in the right place at the right time. However, in my spirit I heard the Holy Spirit telling me that I was all right and that I could trust The Lord to protect me. I have been taught to always heed the still, small voice of The Lord over anything my flesh or mind may be telling me, so I unlocked the passenger door and the stranger hopped in.

As the wind howled, the snow got thicker and thicker. All I could hear was the beating of my heart in my ears and the constant crossover of the windshield wiper blades. Then the stranger spoke.

'This is a word from The Lord your God,' he said. 'You have wondered about the happenings of the last few weeks and here is what The Lord would have you know.'

I must confess that the minute the stranger began to say that he had a word from The Lord for me, my hands started shaking on the steering wheel of the car and I just waited for him to proceed.

'Have you ever been fly-fishing?' he asked.

'Yes, I actually just started taking lessons from some friends of mine that work with me and I have even been given a new rod and reel from a Native American outfitter who is a friend of mine,' I said.

'Good,' he replied. 'Then you must know why the lakes here are so very deep?'

'Yes,' I said. 'It's because a lot of the lakes in Colorado are really canyons that have been flooded.'

'That's right,' he said. 'And because of that, the lakes are very dark and murky, causing the fish in them to struggle to see the bait on the end of a hook.'

I nodded my head in agreement.

'Here's what The Lord wants you to know,' he continued. 'The trout in those kinds of lakes are likened to Satan, and you are a type of bait. The light you carry, because of Christ in you, draws the trout, like a moth to a flame. The only way that the trout knows there is available bait is the ripple effect caused by the bait hitting the water. In other words, the threat of your calling has created a ripple effect that causes the trout/enemy to attack,' he said. 'Do you understand what I've said?'

With shaking hands, I nodded, 'Yes.' He continued speaking.

'It is the Lord's plan that you would continue to learn of Him and seek to know Him more through His word. You have learned much, but there is still more He requires of you. In the days to come, He will be showing you how to deliver His messages to needy souls behind enemy lines, *without causing a ripple effect* and without getting hurt or attacked as you've experienced in the last few months. It is very important that you go deeper with Him in the study of the Word, and that you also get more covering for the assignments He will give you.' I was very concerned by this last statement. I wondered if I had done something wrong. It was like the stranger was reading my every thought.

'The Lord wants you to know that you have not done anything wrong, but that you have operated in your anointing without sufficient prayer cover,' the stranger said. 'You must get more intercessors to pray for you as you continue on in the things that The Lord requires of you. He will show you how to gain more support, and who is to be in this group of intercessors.'

I was instantly reminded of what the witch had said to me in the restaurant and what she was referring to. Timing and great discernment are so crucial when operating under the Lord's anointing!! It can never be stressed enough. Up until that moment, I had not thought very much about the events of the previous year and what the spiritual or supernatural ramifications of my calling really were. That was all about to change.

The lone stranger stopped speaking and asked me one more time if I fully understood the message he had spoken. I knew that there was so much more to what he had said but I nodded my head yes anyway.

I remember looking down at my hands. They were really shaking now. I looked to my right and the stranger moved, like he was getting ready to leave. I turned to him and said, 'Wait! You haven't told me your name.'

He turned back around to look me square in the face and said, 'You can call me Michael.' I froze right there and instantly thought, 'Really, Lord?? Could this man be none other than one of your chief angels? The Warrior Archangel Michael?!' I looked through the windshield and pondered this for a moment. When I looked to my right again, the lone stranger was gone and the passenger side door never opened! He had vanished into thin air and I was left alone with my thoughts and shaking hands. All I heard in that moment was the constant whirring of the wiper blades. There was no doubt in my mind that I had been visited by one of God's chief angels to sort out the crisis of faith going on in my mind at that time.

The next thing I heard was the Holy Spirit telling me that it had definitely been a word from Him, sent by a heavenly messenger. He said that I must drive home carefully in the snow and take the time to record every single word of what had been said to me.

When I got home, I remembered that the power was out and I had to light some candles. I put on my pajamas and sat in my living room by candlelight. I decided to put some logs on the fire as I wrote in my journal all that I have just shared. I felt very encouraged by the events of that night, yet pondered in my heart what my next 'training' at the Lord's feet would look like. He was there with me in the stillness of that very snowy night and I knew that He would always be with me ---no matter what happened to me. He will do the same for any and all of His children.

"For I am convinced that neither death nor life, neither angels nor demons, neither the present nor the future, nor any powers, neither height nor depth, nor anything else in all creation, will be able to separate us from the love of God that is in Christ Jesus our lord."

Romans 8:38-39

The Corner and The Convict

Throughout my life, The Lord has allowed me to learn many things from Him as I travel or even just leave my doorstep to 'go' and do something. It has proven to me time and time again that His children really are carriers of His power and authority. I must add that being a carrier of His Presence and authority has nothing to do with age either. It is all about faith in what you believe and whether or not you have your identity wrapped up in Him.

By the time I was sixteen years old, my parents had already been divorced for four years. My mom had received custody of my sister and me and we moved to Colorado from Indiana to start again. Besides our three beds and our clothes, all we had was Jesus. As it turned out, He was *all* that we needed. In the absence of my earthly

Father, Jesus became the head of our household. Whenever we had needs, and they were many, we had to turn to The Lord. I grew up in a house where we lived by the miraculous, wonder-working power of Jesus. Though there were hardships, we three rejoiced in all that The Lord continually did in our midst. He let us know how real He really was and that *nothing* was too difficult for Him.

During that time in our lives, we didn't have a car to use and so our only real transportation was by public transport or the bus. Occasionally, friends gave us a lift, but more times than not, we relied on the bus system.

Every summer, our world famous charismatic church in Denver, The Happy Church, had a big event called a 'camp meeting' that really did reflect the same signs and wonders of the big tent revivals held by the likes of Oral Roberts and Billy Graham. During that event, many marvelous men and women of the faith would descend upon Denver for a glorious week of meetings where the power of Jesus shown forth in so many ways. I loved it, and our family was very much involved in church life there. My mom was one of the main nursery workers and my sister and I always assisted her.

One night we were traveling back across town to where we lived and we always took two different buses to get to our church. The journey was long and never dull because the routes went through the main drag and the longest continuous road in the state, Colfax. Colfax also ran through the red-light district of Denver and past all of the large adult entertainment establishments. As a family, we had experienced several incredible encounters with the 'ladies of the night' and various drug addicts.

So there we were one night, waiting at the base of the State Capital steps for our second and final bus home. The stop was a big one and there were lots of benches where all sorts of people were waiting for a myriad of buses. It was a busy transfer point. It was very dark and we huddled close to each other, discussing all that we'd seen and heard at the camp meetings that day.

Soon, a man who was obviously high on some sort of drug and reeking of alcohol, came to ask my mother a question.

'Hey, Mama. What's your sign?' he asked in his stupor, hardly able to stand up.

My mother knew he meant for her to give him the zodiac sign she was born under. She had a different response than the one he was expecting.

'My sign is Jesus,' she said with great confidence. The inebriated man instantly sobered up. At that moment, our bus came and we got up to board it. The man followed us onto the bus and soberly walked up to us to say, 'You ladies have a good evening.' The astonishing thing was that he seemed absolutely sober! He was not staggering down the aisle either as he walked past us. I remember turning around in my seat to look at him as he walked to the back of the moving bus. As I turned back around in my seat, I asked my Mother why he seemed to be so sober when just moments before he looked to be out of his mind. I'll never forget her reply as long as I live.

'Girls, just the name of Jesus spoken with authority will order *any* situation you find yourselves in,' she said. 'Now, this is very important for you both to know because I may not always be traveling with you: Jesus will always be there right beside you and in you. You don't need mace, pepper spray, a knife, or anything else but the name of Jesus. Can you remember that?' Both of us nodded our heads and went on with our chatter about the evening.

Right after that night, my sister was traveling on her own across town to church to help out in the nursery for one of the special meetings. As the bus she was on traveled through the red-light district, it stopped in front of an infamous adult entertainment emporium where there was a bus stop.

At the stop, there was a man standing on top of the bus bench. That made him level with the height of the bus window that my sister was sitting near. She had a Walkman in her ears and was oblivious to the man. He didn't get on the bus, but because it was summertime and very hot, her window was cracked. As the bus pulled away from the stop, he man reached in through the window and tightly grabbed my sister by the neck! He wouldn't let go and was hanging onto her. She was absolutely frightened and so alarmed by what he'd done. As the bus picked up speed, the man finally let go. But she was *very* upset by his actions and crying her eyes out by the time she got to our church. My mother was working somewhere else that day, but I was onsite in the church offices, so the nursery workers called me to say what had happened to my sister and how upset she was. They called the police and made a report, and I went to the main church building to talk to her. Needless to say, she was determined not to ride the bus alone across town ever again. She was so shaken. Scripture is very clear about the workings of our enemy.

"Be self-controlled and alert. Your enemy the devil prowls around like a roaring lion looking for someone to devour."

1 Peter 5:8

My sister found out about that firsthand on that day. It only served to make me really angry at the enemy, on my sister's behalf. I had no idea what was about to happen to me next.

The next week, it was my turn to help out in our church nursery, and I had to take that same bus across town, on my own. It was another hot summer day in Denver. I made it all the way to the corner of Broadway and Colfax, where I had to transfer to the bus that would take me to my church. The bus stop was right in front of a huge fountain. There were several people standing there, waiting for their buses.

While I was standing there, a man, about 6'7' in height, came up and grabbed me from behind. He bent down and whispered in my ear that he'd just been released from prison and that he had been watching me since I got off my first bus. He had all kinds of terrifying plans for me and told me that if I screamed, he was going to kill me. He was squeezing me very tightly and leading me down the street and into his car. I wondered if he had a gun or switchblade in his jacket. Needless to say, my mind was reeling.

Instantly I remembered what I'd heard my mother say to us at the bus stop and that police say that the farther away you go from the place that you are abducted, the harder it is to pick up the trail of your abductor. I knew I had to think fast and lean into Jesus if I ever wanted to get out of this frightening situation I now found myself in.

As we traveled down Broadway, I kept hearing my mother's words in my head, clear as a bell. 'The name of Jesus, when used with authority orders every situation you may find yourself in.' I needed some Holy Spirit courage. It was now or never, so I asked Jesus to give me strength and I opened my mouth.

'Do you know Jesus?' I quietly asked the convict as he drove.

He turned to look at me with crazed eyes and growled, 'No!'

So I asked him again, with a bit more courage, 'Do you know Jesus?' Again, he looked at me and said with rage, 'No!!' The voice I heard definitely sounded like he was demon-possessed. I'd heard voices like that before in my Mother's house group. When people need to be delivered of demons controlling their lives, they use voices that are eerie and not of this world. Just think of something evil from J.R.R. Tolkien's *Lord of the Rings* Trilogy and you'll know what I mean.

As the name of Jesus began to fill me with more and more courage, I asked the convict the same question for a third time: 'Do you know Jesus?"

This time, he brought the car to a screeching halt, turned at me and really growled this time: 'Noooooo!!" He leaned across me, opened the passenger side door, and shoved me out onto the roadside, speeding off down the street.

I collected myself and jumped up off the ground saying, 'Thank You, Jesus!!' over and over again. I called the police to say what had happened to me and they immediately sent a squad car over to take my report. The police were absolutely blown away by my story. They kept telling me how very lucky I was to be alive without one scrape on me. I was so glad to tell them what Jesus had done for me.

When the police had gone, I realized that the other part of what my mother had told us that night at the bus stop was equally as true as what she'd told us about the power of the name of Jesus. She had also told us that if we used the name in the presence of unbelieving people, they would either bend their knees in allegiance to Jesus or they'd run away, not interested in knowing Him. The convict clearly didn't want to be set free of the forces that had held him captive. It dawned on me that he was free from prison but not a free man. No one said it better than Jesus:

"So if the Son sets you free, you will be free indeed."

John 8:36

You may be wondering what I did after that whole ordeal. I went on my merry way and got on another bus to go and work in the nursery at church. No way was I going to let the enemy of my soul spoil the day that my Lord had made! I couldn't wait to share what happened with my friends at church.

I knew that my mom and sister would be thrilled to hear the news, too. What a blessing to have been raised in a God-fearing home where the name of Jesus is spoken all the time with reverence and joy! I am forever grateful to my mom for choosing to go the extra mile as a single mother, raising us to know Jesus intimately.

My Great Escape

The previous story was the first kidnapping attempt I lived to tell about. There is another one. In the story that I am about to share, I knew that I shouldn't get into my assailant's vehicle. I was older this time and wiser. My great escape happened one summer about eight years ago.

I was not living in the US anymore and had made the move to be a resident in the UK. It was time for my furlough back home in Denver, Colorado. My sister had just picked me up from Denver International Airport and drove me to the townhouse that she shared with my Mother. She parked her car and went into the house. I took a little bit longer, deciding what bags to take in first.

While she was in the house, I decided to take one of my big suitcases out of the trunk first. As I pulled it along the sidewalk, I looked up and heard someone in a white van calling the name 'Charlie'. I was the only person walking down the sidewalk and that happened to be one of my nicknames. So I looked at the person in the approaching van, wondering if I knew them.

The van stopped along the sidewalk and I could see that the driver who had called out to me was definitely not someone I knew. He was dressed in Arabic clothing and had a foreign accent. He didn't mince his words and instantly told me to get into the van. I couldn't believe my ears and refused to do it.

The van driver threatened to hurt me and said that he knew more about me than just my nickname. He proceeded to tell me what my British Airways' flight number was and where I'd come from. At that point, my mind began to race, trying to think of the best thing to do. I didn't want to run into my mom's house because then the driver would know which of the row of houses was where my mom and sister lived. I needed back-up assistance from Heaven, and fast. 'I need You, Jesus!' I prayed.

At that moment, cars behind the van began to honk their horns to get the driver to move on. He looked in his rear-view mirror and knew he had to move his car. In that moment, I swiftly pulled my suitcase down the sidewalk and went into my mom and sister's house, quickly telling them what had happened. I grabbed the keys to my car that was parked in my mom's carport, put my suitcase in it, and drove away to a friend's house. I didn't think it wise to stay with my mom and sister. They might be in danger.

As soon as I got to my friend's house, I made a call to a Homeland Security officer that I knew. When he heard my story, he told me that I'd done the right thing and that I definitely should not go back to my mom's house, just in case her house was being watched. He also told me that if the Arabic man really wanted me that he would probably be back the next day. My friend told me to ask my sister to look the next morning and see if there were any vans fitting that description parked on their street.

When I called my sister the next day, she went upstairs to the front bedroom window and took a sneak peek through the blinds to see if a van fitting that description was anywhere on the street. Sure enough, there was an unmarked, white van parked diagonally across the street with a man dressed in Arabic clothing sitting in the driver's seat! She said there was no license plate on the front, and I distinctly remembered that he had no license plate on the rear of the van either. I also remembered that across the back windows of the van there was a flag with Arabic writing on it. She saw the same flag in the rear window of the van.

I called my friend back at Homeland Security and told him what my sister reported to me. He advised me to stay somewhere else for the duration of my stay in the States. The best thing about it is that, once again, my calling on the name of The Lord spared me from sudden danger. The Lord is so faithful to His children! Whenever we call on His name, He answers. He is the God who will make a way for us when there seems to be no way. When you need a hero, make sure you call on the name of Jesus. He is the ultimate Hero! Listen to this:

"He rescues and He saves; He performs signs and wonders in the heavens and on the earth."

Daniel 6:27

Up, Up, And Away!

Years ago, a popular American singing group called The Fifth Dimension had a hit song called 'Up, Up, And Away!'. It was all about taking a trip in a beautiful hot air balloon. The song came out when I was a little girl and its words always made me wonder what taking such a trip would really be like.

The Lord knows us better than we know ourselves and He knows our thoughts before we even think them. He even knows the secret desires of our hearts.

"O Lord, You have searched me and You know me. You know when I sit and when I rise; You perceive my thoughts from afar."

Psalms 139: 1-2

"Delight yourself in The Lord and He will give you the desires of your heart."

Psalms 37:4

What a mighty God we serve! He is so relational that every detail of our lives is important to Him.

During one of my trips back to the US from the UK, I was invited to teach in a neighboring town north of Denver. I was invited by a small group of friends who wanted a workshop on hearing God's voice. After I taught the last session, the ladies asked if they could pray for me. I welcomed that offer.

Each lady present spoke a blessing over my life and my return trip to the UK. The last woman had a card for me in her hand and she also spoke a blessing. It is a blessing that I will never forget! She told me that she had a prophetic picture of me in a hot air balloon. The balloon was striped with all the colors of the rainbow and she could see me smiling, high up in the clouds. As she spoke over me, she wondered if the picture The Lord had given her for me was figurative or literal in meaning. The card she gave to me was of a woman in a rainbow-colored hot air balloon!

When you are learning about how to interpret things prophetically, you learn that each person will receive a prophetic vocabulary from the Holy Spirit that has words and symbols that mean something specific and personal to the person receiving prophetic words. Rainbows and things that fly have always meant something special to me about my ministry. Rainbows always speak to the promises of God. To say that I was excited about receiving this word was putting it lightly. I would dutifully weigh and test it as I put it into my Prophetic Words Journal for safekeeping.

I soon returned to the UK, and a week after the balloon word had been given to me, I received a phone call from a British couple that I had ministered to. They called to say that they really wanted to thank me for all the ways that they had been blessed by my ministry. I thanked them for calling and told them it was a pleasure to serve them. The husband asked if I could meet him and his wife at the church they attended two weeks from then. I looked at my calendar and said that would be fine.

They had asked me to meet them behind the church. I had no idea why. So on the day we were to meet, I walked behind the church as instructed, and before I even got to the back of the church, I could hear a strange sound like something was being blown up. Something *was* being blown up! It was a huge hot air balloon that belonged to the couple! As it turned out, the husband had a pilot's license and their thank-you to me was a ride in their hot air balloon, complete with the traditional champagne brunch afterwards! And yes, the balloon was rainbow-striped!!

I don't know who was more excited that day—me or them! I happened to have my camera in my handbag and I began to snap photos of the entire process of blowing up a passenger balloon. It was a glorious sight. The sounds were amazing, too.

Soon, it was time for me to climb into the basket and I wondered if my stomach would feel anything as we climbed up into the atmosphere. As I talked to Patrick, the pilot/owner of the balloon, I hadn't even noticed that we were slowly climbing up into the atmosphere! When Brenda, his wife, called to me, I looked over the side of the basket and realized we were drifting upwards! I hadn't felt a thing. It was such a smooth feeling. I was delighted and I had absolutely no idea where we were flying away to, but I knew it was going to be some flight!

In my mind and spirit, I kept on thanking The Lord for making that prophetic word I'd received a reality. The word had been given three weeks before my magical ride! Incredible.

I now call moments that personally bless us 'kisses from God'. God is so incredibly loving and thoughtful that He sometimes gives us things for no reason other than He knows what is in our heart of hearts and what will delight us. It gives Him pleasure to bring us pleasure! This is what Jesus said:

> *"Do not be afraid, little flock, for your Father has been pleased to give you the kingdom."*
>
> Luke 12:32

I don't know about you, but this kind of love astounds me. It is so overwhelming to know that the Master of the Universe wants to serve us!

> *"It will be good for those servants whose Master finds them watching when He comes. I tell you the truth, He will dress himself to serve, will have them recline at the table and will come and wait on them."*
>
> Luke 12:37

What Master seeks to serve His own servants?! Jesus. He never lies and is the epitome of humility. He chooses to stoop down and serve us. What love!

Salvation At 35,000 Feet

The Presence of God follows us wherever we go. This is what God's Word says on the subject:

> *"Where can I go from Your Spirit? Where can I flee from Your Presence? If I go up to the heavens, You are there; if I make my bed in the depths, You are there."*
>
> Psalm 139:7-8

So there is the proof that God's Presence will even be with us as we travel up in the air. Because of this fact, every time I get a ticket to travel by plane, I get excited in my spirit, knowing that The Lord will indeed meet me in the air! Yes, even before the Lord's return to bring us home (1 Thessalonians 4:17), we can experience His Presence in flight on an airplane.

One of the reasons I love to travel by air is the fact that there is a captive audience for any and everything The Lord might do. I've noticed some unique differences about the workings of human nature on a plane. The people involved have absolutely nowhere to go! They can't escape. Trips by plane also tend to be very long. There is much room for thought and discussion with someone you meet on a flight. Another thing I have noticed is that on a plane, folks are more likely to be honest and transparent because the chances of running into you again are almost nil. So people tend to really 'let their hair down' without guilt or fear. They seemingly have nothing to lose when sharing the matters of the heart at 35,000 feet above the earth. It is the perfect climate for the Holy Spirit to have His way.

On one flight coming from Heathrow into Denver, I sat next to a lady named Marla. She'd had a lovely time in the UK and was looking forward to returning to Colorado where she was from. Everything was going smoothly until we began to make our descent into Denver airspace.

Most Denver locals are familiar with the turbulence that you often feel once you get close to landing at Denver International Airport (DIA). That part of the state is notorious for high winds and tornadoes. As a result, it can be quite bumpy for planes that are trying to land.

On this particular flight, we were having lots of turbulence. My seat partner Marla began to look *very green*. She leaned over to me and told me that she wasn't feeling well and that she might 'lose her cookies'. In fact, she was reaching for the traditional barf bag as she spoke.

The plane was pitching left and right and we kept hitting some deep air pockets. I am always excited by such occurrences and have never been scared by them, but I know most people get twitchy when such events happen. It just makes me pray calmly.

As Marla held the bag in her shaking hands, I sensed the Holy Spirit telling me to get ready to take His lead in the situation. The flight attendants were doing the cabin cross-check to see that all passengers had their seat belts on and then the Captain told them to take their seats and buckle up as well.

While I stayed in the attitude of prayer, the Spirit said that I should tell Marla that I was a minister who believed in healing and that I would be happy to pray with her if she wanted prayer. By this time, Marla's head was between her knees and she clearly was doing everything she could to not use the paper bag. She instantly nodded 'Yes' to my offer. I then asked her if it was all right for me to put my hand on her shoulder. She nodded in agreement again.

So I put my right hand on her shoulder and asked The Lord to come and heal her and bring peace to her entire body. I also asked The Lord to take all fear from her mind. Marla was instantly healed!

As her head bounced up from between her legs, she said, 'How did you do that?!!'

'Jesus did it. I can do nothing without Him. But with Him, all things are possible. When I prayed for you, His healing power flowed through my hands to your body,' I told her.

Marla sat in amazement next to me and began to ask me a flood of questions about Jesus. She really wanted to know Him like I did. So I asked her if I could introduce her to my Best Friend, Jesus Christ. She said she wanted that very much and I prayed with her to accept Jesus. I'll never forget the joy on her face!

After that precious moment, she decided that we must stay in touch. Marla wrote out her address and phone number. I gave her mine, too.

At the baggage carousel, Marla gave me a hug and walked away promising to write. I encouraged her to find a solid, Bible-believing church to attend and promised to send her a Bible and some resources to help her get more acquainted with her Lord and Savior.

All I kept thinking was this: If that's what happens on a flight where there is turbulence, Lord, sign me up for more of the same! That was so much fun and I could hardly wait for the next flight.

We don't have to do anything but be available to the Lord's plans in such a situation. It is not work, but real fun to witness something like that and be used to bring life, light, and joy into someone's life. And guess what? There is a whole world out there just waiting for you and me to take the life and joy of Jesus to them! If we don't do it, who will? This is what the Apostle Paul said we are supposed to be like to the world:

"You show that you are a letter from Christ, the result of our ministry, written not with ink but with the Spirit of the Living God, not on tablets of stone but on tablets of human hearts."

2 Corinthians 3:2

Such a precious thing to consider. Our witness to the world is being read every day, whether you know it or not. Someone is receiving a message from our lives. What message are we transmitting to the world around us? Let's make sure that it's one that leads others to a hunger and thirst for Jesus Christ.

British Airways Flight 219

I'm used to being a part of God's plans to hijack someone in the air, but what's it like to be on the receiving end of something God has created? You never know what God is up to. He is full of the most delightful surprises! To be in partnership with Him, you must be willing to go with the flow and move with His spontaneous calls to action. His working with, in, and through us is all about the fulfillment of His plans and purposes for us and those around us.

In this next story, I was totally caught off guard by what The Lord had already begun to work out in someone's life before I even got on the plane! Scripture says this about the workings of God's mind in such instances.

"No eye has seen, nor ear has heard, no mind has conceived what God has prepared for those who love Him."

1 Corinthians 2:9

God always knows what is best for us and we must do our best to trust Him at all times. Even on days when things are not seemingly going your way. That's what was happening to one lady who had just completed all of her business in London and was making her way home via British Airways Flight 219.

The flight was fully booked and filling up quickly. The Lord had told her that she would be meeting a 'friend for life' on her flight home to Denver. As she made her way down the aisle to her seat, Janet saw a woman sitting in her row, in the aisle seat, with an alcoholic beverage in her hands already. The plane wasn't even in the air yet and folks were already drinking. She saw a black woman sitting in the window seat of her row looking out the window. That black woman was me!

She put her carry-on bag in the overhead locker and wondered who The Lord was about to introduce her to. As she pondered these things in her mind, she decided to go to the restroom before the flight got underway. While there, she heard The Lord say to her that everything would be revealed to her if she would be still and write to Him in her journal. She wondered what was going to happen next but decided to obey what The Lord had said to her.

So she sat down in the middle seat that she'd been assigned and reached down to take her journal out of her bag. She opened the journal and began to write in it. At that moment, I turned toward her and discreetly looked to my left at her journal and happened to catch a glimpse of the page Janet was writing on. With joy, I realized that there were crosses on all the pages of that journal. I wondered to myself if I was sitting next to a fellow sister in The Lord.

Without a moment's hesitation, I whispered to her, 'Are you a Christian?'

Janet turned to me instantly and said, *"It's you!!"*

I started laughing out loud and so did she. I wondered what in the world she meant by that. I had never seen her before in my life! What did she mean by that statement?! I was about to find out.

As it turned out, Janet was indeed a Christian. She told me what God had told her before the flight about meeting me. She told me that she was a lawyer who was married with four sons. From Heathrow to Denver, Janet shared with me her heart for creating a ministry that would have the ability to be a blessing and a resource for women everywhere.

I shared with her that I am a minister, and that I often work with people about God's plan for them in the walking out of the vision and purpose for their lives. I told her about the book I'd written called *True Grid: God's Custom-designed Blueprint For You* that is a tool for assisting people of all ages in the fulfillment of the vision God created for them since before the beginning of time.

"For we are God's workmanship, created in Christ Jesus to do good works, which God prepared in advance for us to do."

Ephesians 2:10

It is a 10 hour flight from Heathrow to Denver, so we had loads of time to share our hearts with each other. I had found a kindred spirit for sure! And God had kept His word to Janet about what was going to happen on that flight.

Once again, I found myself giving my contact details and a copy of my book to someone who was a stranger but was now a newfound sister in Christ. Before we left the plane, we promised to meet up for a coffee at Starbucks in downtown Denver. Neither of us knew it then, but we would do that for several years to come and form a solid sisterhood in Christ. Janet has even visited my home on the South Coast of England and introduced me to other Christian women who are ministry leaders. So much came out of one flight to Denver! God planned it all. Every single bit of it. Amazing.

Janet's dream of creating a resource for Christian women did become a reality and many are the blessings that have been received by women because of it. God is so kind and loving to us! He says that what He starts, He finishes. Man may lie but God never lies.

"God is not a man that He should lie, nor a son of man that He should change His mind. Does He not speak and then not act? Does He promise and not fulfill?"

Numbers 23:19

Our God is so mighty and true. There is no one like Him. How comforting to know that we can depend on God 24/7! He always keeps His word. He never changes.

"Jesus Christ is the same yesterday and today and forever."

Hebrews 13:8

God's Tangible Presence

God wants to be everywhere that we are. Because He has made us the temple of the Holy Spirit, we carry that Presence wherever we go. It is an awesome thing to consider and not something to be taken lightly.

"Don't you know that you yourselves are God's temple and that God's Spirit lives in you? If anyone destroys God's temple, God will destroy him; for God's temple is sacred, and you are that temple."

1 Corinthians 3:16-17

"....For we are the temple of the Living God. As God has said: 'I will live with them and walk among them, and I will be their God, and they will be my people.'"

2 Corinthians 6:16

I think we sometimes forget this truth because we are so easily distracted by the world in which we live. This next testimony gives evidence of the previous verses.

In the summer of 2013, I was on the Heathrow flight to Denver for my annual stay in the States. We'd been in flight for about two hours. I'll be honest with you. I felt it very strange that I hadn't had a 'God-incident' yet on that flight.

As I was mulling this over in my mind, I heard The Lord tell me to get up out of my seat and walk to the back of the plane where the toilets were. I really didn't need to use the bathroom but got up out of my seat in obedience anyway. I stood there, stretching my legs and periodically bending down to look out of the small window at the earth below. No one was there but a couple of flight attendants in the galley beyond where I was standing.

I turned away from the window and suddenly saw a young, college-age guy looking at me. I noticed that he had a Colorado State University T-shirt on. So I smiled at him and asked him what he'd been doing in the UK.

His name was Justin and he was traveling with a group of other students from the same university. They'd come from South Africa where they'd been on a missions trip for Campus Crusade for Christ. Here was my 'God-incident'!

I told him that must have been very exciting. He said it was and that it changed his life. As he continued to share his experiences in South Africa, he told me that he could 'feel' the Presence of God all around me and asked what I did. I told him that I was a minister, called to minister in the United Kingdom and beyond. He was so excited and said that he just felt drawn to talk to me.

On my end of things, I got a strong sense from The Lord that He had a calling for this young man. I felt that I was supposed to send him a copy of my *True Grid* book. He was the only believer in his family and had such faith in The Lord! I was deeply moved by his testimony.

Once again, I exchanged addresses with someone who only moments before had been a total stranger to me. God was definitely working in and through our conversation. I just love encouraging the Joshuas of tomorrow. I believe Justin is one of them for sure.

This story doesn't just end there. Once we got off the plane and Justin rejoined his group, he told them about our discussion and several of them gathered around me at immigration and customs in Denver. I wondered what else was going to happen. I smiled and waited for these lovely children of God to speak.

One beautiful black girl came over to me with a leather journal in her hands. She said they all wanted me to have it. I asked why and she said that it was a journal that was started by a missionary in another part of the world for the express purpose of being handed to the next missionary to write testimonies in. The idea is that when the journal is totally full of testimonies of the Lord's exploits, the last missionary to write in it would then send the journal back to the original missionary at the return address in the back cover of the journal.

Well, I had never heard of such a marvelous thing as that! I loved journaling and could hardly wait to write in this blessed book. Once the whole missions team had heard about me from Justin, they unanimously agreed that I would be the next missionary to scribe in the journal. I blessed them all and said I'd see them all in heaven one day, if not before. They agreed and we parted ways at the immigration desks.

There is *so* much power in our testimonies of Jesus' wonder-working power in our lives! We must always have something great to share about Jesus. It is one of the best tools of warfare against the enemy of our souls and the accuser of the brethren.

"They overcame him by the blood of the Lamb and by the word of their testimony..."

Revelation 12:11

Every time we boast about something The Lord has done, there is much blessing in that.

"But, Let him who boasts boast in The Lord. For it is not the one who commends himself who is approved, but the one whom The Lord commends."

2 Corinthians 10:17-18

In case you are wondering, I wrote in the leather journal that summer just before I returned to the United Kingdom and gave it to a mighty missionary to China who is Japanese. Justin is now doing some short-term studies in Europe and stays in touch with me via email. He is still actively involved in his Christian campus activities, with a strong desire to do more missions activities in Africa.

My Con Air Experience

A few years ago, Hollywood came out with a movie called *Con Air* that starred Nicolas Cage and a host of other well-known movie stars. I am instantly reminded of that film when I think of this next testimony of mine. The Lord gives me so many supernatural experiences every time He sends me on a journey by air. This story is actually the end story for what I shared earlier about my anointed sabbatical trip to Florida that featured encounters with angels and rabbis.

I was sitting in the gate lounge for the return flight from my 30 days at the beach house in Miami. This trip was truly the gift from God that kept on giving. I couldn't stop pondering over the incredible benevolence of my Florida hosts. The owner of the beach house had just given me a delicious send-off lunch at one of my favorite American restaurants. And if that wasn't all, the wife of the owner gave me a new handbag with a cheque inside for $500! I went to Florida with nothing but my desire to obey Jesus and He caused my cup to run over! These verses instantly sprang to my mind:

"Give and it will be given to you. A good measure, pressed down, shaken together and running over, will be poured into your lap. For with the measure you use, it will be measured to you."

Luke 6:38

"...You anoint my head with oil; my cup overflows. Surely goodness and love will follow me all the days of my life, and I will dwell in the house of The Lord forever."

Psalms 23:5-6

Soon it was time to get on board the flight and I knew that because I normally sit in the back of flights, near the galley, I'd be called to board first. The airlines tend to board from the back of the plane first. Well, I thought something was a little bit odd as I made my way to the back of the plane. There were already several men sitting across the back of the plane in two rows. They were sitting in the row that I was supposed to be in. My assigned seat was the only empty seat on the end of one of the rows, putting me on the aisle.

I put my carry-on bag in the overhead locker and took my seat, buckling myself in. In a moment, I knew that I was not sitting with normal tourists or business travelers. I was sitting amongst an entire row of ex-convicts! Their law enforcement companion was a US marshal on the other end of the row.

Almost as soon as I realized who I was sitting with, a very nervous flight attendant asked if I'd like to change my seat. I told her that I was fine, even though I had heard the lewd comments the ex-cons were making toward the flight attendant. It seemed like a real opportunity for The Lord to move. I begin to pray in the Spirit for His wisdom and discernment in the situation I now found myself in. I reminded myself that I fear no one but Jesus Christ.

It wasn't long before the men got tired of teasing the flight attendant. The marshal let them know that he was not the least bit impressed with their verbal skills. They got quiet for a moment and then turned their attention to me. I was the only woman in the row. I knew that this was God's open door.

Groups like this always seem to have a ring leader. He happened to be the ex-con seated on my right. He asked where I'd been and where I was going, so I told him that I'd had some time off with The Lord and that I was a minister traveling back to my UK assignment.

That's when he began to tell me that he believed God had given up on him a long time ago. I told him that I begged to differ. Man, oh man, was that door swinging wide open for God to move!

The ex-con began to tell me that he'd really messed up his life and that even though he and the men sitting around me had a long way to go, they really were trying to turn their lives around. I told him that was great and that God would love to come along for the journey with them. I told him about the Jesus I know who happens to be my best friend. The ex-con said he'd never heard anyone talk about Jesus like that. He only knew Jesus through profane speech.

I told him that the name of Jesus is a powerful weapon against the forces of darkness when used with the authority that God gives His children. The ex-con was very intrigued. He asked me why I wasn't afraid of him and was willing to answer so many of his questions. I told him that Jesus loved him and that there is no fear for anyone who knows Jesus.

He asked how Jesus could love an ex-con like him who was still pretty messed up. That's when I told him about Jesus and the convicts on the cross. The ex-con sitting next to me began to cry and was somewhat embarrassed because he was sitting in such close proximity to his friends. I continued on anyway and handed him a tissue for his streaming eyes. This is the story I told him about the day of Jesus' crucifixion:

"One of the criminals who hung there hurled insults at him: 'Aren't you the Christ? Save yourself and us!' But the other criminal rebuked him. 'Don't you fear God,' he said, 'since you are under the same sentence? We are punished justly, for we are getting what our deeds deserve. But this man has done nothing wrong.' Then he said, 'Jesus, remember me when you come into Your kingdom.' Jesus answered him, 'I tell you the truth, today you will be with me in paradise.'"

Luke 23:39-43

There were so many things the ex-con asked on that flight. I just prayed that nothing but God's wisdom and love would come out of it all. Amazing how at the name of Jesus, all vulgar speech stopped coming from these men! Such power in the Name Above All Names.

As I prepared to get off the plane, the ex-con shook my hand and thanked me for taking the time to answer his questions. He said he would think long and hard on our discussion and said that he wished his girlfriend had been there to hear it all. I told him to be sure to share with her all that I had shared with him. He promised he would. He gave me a hug as I turned to leave and I said to him, 'I hope that Jesus and I see *you* and your girlfriend in paradise!'

This was one of those moments in life where I'd have to wait until I get to heaven to find out what happened in that ex-con's life! It was such a blessing to be able to share the love of Jesus and the truth of Jesus with those men. I realized that some people will actually meet Jesus at 35,000 feet in the air *before* His return to earth; as long as there are believers who are free to share the Gospel message on flights, this will be true.

Shocked By The Sheriff

I would be remiss if I didn't put this next testimony in this book, in this particular section, as a follow-up to my *Con Air* story. So many amazing things seem to happen to me whenever The Lord sends me to Florida. It's like some heavenly vat of blessings begins to pour into my life at the mention of my intention on making any trip to Florida. It is all quite shocking to me, yet we know God can and will do whatever He wants to do in and through our lives. So without further ado, let me tell the tale.

In the summer of 2012, I'd just finished doing a weekend at Whisper Crossing Ranch in Kiowa, Colorado. During the weekend I was there, I had the honor of meeting the sheriff of the county. He and I spoke at a meeting of believers that weekend and had the opportunity to chat afterwards. We exchanged business cards and we both said how much we enjoyed each other's talks. Once the weekend was finished, I packed my things and headed back to Denver to pack for a flight to Miami, Florida. I was going to minister at my aunt and uncle's church there and my Mom was going to accompany me.

There was only one problem. Mom had her ticket but I had not received mine from the church yet! Once I got back from the ranch, I only had a few hours to re-pack and get ready to go to Miami because I had been booked on the 'red-eye' flight from Denver. My Mom had even called a cab to come and take us both to the airport. As I got dressed and ready to go, I kept checking my email and still there was no ticket. I began to pray.

While I was praying, I realized that my cell phone was blinking and letting me know that I had a message on it. The message was from the sheriff I'd met during the ranch weekend in Kiowa! I could hardly believe my eyes. The sheriff had sent me a message that simply said he was praying for me at that very moment and that he felt led to ask me, in true police speak, if I needed *back-up*? I just laughed out loud and wrote back immediately that I was meant to be on the red-eye flight to Miami but my e-tickets hadn't come through yet. It was about 3am in the morning when I got his message. I accepted his offer for some back-up prayer, and within the hour, my e-tickets appeared on my computer screen! I was overjoyed and sent a message back to the sheriff right away. The cab my Mother had ordered was on-time and so were we! Both of us made our red-eye flight to Miami and had a most enjoyable flight and time of ministry with our family there.

In my world, what the sheriff did was a very prophetic act. Especially when you think what time of day his message was being sent. He stepped out on a limb with his question to me. And he was right on the money. Christ in him, the hope of glory showed up big time (Colossians 1:27)!

I should not have been shocked at all by the behavior or character exhibited by this law enforcement official. What can you expect from a sheriff that has this verse over his door:

"He has shown you, O man, what is good. And what does The Lord require of you? To act justly and to love mercy and to walk humbly with your God."
Micah 6:8

You can expect exactly what I got! A word of knowledge fitly spoken by a God-fearing sheriff who knows how to hear and obey the still, small voice of God. His job is to 'protect and serve', but what he'd done by serving me that day in the wee small hours of the morning was above and beyond the call of duty!

"A word aptly spoken is like apples of gold in settings of silver."
Proverbs 25:11

The Lord wants every man, woman, and child in any and every walk of life to be able to have intimacy with Him every day. We were designed to have everything that Adam had. He walked and talked with God in the Garden of Eden in the cool of the day, and was naked and transparent before God, without shame. This is the kind of relationship we were designed to have with Our Maker. We can have it today, if we will choose to listen, and when we hear, obey Him.

"You were shown these things so that you might know that The Lord is God; beside Him there is no other. From heaven He made you hear His voice to discipline you."

Deuteronomy 4:35-36

And we know that The Lord only disciplines those that He loves and those who are His children. He is so much in love with us and wants nothing but the best for all of us! We must choose as an act of our wills to hear *and* obey God's voice of love. The Sheriff has learned this valuable lesson and is used by The Lord to help others through law and order. I got blessed as a result.

"Because The Lord disciplines those He loves, and He punishes everyone He accepts as a son. Endure hardship as discipline; God is treating you as sons. For what son is not disciplined by His father? If you are not disciplined (and everyone undergoes discipline), then you are illegitimate children and not true sons."

Hebrews 12:6-8

Travelogue Thoughts

1. Have you ever volunteered your services to The Lord before a trip? If yes, what were the results?

   _____

   _____

   _____

2. Have you ever encountered a heavenly messenger? What happened?

   _____

   _____

   _____

3. What's your favorite mode of travel and why?

_____
_____
_____

4. Have you ever experienced one of God's 'suddenlies' ? Write about it.

_____
_____
_____

5. Have you ever received a 'kiss from God'? What happened?

_____
_____
_____

Charlynne M. Boddie

2

EXPLOITS IN ENGLAND

"A pessimist sees the difficulty in every opportunity; an optimist sees the opportunity in every difficulty."
Winston Churchill

"You can have anything you want in life if you just help enough other people get what they want."
Zig Ziglar

"A woman is like a teabag. You never know how strong she is until you put her in hot water."
Eleanor Roosevelt

"When you get into a tight place and everything goes against you, till it seems as though you could not hold on a minute longer, never give up then, for that is just the place and time that the tide will turn."
Harriet Beecher Stowe

"Sometimes struggles are exactly what we need in our life. If we were to go through life without any obstacles, we would be crippled. We would not be as strong as what we could have been. Consider the butterfly that struggles to free itself from its cocoon. The struggle gives strength to what was once just a worm, so that it can spread its wings and fly away."
Unknown

"Hope is the power of being cheerful in circumstances we know to be desperate."
G.K. Chesterton

It was during the summer of 1988 that I took my first overseas flight outside of America. I had been tasked with leading a small, Christian mime troupe to the United Kingdom for the majority of that summer. All of us on the team were Oral Roberts University (ORU) graduates or students. I was one of the grads and had heard The Lord call me to do this mission in one of our last campus chapel services at ORU. I had a serious aspiration to go to Hollywood and beyond to shake up the media world for Jesus. And in my heart, I promised The Lord I would just do this 'one little missions trip' for Him. I had *no* idea what The Lord had planned for me with just one trip to a foreign land. If you have not already found this to be true, our God is not only an awesome God, He is extremely sneaky, too!

That summer changed my life forever! Who knew that I would see so many miracles in just 90 days! But I surely did. God put some incredible supernatural bait on His heavenly hook and then He reeled me in to His plan for me to get the 'Missions Bite'. The next three testimonies come from that miraculous first time that I was in England. My team and I were hardly in the country for a week before the son of one of our host families took us aside and prophesied over every one of us. The words that were spoken over me opened the door for me to understand the calling of God on my life to be a *prophetic evangelist to the nations*. The prophet who spoke over us became my first mentor, and he and his colleagues in the UK solidified for me what God wanted me to do in the UK, with great confirmation in the decade that followed.

Double-Decker Dinah

One of the most amazing things that we did as a team that summer of '88 was participate in the first street evangelism course of something called *T.I.E. Teams* or 'Training In Evangelism'. There was teaching first and then the students were put into groups that were sent to various places in the UK to evangelize on the streets. My teammates and I trained in Clapham, just on the outskirts of London, and we lived in a church there. We practiced what we learned and did our miming on the streets before we were sent to another city.

During that time, I remember going sightseeing in London on a double-decker bus one day. The Americans with me were so excited to see the City via this famous mode of travel. We also had some

British TIE Teamers with us. One of them was an older woman named Dinah. She and my US team decided to go and find seats on the top level of the bus. It was a hot summer day and lots of people from all over the world were doing exactly what we were doing.

There was so much chatter on the bus, with our tour guide telling us what we were seeing and the history of things as we went along, but I was also hearing Someone else speaking to me. It was the Holy Spirit. He was giving me a download of something for Dinah. It made no sense to me, but The Lord was prompting me to get up and tell her what He had just given me for her.

The bus we were on stopped to let other tourists board, and when that happened, I got up out of my seat and went over to Dinah's seat. She turned to me and I shared with her what The Lord had said. He basically told me to tell her that my university has a great nursing school. Dinah then asked me what school I was from and I told her it was Oral Roberts University. She got so excited!

Unbeknownst to me, Dinah was wanting to go to a Christian nursing school and had been mesmerized by the vision of Oral Roberts to build a university that would teach its students to be Spirit-led and Roberts' dream for a Christian hospital that would marry prayer and medicine. She asked The Lord for confirmation about where she was supposed to go. When I went up to her and told her that one thing, she began to cry and couldn't stop praising God! I knew nothing about Dinah except her name, but God knows us better than we know ourselves. Dinah asked me for our school address. I gave it to her and she was bouncing with joy all day.

What happened on that bus was just a taster for what was to come. Signs and wonders follow those who believe.

"Now to each one the manifestation of the Spirit is given for the common good. To one there is given through the Spirit the message of wisdom, to another the message of knowledge by means of the same Spirit, to another faith by the same Spirit, to another gifts of healing by that one Spirit, to another miraculous powers, to another prophecy, to another speaking in different kinds of tongues, and to still another the interpretation of tongues. All these are the work of one and the same Spirit, and He gives them to each one, just as He determines."

1 Corinthians 12:7-11

God Gets A Gang Leader

While we were still being trained in London, we were asked to do a praise march right through the center of London one evening. We had musicians and the students all praising God together as we walked along. It was fantastic! Every few blocks, my teammates and I would stop and do some street skits for the crowds that were in various squares we happened upon.

Most of the people enjoyed watching us perform, but by the time we were getting closer to Leicester Square, we noticed that there was a gang of kids heckling and mocking us. Some of them even threw things at us as we praised The Lord.

When we stopped to perform, this gang kept on heckling us. We didn't let it get to us at all. In fact, this is when the Holy Spirit gave a download to one of the guys on my US team. As Mitch was performing, The Lord caused him to notice a young man who seemed to be the leader of the gang that was heckling us. When our skit was over, Mitch walked up to the gang leader and introduced himself to him. The gang leader was pretty gruff and just stood there amongst his friends, snickering. So Mitch asked him what his name was. The gang leader told him it was Steve.

That's when Mitch whispered a question to Steve. He asked Steve about a time when he was a little boy, all alone in his bedroom, crying out to God and asking for God to show that He was real. With that word of knowledge, Steve stopped snickering and fell to his knees, crying! Right there on the spot, in front of his friends. They became silent and watched in wonder. Mitch went on to tell Steve that God had sent him across the miles to tell him that God loved him and knew everything about him. Then Mitch asked if Steve would like to be introduced to Jesus. Steve said yes, and while kneeling down, he gave his heart to The Lord! It was such a magical moment for all of us. Because of what Steve had done, several of his friends in the gang came forward to meet Jesus! Incredible. These are the joys of doing street work for Jesus. After my team prayed with everyone who wanted Jesus, we gave them information on what to do next and how to get plugged into a local church.

We all continued our praise march through the streets of London's West End with great rejoicing. There is nothing dull about being a true follower of Jesus Christ!

My God's Stronger Than Yours

When our training was over in London, the leaders decided to send the student team I was on to Worthing to practice all that we'd learned. Worthing is located in sunny West Sussex, right on the southernmost coast of England. Everyone was very happy that we were selected to be so close to the ocean. Our long, hot summer continued.

In keeping with everything we'd learned in London, we all got settled in with our respective host families and then decided to perform a sort of spiritual 'pulse check' on the city of Worthing. To do this, we decided to do a prayer walk through the neighborhoods one evening. When we were walking the streets, we were amazed to see how many supposed 'toy stores' carried so much information on the black arts and witchcraft for children. We began to pray for the people of the city to open their hearts to Jesus and see with spiritual eyes what the deception from the enemy's camp was all around them. Concerted prayer like this with people of like minds puts the enemy and his forces to flight. We did this at night and during the day. We didn't perform any of our skits until we felt the leading of The Lord to begin. The last place where we prayer-walked was the center of the shopping district, one hot, sunny day.

What I have not shared with you is the fact that before I left the States to come on this mission trip, an English prophetic voice told me that the witches of England were expecting me and would make their presence known to me at some point during my trip. When I received that word, I sensed in my spirit that it was a word from The Lord and that I should be alert and keep my spiritual armor on at all times.

I praise God for that prophetic warning because on the day that we prayer-walked the shopping district, I was walking and praying in front of a row of shops with a US teammate, when I passed an older woman and a young girl about my age and instantly felt a shiver run down my spine. The next thing I heard was the Holy Spirit telling me that I'd just crossed the path of a witch. I began to pray in tongues and told my teammate to back me up in prayer.

As I turned around to look at the back of her, the woman turned around and stared at me, with a hiss. She and the young girl walked up to me and told me that I needed to leave because 'the dark prince wanted me to go'. With the power of the Holy Spirit rising in me, I told her that *The Prince* of the entire universe, Jesus of Nazareth, had sent me, and that no weapon formed against me would prosper. I said I wasn't going anywhere, and that if she didn't want to bend her knee to Him, she was the one who would have to flee.

With that, the older woman and her companion ran across the square, grabbed their chairs and tarot card table, and ran as fast as they could. I remember several townspeople coming over to me and my friend, saying that I needed to watch my back because she was the head of the witch's coven in that area. I told them that the only person I fear is Jesus Christ and that He is my Defender. I could tell that they were very frightened.

The next day, the witch's companion came up to me while we were out on the streets performing one of our skits. She was blonde and about my age. She asked if there was somewhere we could talk in private. I saw a nearby McDonald's, so we went there and grabbed a table.

This young girl was in training to become a witch. She had never seen anyone stand up to her mentor. She had never been without fear in her whole life. She wanted to know what or who made me so strong. It was my joy to share with her about Jesus and the fact that He came to save all of us. I told her that His great love for us casts out all of our fears. She asked me to introduce her to Him, and when I did, she gave her heart to Him. What a thrill!! My mom's words rang true --at the name of Jesus, people will either run from Him, or run to Him. This young witch decided to run to Jesus and traded in her old life for a crown of glory and eternal life. Her mentor ran from Him and all that He offered to her. She was *so* deceived!

I knew that unlike the gang leader in London, we would have to put this young lady in a safehouse for discipling and protection. The enemy would not like this conversion, and she needed the Lord's protection while she grew up in the knowledge of Him.

If you are wondering what became of this young girl, I can happily tell you that she grew up strong in the things of God and married a good Christian man. They now have two children and continue to walk with God.

The Church must be aware of the enemy's ploys, and at the same time know without a shadow of a doubt that what we have in Jesus

Christ is stronger than any plan or scheme of the enemy. To operate with the power of Jesus against darkness, we must know His Word and operate in His authority. I am reminded of these words from Jesus:

"I tell you, My friends, do not be afraid of those who kill the body and after that can do no more. But I will show you whom you should fear: Fear Him Who, after killing the body has power to throw you into hell. Yes, I tell you, fear Him."

Luke 12:4-5

Oh, the power of the blood of Jesus and His Word! They are both such powerful weapons we have in our arsenal against all that is against the plans and purposes of our God. Wherever and whenever we travel, we must 'pack' the knowledge of Jesus Christ and all of our supernatural weapons of warfare.

There are so many other stories I could share from that first summer I spent in England. But I'll go on and share some of my adventures in other places in the United Kingdom once I began to travel there all the time, and also some stories from all the years that I lived in England as a resident.

Red Shoes and Railroad Ties

God doesn't just let us feel or sense His matchless favor once we reach a certain destination, He can let us sense His Presence on the way to different places as well. On another occasion, in my earliest days of living in England, I needed to be somewhere and my assistant couldn't come. I found myself catching yet another train. Because Europe relies on trains more than the auto-bound United States, I really enjoy going places by train. Just like being on a plane, you have a captive audience on a train for a certain amount of time. To me, each train journey is an opportunity to see something unusual happen that God brings about, as only He can do.

My assistant Elise dropped me off at the train station with two bags on a still, hot summer day. I knew I had to transfer twice and was not looking forward to doing that with two bags on this journey by myself.

Everything was going smoothly until I got to the first station where I needed to change trains. I got there in good time to make my connection and then as I was boarding the second train, one of the red sandals I was wearing fell off my left foot and onto the rails below! My bags were on the train and the stationmaster was blowing his whistle to let folks know the doors were about to close and it was time for the train to go.

I was devastated! I loved those sandals and was wondering how I was going to go the rest of that long journey with just one shoe, lugging around two bags! Now would be a great time for The Lord to show up, I prayed. I didn't know what to do but pray, and I could feel a tear welling up in my eyes.

As the train began to move, it *suddenly* halted. An English gentleman called out to the stationmaster on the platform saying, 'See here, stationmaster, this young woman's shoe has fallen off onto the tracks below. We cannot possibly leave until her shoe has been retrieved!'

All I could think to myself was, 'Lord, chivalry is *not* dead! Hallelujah!'

The train stopped with another sharp blow of the stationmaster's whistle. I was somewhat embarrassed but grateful at the same time to this chivalrous man who had stopped the train on my behalf.

The stationmaster walked into his office and grabbed a stick for picking things up. He calmly walked over to the open door of the train coach where the gentleman and I were standing. He simply reached down with his stick with a claw on the end of it and clamped onto my red sandal. He then lifted it off of the train track and carefully placed it on my bare foot!

As he did it, a tear ran down my smiling, grateful face. When he saw my tear, he said, 'Don't cry, Love. If the shoe fits, I'll marry you!' That made me really giggle. I love Cinderella stories and I really felt like Cinderella in that very moment. The gentleman thanked the stationmaster and I thanked them both.

'Does God really care about even the shoes on our feet?' you ask. Apparently so. He even cares about our tears and the hairs on our heads!

"Record my lament; list my tears on Your scroll----are they not in your record?"

Psalm 56:8

"Indeed the very hairs of your head are all numbered. Don't be afraid; you are worth more than many sparrows."

Luke 12:7

Nothing about any of God's children is trivial to Him. He is that wild about each and every one of us.

Two Dreams For The Price Of One

On one of the trips I took to Scotland with my ministry assistant, Elaine, I remember getting onto the plane and taking a look at the in-flight magazine that you always find in the seat pocket in front of you. I opened the magazine to find an article about one of my favorite American actors, Kevin Spacey. He had just moved to London and happened to be a two-time Oscar winner.

In my time as a film critic, I met over 500 celebrities and viewed countless films, but had never met Kevin Spacey. My sister and I were great fans of his work and had always said we'd love to meet him, but alas, it hadn't happened. So you can imagine my shock to hear The Lord tell me, as I read the article on the plane, that I was going to meet him very soon. It made me giggle and I leaned over and told Elaine what I'd heard. She said she was in agreement with me. I wondered how The Lord was going to make that happen.

About a year before I took that trip to Scotland with Elaine, I'd been invited with some friends to go and hear a Gospel singer in the town where I was living in England. I had not met her before but was blessed by the obvious anointing of her voice and felt that I was supposed to give her a word from The Lord after the concert.

The singer's name was African; she was called Edrey. My friends took me backstage and I introduced myself to her and shared that I was a minister with a word from The Lord for her about her gift. As I spoke the word of The Lord over her, she began to cry. She was very touched and I handed her a piece of paper with my name, date, and the word on it. I also gave her my card.

Edrey and I stayed in touch after that. She told me the word really spoke to her huge, life-long dream of being a professional performer on the world stage. It seemed crazy to her because although she was a born-again Christian, her parents had not believed in her dream and encouraged her to become an accountant for England's Home Office. She was basically a government accountant who sang as a hobby.

Once I got to know her and heard her heart's cry, I asked her if she'd be interested in doing my vision seminar, The X-treme Dream. She said she really wanted to explore the possibility of God's plan for her creative gifts. As a result, she registered for a course I was doing in southern England for 130 people one Saturday in a church building. It was very clear that Edrey really wanted to pursue a professional singing career. So I encouraged her to audition for some West End shows and asked her to consider taking some acting lessons. She knew nothing about acting but did as I advised, and before you know it, she was auditioning for West End shows!

In a very short amount of time, Edrey got one of the lead roles in the smash-hit West End show, *The Lion King!* My friends and I were not in the least bit shocked. All of us were so elated for her and rejoiced with her over what The Lord had done in hardly any time at all.

Edrey began to sing all over the world and with many luminaries in the UK who also recognized her great gifts. Needless to say, she kissed her accounting job at the Home Office good-bye. By the time Elaine and I went to Scotland, Edrey was singing away professionally all over the place.

After the trip, I got a phone call from Edrey saying that she wanted to know if I'd be interested in going to a West End show with her for my birthday, which happened to be later that week. Elaine and I got home on the Sunday and Edrey wondered if I would like to come and do a matinee show on the following Wednesday. I said I'd love to do it!

I never turn down an opportunity to pay my respects to the arts. My mother had raised my sister and I to thoroughly enjoy music, plays, literature, film, and television. Many of my friends enjoy the arts as much as me. And what a thrill it was to have one of my great traveling companions, Cinzia, a 'filly' from Philly, along for the trip up to London to celebrate my birthday that year and see the show with Edrey and me.

We met Edrey at The Old Vic Theatre, and the marquis said that we were going to be seeing Richard III starring, yep, you- guessed it---Kevin Spacey! Cinzia and I were so excited. I could hardly wait for the lights to go down and for the show to begin. It was everything and more than we thought it would be. Kevin's performance was stellar. It was amazing!

Unbeknownst to me, Edrey had sent Kevin a note and asked him to say hello to me between shows. So we went to the side door and there he was. For once in my life, I was utterly speechless! I, who had interviewed hundreds of Hollywood's best and brightest stars, couldn't speak for the life of me! I had just told Elaine that God told me I'd be meeting Kevin Spacey and there I was—only three days later—doing just that!

How did Kevin respond to my speechless behavior? He was a prince. He held my hand and said, 'Just take your time, sweetheart.' Inside, I was kicking myself, and finally was able to release my tongue from the roof of my mouth by saying that my sister and I knew his business manager in New York. We chatted quite easily about her and his performance. Phew! That was a close one. I almost missed my chance to say what I had always wanted to say to him. Before we left him, he graciously signed our programs from the show.

Edrey and Cinzia were laughing their heads off at me. And all I could say to Edrey was thank you and also what God had said to me just three days before the show. I also told her that there was a 'dream board' in my office with a phrase about Kevin Spacey on it, reminding me daily that I wanted to meet him and that it was on my life's 'bucket list'.

This story is yet another proof that God gives His children kisses for absolutely nothing—just because. He is so kind. It pleases Him to make our dreams come true in the most incredible ways.

I got on a plane to hear The Lord say that He was going to fulfill yet another dream of mine, but I boarded a train to get to London to actually see that dream fulfilled.

At the beginning of Section 2 in this book, there is a quote from Zig Ziglar that says, *You can have anything you want in life if you just help enough other people get what they want.'* This is such a true saying. In other words, you cannot out-give God. The more we give to others, the more we'll get in return. This is what God says about all of this:

"Do not be deceived: God cannot be mocked. A man reaps what he sows. The one who sows to please his sinful nature, from that nature will reap destruction; the one who sows to please the Spirit, from the Spirit will reap eternal life. Let us not become weary in doing good, for at the proper time we will reap a harvest if we do not give up. Therefore, as we have opportunity, let us do good to all people, especially those who belong to the family of believers."

Galatians 6:7-10

Caring Cabbies

In Section 1 of this book I shared several testimonies of moments when I didn't have to pay for meals or cab fare. I'd like to share some more stories with you on that subject. This time it's about two cabbies. One is Christian and the other is not.

Since my sister and I were children, we have always had a heart for people who worked in the service industries. That burden in my heart for them has never left. I sense the Lord's love for those who have the most thankless jobs on the planet. That compassion for these people comes back to me in ways that always astound me.

When I first settled down in the UK, I lived in Horsham in the county of West Sussex. I had many friends there and it was quite convenient for me to get in and out of London, where I often was invited to preach and teach, by train.

In those days I didn't have a car, so I went everywhere by train, plane, and rides from friends who were available to drive me here and there. Whenever I took the train, I had to catch a cab to and from the station. I used cabs so much that all of the cabbies in Horsham who worked for the cab company I used knew me by name. I stood out like a sore thumb as the only Black American in Horsham. They all knew I was a Christian and often asked my opinion on various subjects and current events. Needless to say, there was never a dull moment on those trips to and from the station, whether the driver was Hindu, Muslim, or Christian.

While I lived in Horsham, many visitors from all over the world came to see me for prayer or ministry of some sort. Horsham's proximity to London and Gatwick Airport made it easy for people to get to me by train. The cab drivers got my address given to them so many times that they began to call my house Jesus' House!

One cabbie in particular was a Christian called Chris. He was a precious brother in The Lord and we always talked about what was happening at his church and in his life. He even invited me to visit his church and meet his friends and his priest. It was a rare day when Chris would accept cab fare from me. He almost always told me to just get out of his cab when we reached the destination I needed to be dropped off at. This cabbie also sowed into my ministry. What a blessing he was to me during my years in Horsham!

The flip side to the story is that on one trip to London, I took the train from Horsham to London and had to catch a cab to meet a friend at the famous Savoy Hotel in the Strand. The drive from London Victoria to the hotel was very pleasant because of all that the cabbie and I discussed on the way to the hotel. He asked me all sorts of questions about my work and what I believed about God. I was amazed at how much he packed into that 15 minute trip! It seemed like we had the entire world sorted out in that amount of time.

When I got to the hotel and the doorman opened the cab door for me, I reached into my handbag to give the driver some cash for my lift. Guess what? He refused me just like Chris almost always did in Horsham! When I asked him why he did that, he simply said that his drive with me was the 'best fare he'd had all year!' He went on to say that he felt like giving the real Jesus a try for the first time in his life. He thanked me for sharing all that I did and I thanked him for his kindness and blessed him as he pulled away from the hotel's circle drive. The doorman shook his head in amazement at the conversation he'd heard between me and the cabbie.

This testimony shows us the power and the value of 'the word of our testimony'. The name of Jesus is so powerful!

"Therefore God exalted Him to the highest place and gave Him the name that is above every name, that at the name of Jesus every knee should bow, in heaven and on earth and under the earth, and every tongue confess that Jesus Christ is Lord, to the glory of God the Father."

Philippians 2:9-11

"And whatever you do, whether in word or deed, do it all in the name of The Lord Jesus, giving thanks to God the Father through Him."

Colossians 3:17

Pennies From Heaven

There are so many cab driver stories for me to share that it was really hard trying to figure out which ones to share and which ones to hold. Here is one more for you to consider. This happened when I was living in Horsham. There are so many things that spun off from this story as a result of the miracle that God pulled off on this particular day.

It was a normal day when I got up that morning in Horsham. I had my quiet time with The Lord and got dressed and ready for what was in my book to do that day. As soon as I got dressed and ready for the day, I got an urgent call from someone I had led to The Lord that was going to be admitted into a rehab center for addictive behavior. They had previously asked me to come and pray with them before they were driven to the special facility, where they would be for a long time. I needed to go before it was time for this person to be admitted.

I said I was on my way and immediately called my trusty cab company to come to the rescue and take me to the person in need. The cab company would be with me in a matter of minutes. As soon as I saw the cab in my driveway, I put my shoes on and grabbed my handbag and Bible, ready to go.

Then I realized that I didn't have any cash on me to give the cabbie! I had promised to pray with this person and hadn't been to the bank to get any cash. Oh dear. I needed The Lord to listen to my quickie prayer post-haste.

Right at the moment that I shot that arrow prayer to God's ear, I looked out the window and saw a blue car stop in the middle of my driveway and a Caucasian woman get out of the car. She ran to my front door and knocked on it. I opened the door, and before I could say anything, she put 40 pounds cash into my hands and said this: 'Can't talk now. I gotta go.' Then she ran down the driveway, hopped into her car, and drove off just as the cab I'd called turned into my driveway!

I grabbed my handbag and hopped into the cab with the biggest grin on my face that the cabbie, who knew me, had ever seen. The Muslim cabbie said, 'Why are you grinning?'

I told him that God had performed an instant miracle so that I would have the 'dosh' to pay him the fare for this journey. He wanted to hear what happened as he pulled out of my driveway. He shook his head, saying to me, 'Your God always does such amazing things for you!' I agreed with him.

It was like the money just fell out of the skies and into my open, needy hands! I couldn't stop laughing as I got out of the cab and paid the cabbie with the money God had just provided. This is but one of the reasons why God is called *Jehovah Jireh* or *God Our Provider* (See Genesis 22:14).

The person who received prayer from me that day was so grateful for the ministry that was provided that they later blessed me by *providing* private medical attention for me that I desperately needed in order to unravel something that had been troubling me for years. The person paid for my care and that led to my being looked after by a nationally-known surgeon, who ended up successfully bringing me out of a life-threatening surgery that makes me a walking miracle today. Ministering to *one* person by the hand of my audience of *One*, the Living God, brought health and healing to my body and to the person I prayed with that day!

Did the person recover through their rehab experience? Yes! They are living a very blessed life today. God turned their entire situation around through a series of events that I witnessed.

If we will do what is uppermost on God's mind and heart in a situation, He will most assuredly look after our every need. He always keeps His word to us and it is so important that we keep our word to Him and those we make promises to. God is concerned about the character we exhibit to others because it reflects Him or our lack of Him in our lives.

"But seek first His kingdom and His righteousness, and all these things will be given to you as well."

Matthew 6:33

Emergency Prophecy

Is it possible to hear the voice of The Lord for someone on the spur of the moment? Absolutely! God knows everything that is happening in our lives before it happens because He is the Alpha and the Omega. He sees the end from the beginning of any and every thing that can happen to us. In other words, *nothing* surprises Him. In fact, I think God likes to see what we'll do in crisis because we are typically out of our comfort zones and so in need of a Savior that we just have to fall into His arms and trust Him for His help.

One day, my colleague, Lesley, and I were invited to go and pray with a leader in London at her home. We set out after rush hour and arrived without incident to pray for the ministry that this dear woman led. When we arrived, we noticed that her assistant was not there. We assumed that she was running late and we didn't think too much about it. But as time marched on, we could see that our hostess was beginning to wonder if things were okay with her missing assistant.

As we waited patiently, sipping our teas and coffees with the others who had assembled for prayer, our hostess received an urgent phone call from her assistant, Camille. She had called her boss, weeping into the phone with her crying infant on her hip. It seemed that a real mess was unfolding, but she was coming, though what state she'd be in once she arrived, we didn't know. We all began to pray for her. Lesley and I shot an arrow prayer up to the Holy Spirit and asked Him if He wanted us to be ready to pour out a prophetic blessing on Camille when she arrived. We waited on that familiar still, small voice of The Lord and wrote down a few things that He dropped into our spirits. We didn't say a word to each other about what The Lord was speaking to us.

In a few minutes, Camille and her infant son arrived. Tears were streaming down both of their faces. Someone got Camille a calming, hot drink and someone else held the baby for her as she told us about her awful morning commute.

She had woken up knowing that she and the baby were coming to her boss's house for prayer. On the way to the train, she was going to go to a cash point and get some cash for their journey and some baby supplies that she needed. Everything was fine until she got to the cashpoint. When she put her card in to get some cash, the card was declined with a note saying that there was nothing in her account!!

Apparently, this had happened to her before and she couldn't take it another time. She just fell apart. Camille revealed to us that she was married to a gambling addict. She was hurt, ashamed, and exhausted. Because this stressed her out, the baby was stressed. We all knew that only Jesus could sort out what was crooked and make it smooth.

So we all gathered around her and began to pray for God's peace to come to her and the baby. Soon the baby was calming down and Camille was able to just 'be' and receive some much needed ministry. With the other people in the room praying quietly, I began to share with Camille what The Lord had dropped into my spirit for her.

This is what I saw: I saw a picture of a large industrial-sized kitchen with a big stove that had a pot on every burner. They were boiling over and the pressure cooker pots that were about to explode. There was a man in the midst of it all in full chef's attire trying his best to manage all of the boiling pots. It was hard for me to watch because it looked like someone in a magic show trying to juggle china plates on sticks. I had a feeling that something very bad was about to happen. Soon, all of the pots exploded! It sounded like several guns firing within seconds of each other. The chef had all kinds of food splattered all over his once-clean uniform. There was food dripping down the walls and ceiling and pooled all over the floor. The chef was crying in a heap on the floor.

The next thing I saw was that the swinging door to the kitchen opened and a huge Master Chef walked in. He surveyed the huge mess and the assistant chef sitting on the floor, who looked at him with shame and disgrace. He was clearly afraid of what the Master Chef would do. Unlike what the celebrity chefs on TV would say or do, this Master Chef came in and cleaned up the entire mess! When He was done with that, He sat down with the assistant chef in the middle of the floor and lovingly cleaned him up, too! Then He held the assistant chef in His big, strong arms and told him that He had a plan for how to get him out of this mess he was in.

Then The Lord gave me the interpretation to the picture. He told me that the man in the picture I'd seen was Camille's husband. I told this to Camille and she was crying and smiling at me, all at once.

When she calmed down enough to speak, she told me that the man in the picture I'd received from the Holy Spirit was absolutely her husband. She knew it was him because her husband was a sous chef in real life!!! She couldn't stop smiling. In that moment, it became clear to her that The Lord of Lords could see her and was intimately aware of all of her woes.

Camille also told all of us that her husband was a gambling addict and that she had no money to her name and had been in that spot so many times before that she was flat-out discouraged. That is why she had come in so upset; she didn't know what to do.

We then prayed for her and explained how I'd received the picture from the Holy Spirit for her desperate situation. I wrote it all out for her and encouraged her to share it with her non-Christian husband. She did that night, and today he is now a believer who has been able to get help for his addictive behavior. They are still married and their son is in school now. The Master Chef in the picture came to this couple's rescue and really and truly saved them all. The Master Chef is none other than King Jesus. His name means 'salvation'. We are all mightily blessed because of all He has done for us. There is absolutely *nothing* too difficult for Him! The more desperate the situation, the more we need a Savior!

"The Lord your God is with you, He is mighty to save. He will take great delight in you, He will quiet you with His love, He will rejoice over you with singing."

Zephaniah 3:17

Word For A Waitress

One of the most beautiful things about the Holy Spirit is how spontaneous He is. His ability to move in a person's life is not contingent on us. He knows *everything about everyone in the whole world.* He is big enough to cover the questions of all seven billion plus people on the planet, and He is also sensitive enough to cater to each person, no matter how old or what color they are. The Holy Spirit is the wisest Teacher that you and I could ever have. All we have to be is willing to hear and obey what He whispers into our ears. Then it is up to us to step forward and speak forth what He reveals to us.

The previous testimony proves that the Spirit of God can speak to us in the middle of someone's crisis. This next story shows that we can hear at someone else's prompting—even in a popular restaurant at lunch time.

I live in a lovely fishing village called Selsey, which is located eight miles from the market city of Chichester in the county of West Sussex. I am a 90 minute train ride from London. My town is right on the water and I love living there. The people of Selsey are precious to me and even more so to The Lord.

In the high street, or main street, of the town, there is a popular restaurant called The Riviera, or The Rivvy, as it is affectionately called by the locals. It is styled to look like an American diner from the 1950's. It has big sky-blue and white booths and tables and chairs to match. On the walls there are black and white photos of famous American and British film and music stars. The food is great and they serve plenty of it! The music they play is reminiscent of yesteryear. It is definitely one of my 'happy places'.

I go in at least once a week and have gone more than usual for the completion of this book. It has been a great place for me to focus on the business of writing. I know most of the waitresses by name and credit them with helping to keep me on task for this book you are now reading.

My colleague, Lesley, and I often go there to catch up and share with each other what The Lord is doing in our lives. One particular day in the afternoon, around lunch time, one of my favorite waitresses, Ivy, was running around as usual, looking like she had roller skates on because she was moving so fast. Her arms were laden with three different entrees as she whizzed by us.

The next time she came by with about the same amount of orders to deliver to her tables, she stopped for a second and said: 'Go on, then!' looking right at me.

I stopped talking to Lesley and asked what she meant by her statement. She told me that she wanted me to go ahead and give her a reading. Instantly, I realized that she was referring to me because she knew that I lead a prophetic school, and in her understanding, we are psychics who give out readings!

I told her I understood what she meant and that I don't give readings, but information the Bible calls prophecy. She said she would deliver the food she was carrying and she'd come back to get her prophetic word.

Sure enough, she delivered the food to her tables and came back to our table like a shot. In just about a minute or two, the Holy Spirit dropped into my spirit a picture for Ivy. I saw a myriad of wheels turning and twisting in her brunette head. They never stopped. I went on to say that the wheels were a picture depicting her frustration with her life at that time. She was antsy for change and wondering about many things regarding her purpose in life. I told her there was more to her gifts and talents than what we all saw her doing every day in The Rivvy.

She pondered what I said for a hot moment, looking up at the ceiling, and then said, 'Yeah, that's right.' She then whizzed off to pick up the next order and later came back to tell me that she was wondering if she should leave her job and do something else or stay. The picture showed that God above sees her and is intimately acquainted with her, whether she knows Him or not.

Scripture says that a day is coming when we will see God as He really is although He fully knows each of us. Right now, we only see a part of Him.

"Now we see but a poor reflection as in a mirror; then we shall see face to face. Now I know in part; then I shall know fully, even as I am fully known (by God)."

1 Corinthians 13:12

In our Led By The Spirit School of Prophecy, we call short, sweet words, like what I gave to Ivy, 'popcorn words of prophecy', because they come out fast, short and sweet. Prophetic words can be long and detailed or short and to the point. The Holy Spirit knows what is needed for every situation. All I have to do is be a clean, willing vessel with a renewed mind ready to serve when squeezed into service for whomever The Lord puts in front of me. It really is a lot of fun! Doing this has the ability to change the view that people have of a God Who is far away or doesn't care about them.

To Be Or Not To Be?

One thing that really stirs up my righteous anger toward the enemy is the amount of people who listen to him and take their lives each year through suicide around the world. Something that has caught my attention since I came to live in the UK is the amount of people who commit suicide by jumping in front of a moving train.

UK statistics show that 238 people took their lives in this way in the last 12 months (2012-2013)[1]. That is 238 too many in God's book.

While I have never worked on a suicide helpline, I have talked someone out of committing suicide while I was a resident advisor at Oral Roberts University. The young woman I spoke to that dark night is now a Ph.D. teaching at a prominent east coast university in America. When in crisis, we must always call upon the wisdom of the Holy Spirit. He can see everything from every angle. The Lord has taught me so much about crisis situations and I am so grateful to Him!

About five years ago, I was standing on the train platform in the town of Horsham, West Sussex, waiting for the train to London's Victoria Station. As I stood there, a kind, elderly gentleman began to speak to me and his face lit up when he discovered I was American. He asked if I'd like to sit with him on our journey to London. I said that I most certainly would.

The train arrived and we boarded a coach that had a nice empty window seat for both of us. He set his cane and hat on the seat next to him. I sat opposite him and settled in for the 45-minute journey. As the train lurched forward, I asked him what he was most passionate about. His face lit up again as he told me about his passion for cricket and how he and his girlfriend have traveled all over the world following the sport. Once he was finished sharing about cricket and answering all of my questions about it, he then asked me what my passion in life was.

I began to share with him my testimony about knowing Jesus and the call on my life to come and be a teaching missionary based in the UK but with a global calling to any nation The Lord led me to go to in His name. He was enthralled with the many stories I shared with him from near and far away.

We were in a fairly empty train car and had not noticed that a young woman had gotten onto our coach in Horsham. We were so engrossed in our discussion.

About 15 minutes into my chat about my life and calling, the young woman across the aisle and one seat behind us came running over to our seats! She plopped down right next to the elderly gent and said in a very excited tone of voice, 'I want what you have got!'

---

[1] https://www.theguardian.com/news/datablog/2013/sep/11/uk-rail-suicides-decade-data

She was looking directly at me. This turn of events intrigued the elderly gent, who by this time had grabbed his cane and was now leaning on it with a twinkle in his eye, wondering, no doubt, what I was going to say to this young woman.

I asked her what her name was and she told me that she was called Nadia. We introduced ourselves and I asked her how I could help. She wasted no time telling me that she had gotten on the train with the thought to throw herself in front of the train sometime before the train arrived at Victoria! That saddened me, but I knew that it was now time for Jesus to come in like only He can to save the day.

She went on to say that all that I'd told the old gent made her thirst for what I had in my life—or should we say Who I have in my life. I told her that it would only take a moment to bring her into the knowledge of what life in Jesus is like. She pumped me with questions that I answered as the train sped its way to London Victoria. We made a plan to meet at Starbucks later. She said she needed to ponder all that had been said to her on the train. I agreed to her request to meet her later at Starbucks.

Meanwhile, the old gent got off the train, kissed me on both cheeks and said what a delightful time he'd had on the train journey. He hoped that we'd meet again and then he hugged me and we parted ways.

As I walked to catch a cab to my appointment that day, I prayed in tongues for both of the folks I'd met on the train that day. Especially Nadia who decided not to take her life. I prayed that the enemy would not snatch her life in the interim time there was before we agreed to meet up at Starbucks.

We had set a time to meet and Nadia did show up. I was so relieved to see her walk through that door! The Lord had kept her safe from harm and she was bouncing when she walked over to my table and sat down. She decided that she *did* want to meet Jesus and asked me to please introduce her to Him. What a thrill it was to snatch yet another soul away from the evil clutches of the enemy! We cried together and I hugged her for making that decision. Then I led her to Jesus in a corner of Starbucks. Her life has been changed forever. Hallelujah!

Where is she now? She lives in South Africa and we often get the chance to speak to each other via that wonderful invention called Skype. God is *so* good and kind and faithful to us! He really is the best traveling Companion that ever lived! He is The Living Word and He is always near us:

"But what does it say? 'The Word is near you; it is in your mouth and in your heart,' that is, the word of faith we are proclaiming: That if you confess with your mouth, 'Jesus Is Lord,' and believe in your heart that God raised Him from the dead, you will be saved. Everyone who calls on the name of The Lord will be saved."
Romans 10:8-10, 13

God has given us the freedom to choose life or death. The benefits of choosing life are truly out of this world! This is His promise to us:

"This day I call heaven and earth as witnesses against you that I have set before you life and death, blessings and curses. Now choose life, so that you and your children may live and that you may love The Lord God, listen to His voice, and hold fast to Him. For The Lord is your life, and He will give you many years in the land He swore to give to your fathers, Abraham, Isaac and Jacob."

Deuteronomy 30:19-20.

Each human being has the propensity to give birth to generations of other human beings. The enemy is against us fulfilling God's call to multiply and have dominion over the earth and all that is in it (See Genesis 1:27-28). He despises the thought of God's chief creation ruling and reigning with God forever. That is, in fact, God's plan for all of us who know Him as Lord and King.

I cannot stand the thought of human beings, so full of promise and God's dreams for their lives, taking their own lives without even knowing the truth of the God Who created them! Any time I can be used of The Lord to save a life for eternity, I will be honored to do so for the glory of His name. It has been such a pleasure to see the wonder-working hand of God guide me in the 'rescues' I have retold here. I believe wholeheartedly that life is worth nothing without Jesus!

Dreams Really Do Come True

There's an excellent story in Genesis about a young man named Joseph. He was a big dreamer and the most favored son of his father, Jacob (See Genesis 37: 1-10). Dreams are just one of several ways Scripture tells us God is able to speak to us.

In the early years that I was coming and going from the UK, working toward a more permanent residency here, I met a single mother with one son. The mother's name was Gwendolyn. Gwendolyn met me after hearing me speak in her parish church one Sunday morning. She offered me an invitation to come and have a meal with her and her son, Mitchell.

We set a date for me to come and have dinner. Gwendolyn picked me up from the priest's home where I was staying and told me that her 12 year old son, Mitchell, would be at home before us. He was in school at a boarding school nearby and would take a bus home.

Soon, we pulled up in front of their house and the door opened. There I saw a handsome, dark-haired, blue-eyed boy who looked like he'd just seen a ghost! Gwendolyn had just introduced me to Mitchell and the boy had said nothing but just stared at me with eyes wide open and as big as saucers. Needless to say, Gwendolyn was mortified at his bad manners and immediately began to scold him for not greeting me properly.

I had been a nanny, mainly to boys, in the States and in the UK. Children have always been a favorite of mine and I would say that I have a sort of gift from God with troubled children, especially boys. The response I was getting from Mitchell seemed odd, to say the least. I wondered if I was the first black person he'd seen up close. I was not offended at all, but just wanted to know why he couldn't speak.

Gwendolyn took my coat and said that she was going into the kitchen to check our dinner. I sat down in the lounge with Mitchell. I quietly asked him what was going on.

Mitchell came over to me, and in a whisper, said, 'I saw you two weeks ago in my dreams!!'

'Oh, boy', I thought. That explained it all. Mitchell had a prophetic dream that had actually *come true!* I asked him if he'd told his mother about the dream when he'd had it and he told me that he hadn't because they didn't know any black people. When I walked through the door, the dream came tumbling back to his memory and he just couldn't believe what had happened.

I told him that it would take the heat off of him if he told his mother what he'd just told me. I told him that what happened to him had happened to a young man in the Bible, so he was definitely in good company.

I explained that God sometimes chooses to speak to us in dreams. When Mitchell asked why, I told him that when we are sleeping is one of the times when we are most still in our whole lives. God doesn't get interruptions from us when we are asleep. Mitchell was quite perceptive and very excited about the whole thing. He had a huge grin from ear to ear as he told his mother about his first prophetic dream. From that night onwards, I knew that Mitchell and I would be good friends. As time wore on, we discovered that God had given Mitchell a prophetic gift of perception about supernatural things.

God says a lot in His Word about dreams. Dreams happen when our body is asleep but our soulish realm or mind, will, and emotions are awake. Our dreams are about the supernatural realm and give us messages about God's plans and purposes for us and others, too. They must be weighed and tested with mature believers so that we can know if they are truly wisdom from God or just a bad piece of pizza we ate the night before.

"I slept but my heart was awake."

Song of Songs 5:2a

"He (Jacob) had a dream in which he saw a stairway resting on the earth, with its top reaching to heaven, and the angels of God were ascending and descending on it. There above it stood The Lord and He said: 'I am The Lord, the God of your father Abraham and the God of Isaac. I am with you and will watch over you wherever you go, and I will bring you back to this land. I will not leave you until I have done what I have promised you.'"

Genesis 28:12-13,15

It was one of those moments where a child had something very significant to say. It also confirmed for me that I was right smack dab in the middle of where The Lord wanted me to be at that moment in my life. He used a child to let me know that. How comforting it was to me and this dear mother and son! I encourage you, dear Reader, to consider the dreams you may have had in your life. Ask The Lord what He may want to share with you through the messages they carry. Remember that it is never about the age of the receiver, but the content of the dream. Be sure to write *everything* down from your dreams and record them in a journal. Our God is a God of specific intent. God is definitely in the details. In the days ahead, your recorded dreams will become a real treasure to you and those they are shared with. You may just be in line to get blessed beyond measure!

Children of Light

When you come into the family of God, you become the holder of many different titles that can be found in the Word of God. One of the names of God that really fascinates me is The Father of Lights. Because God has this title, we become His children of light.

"Every good and perfect gift is from above, coming down from the Father of the Heavenly Lights, who does not change like shifting shadows."

James 1:17

"You are all sons of the light and sons of the day. We do not belong to the night or to the darkness."

1 Thessalonians 5:5

"But we all, with unveiled faces, beholding in a mirror the glory of the Lord, are being transformed into the same image from glory to glory, just as by the Spirit of the Lord."

2 Corinthians 3:18

We can know something is true in the Word of God, but does it transfer from the supernatural into our real life? Have you ever wondered about these Biblical truths and if they are visible or invisible in real life? The telling of my next adventure will let you decide.

My ministry teammates and I have had many invitations to minister in the great City of London and its many boroughs. On one occasion, we were invited to teach our school of prophecy on the outskirts of London. We had made good time and were early. So

Lesley decided to pull our van over and let us all out to stretch our legs and get a snack and something to drink. In the van were myself, Lesley, our able driver, her son Graham, and a friend named Vera.

Lesley decided to stay put in the van and asked me to get her a latte, her hot drink of choice. Three of us went into the Esso On The Run convenience store at the petrol station. We found something that tempted us, ordered our drinks, paid for it all and went back out to the van. We would eat there and then go on to our class in Crystal Palace.

We had just been back in the van for about two minutes when the young Hindu man behind the till who had rung us up came running out of the store, screaming about a white light he saw on us! He kept on screaming about the light and pointing at us. Everyone in the van was speechless. Lesley stopped mid-slurp on her latte, shocked at what this guy was saying. No one said a word.

Suddenly the Holy Spirit told me to get out of the van. By this time, everyone who was filling their cars with gasoline was looking at us and wondering what the commotion was all about. I bet they thought we'd taken something without paying for it!

As I stood beside the van, waiting for the Spirit to tell me what to do, the Hindu man was now kneeling on the ground, shaking. He seemed to be bowing before me and I instantly thought of how Paul and Barnabas must have felt in Acts 14 when they had to tell the people of Lystra not to worship them after someone they prayed for was healed.

I asked the young man what his name was. He told me it was Darren. I begged him to please get up off the ground. He kept saying that the light he saw around us was too bright for him to look at us. I asked him if he would like to meet the Source of the Light he was seeing. He said that he would. I then shared the Gospel with him and he got saved—right there near the gas pumps!

He wanted to know why the light was on us. I told him that when you spend time with Jesus, the light He carries comes off on His followers. That is exactly what happened to Moses on the mountain of God. When he came down off of the mountain, he had to wear a veil over his face because it glowed so brightly before the people.

As we chatted, we found out that Darren was planning to finish work that day at the gas station and then go and kill himself. He was a gambling addict and he had no money left for him and his wife to live on. His wife was a Buddhist and they had no children. He felt his life was over until he met Jesus. His plans were seriously interrupted that night!

Darren wanted to know where we were going that night. I told him that I was a teaching missionary for a school of prophecy. He said he wanted us to stop and pray with him each Wednesday night at that station! He walked away floating that night and had no desire to kill himself.

After that, every Wednesday night that we drove to London for class, we stopped at the Esso Station to encourage Darren in his faith. He found a good Indian-Christian, on-fire church, and he began to invite all of his non-Christian Asian friends to meet with us in the gas station each week! We were having church in the convenience store each time. It was absolutely incredible what God did in the gas station. Darren's Buddhist wife even got saved during that time.

Within a year of Darren coming to The Lord, his wife became pregnant and she gave birth to a little baby boy that they decided to name Jeshurun. That Old Testament name is a name of endearment for Jerusalem. Now Darren is a prophetic voice who regularly preaches in his church. He has a strong anointing and often prophesies words of knowledge to me over the phone that are extremely specific about things that are actually happening in my life! What a precious brother in The Lord he has become. There really are *no* strangers to those who know The Lord, only people who have not been properly introduced!

Perception Runs In The Family

In my experience as a prophetic school teacher and prophetic voice, I have seen God do many amazing things in families. I often share with my students that the perceptive or prophetic ability is part of a person's 'spiritual DNA'. By the physical DNA in my parents, I am part Black, Native-American, and Scottish. They are physical traits that I carry. Spiritual DNA works in the same way. My colleagues in the prophetic realm and I have witnessed this fact to be true and will tell you that when a person is prophetic or able to hear God's voice as a lifestyle, the likelihood of other members of the same family having the same ability are extremely high.

In the Word of God, we can see that Jacob was a dreamer (Genesis 28:12-15). He was also the father of another famous dreamer, Joseph. That is an Old Testament proof of spiritual DNA. We are told that Philip the Evangelist had not one but four unmarried daughters who all prophesied in Caesarea (Acts 21:9). On the UK prophetic team that I lead, we have had several instances of this occurring. It is really fun to witness how God moves uniquely amongst members of the same family! My next adventure shows how God uses the same perception gift in a family I didn't know, all in one day.

On one of my road trips with my team, I'd been invited to minister on a Sunday morning in a Baptist church. It was a full house that day, and while I could sense the Presence of God in that place, I had no idea how His Presence was affecting those who were seated in front of me!

I did an altar call for prayer and many people came forward from all walks of life and every age group imaginable. In moments like that, I do my best to follow the Holy Spirit's lead in how He'd like me to minister to each person that comes forward. This morning was no different.

An older woman came forward named Angelica. She asked me to pray for her granddaughter who was autistic. I prayed for the grandchild and Angelica told me that the child herself had asked to come forward for prayer! Angelica told me that this was very unusual for her grandchild to be so drawn to a total stranger in this way. She then went on to say that she wondered if her grandchild could see 'the bright, white light' that was emanating from me! I asked Angelica if she could still see the light and she said yes.

I wondered what else The Lord had up His sleeve as I continued to pray for those who answered the call. I kept praying for folks and some were so overcome by the power of the Holy Spirit that was in that place that they ended up on the floor. I kept praying for people. One lady came forward called Finola. She asked for general prayer and then asked me if I was aware of 'the bright, white light' that followed me as I was preaching. I asked her to tell me exactly what she saw and she said that the light followed me as I moved back and forth on the platform. I told her that we were all experiencing the evidence of God's Presence that day, His shekinah glory in Hebrew.

Then, a few moments later, someone younger than Finola said the same thing. Later, I heard from the pastor that the folks who had spoken to me about seeing 'the light' were all in the same family! I have a real heart for prisoners and seeing anyone behind bars find freedom in Jesus. Apparently each of them had served time in prison and now they were free—really *free*! There is nothing like the freedom the Spirit of The Lord brings!

"Now The Lord is The Spirit, and where the Spirit of The Lord is, there is freedom. And we, who with unveiled faces all reflect the Lord's glory, are being transformed into His likeness with ever-increasing glory, which comes from The Lord, Who is the Spirit."

2 Corinthians 3:17-18

Wonders in Waitrose

We really are God's children of Light! His Presence goes wherever we go, no matter how mundane. In the days that we are living in, The Lord wants His Presence to be known to all of creation.

Case in point—there is a luxury grocery store chain called Waitrose in the United Kingdom. Everything they do tastes extra special and I really enjoy their in-house brand of yogurt. While I may not do all of my shopping there, occasionally if we are in the area, Lesley and I will drop by just to get a few yogurts for a breakfast treat.

On one of these special occasions, we were at the checkout line in Waitrose, bagging my yogurt. The elderly lady who was slowly putting her things into her cart before us took her time, and when she turned around to leave, she stopped in her tracks and said to me, 'What's that white light on you?' Oh dear, I thought. Here we go again, Lord. I was used to this happening by that time, but it is really wild when you are a Black person and people who are Caucasian don't see anything but God's white light on you!!

I heard Lesley say, 'Oh, oh, it's happening again.' I turned to this dear lady who looked bewildered and I told her that I was a Christian minister and that the glow she was seeing is what happens when Christians encounter the Presence of God on a routine basis. She just said, 'Is that what that is?' I assured her that it was normal for God's children to experience things like that. She seemed satisfied with the answers she received and pushed her cart out of the store.

We giggled all the way to the ministry van because once again The Lord had shown up in His glory. That lady got more than she bargained for that day—the glory of God in checkout lane two!

"Then your light will break forth like the dawn, and your healing will quickly appear; then your righteousness will go before you, and the glory of The Lord will be your rear guard".

Isaiah 58:8

The Light of Prophecy

If you are like me, you may have wondered how prophetic people know when or how God shows them who to prophesy over or 'call out' in a meeting. Some prophets will tell you they had a prompting from the Holy Spirit about who to call out and prophesy over. A Seer prophet will tell you that they 'saw' with their spiritual sight the person or persons that God wanted them to prophesy over *before* meeting them. They receive information from the Spirit differently than a prophet. They actually see who they are to speak to on the Spirit's behalf.

A few years ago, a few of my teammates and I took a road trip to go and hear two internationally-known prophetic voices to our generation: Paul Keith Davis and Marc DuPont. I respect them both and we were so delighted to be able to go and see both men in Exeter, England, for a whole weekend.

At some point in the meeting, Paul Keith Davis called me out. When I went down front to receive what the Spirit was saying, Paul Keith mentioned to me that he'd seen a 'white light' appear over my head. He said that was his sign from the Holy Spirit that he was supposed to call someone out and prophesy over them. That was the first time I'd heard a prophetic voice share something like that. I asked him if he could still see the light on me as we were talking and he said yes.

Looking back on that event, I remember thinking that God's light resting on a person who belongs to Him is a sort of neon sign that says, 'This person is mine and is ripe to receive a word from The Lord.' It is a handprint of God on you and me. God chooses the most incredible ways to connect with us and let us know that we are His—His children of light. He is that crazy over us. Isn't walking with The Supreme Master of the Universe amazing? There is no one like our God. *No one.*

"Moses replied, 'It will be as you say, so that you may know there is no one like The Lord our God.'"

Exodus 8:10

Miracle on the Cricket Pitch

These next few events I'm going to share are all focused on the many and various ways that God chooses to bring healing into my travels away from home. Yes, even on a cricket pitch. (For my American readers, this is a field where people play cricket.)

Where I live on the south coast of England, everything I need is literally a hop, skip and a jump away from me. Selsey used to be an island until they connected it to the mainland of England via a two-lane country road. We are eight miles from the nearest city, so having banks, grocery stores, restaurants, a post office, printers, and other shops within walking distance of my front door is one of the benefits of living near a town high-street. I love it, and I often do some prayer walking and use it as an opportunity to get to know my neighbors.

One day, almost two years ago, I had an appointment at the doctor's office, or surgery as we say in the UK. It's building bordered one side of our town cricket pitch. My house sat on the western border of the pitch. All I had to do was walk across the country lane at my front door and walk across the pitch to go see my doctor. I had finished my appointment and was walking back to my house, crossing the pitch on a warm, sunny day.

Half way across the pitch, I saw an East Indian woman coming toward me, so I greeted her and said, 'Hi, and how are you today?' She stopped and told me that she was in pain and on her way to the doctor's surgery. She told me that she was really suffering with an awful ear ache. I could relate because that used to happen to me quite a bit as a child.

The Holy Spirit prompted me immediately to tell her that I was a Christian minister who liked to pray for the sick and watch God heal them. I asked her if she'd like for me to pray for her. In true Spirit-led fashion, I asked her permission to lay hands on her. That's when she told me that she was not in a church and wanted to be closer to God.

I told her that I'd be happy to pray for her on those issues as well. She happily said, 'Yes, please!' She closed her eyes and I prayed for her issues and asked The Lord to heal her ear ache as I laid my hand on the ear that was hurting her. She opened her eyes after I prayed and was full of joy. Her ear was totally healed and no longer in pain!! She was so excited that she hugged me and said she didn't need to see the doctor.

We continued to chat and praise The Lord on the cricket pitch. Before we parted ways, she and I exchanged names and cell phone numbers. I had a feeling that we would see each other again. Her name was Ava.

What had happened that day made me think of the many encounters in the New Testament where whoever was healed walked away with joy. There truly is nothing like knowing Jesus and being in partnership with Him on a daily basis! Such occurrences cause us to understand what having the 'joy of our salvation' is all about. She went away with a bounce in her step and so did I.

Miracle At The Riviera Diner

In the previous story, I said that I had a feeling that I would see the East Indian woman again. That inner hunch from the Holy Spirit was so right! Within a month of that divine appointment on the cricket pitch, Ava texted me to ask if she could come and see me at my home. I told her I'd be delighted to have her come for a visit.

When she came for that visit, she told me her whole life story and that she was once the wife of the most well-known drug dealer in all of the Caribbean. He was now dead but she told of how horrendous her life with him had been. She had often feared for her life. She had children from that marriage and was now married to another man in the UK. This marriage was troubled too and she wanted to rekindle her relationship with Jesus. That day, we prayed together about all that she had shared. I also gave her some of my preaching CDs and invited her to come to church with me anytime that she wanted to go. Again, she hugged me and thanked me for being so kind to her.

She promised to stay in touch and asked me to come to her house next.

Several weeks passed by and both of us ended up having some serious health issues to sort out. I had major surgery and she was diagnosed with cancer. My surgery went well and I was told that I was a walking miracle. While I was off work for about four months, I made a point to go see her at the boarding house where she and her husband lived.

I was struck by the genuine joy that she truly had, even though her living conditions were very hard. She had to walk everywhere and was often alone for the treatments she had to have at the hospital. Her husband was a bus driver and they were often apart. She kept saying that since meeting me that day in the cricket pitch, she had fallen in love with Jesus all over again. The only thing she cared about was 'her Jesus'.

Whenever we met, we caught up on each other's lives and prayed together. I could see that she was definitely back on track with her personal walk with Jesus.

After I recovered from my time of healing from major surgery, I went back into my normal schedule of full-time ministry. My new friend stayed in touch via text messages and stayed positive in Christ. She was unable to come to church with me because of all the symptoms she was experiencing with her cancer treatments. I just spoke with her on the phone and prayed with and for her continually.

At the beginning of 2014, I began to write this book and often found myself sitting in a private booth at The Riviera diner with my trusty iPad in tow. While I kept in touch with Ava, I had not seen her in several months. It was on one of those writing days at The Riviera when that changed.

It was a busy lunch time at the Rivvy. Most of the booths were full and the wait staff was racing around the booths, delivering lots of great food to a constant stream of hungry patrons. All of the sudden, Ava came around the corner of the diner and saw me. She was so excited to find me! She had never been into the diner and was so glad that she had decided to check it out that day.

As soon as I saw her, I knew that she would want to sit down and chat for a while because we'd not seen each other for a very long time. I cleared my table of all of my notes and reference materials so that she could sit down.

Immediately, we hugged each other and I asked about how she was feeling. Once again, she told me that she was on her way down the high-street to go to the pharmacist to ask for something she could take to relieve her pain.

I found myself dealing with some inner turmoil in my flesh. I wanted to lay hands on her in the diner, yet I was very aware that it was full of people and a place of business. I also was 'on a roll' with my writing and didn't feel I could afford to stop and have a very long chat. My mind was saying one thing and my body something else. Both were vying for my attention and urging me not to minister to Ava. The Holy Spirit's still, small voice won out!

The Spirit urged me to ask Ava, once again, if she would like for me to pray for her pain to go away. I soon found out that she was not just dealing with chemo pain but she also had some dental pain, too. She was in great discomfort and her head was very swollen. I asked the Holy Spirit what to do. He said to ask Ava to lean forward so that I could lay hands on her head and pray so that she could hear me above the diner noise. I always travel with anointing oil for the sick I may encounter on my travels, so I reached into my handbag and put some oil on my right hand and laid hands on her head and prayed.

Once again, The Lord moved! This time Ava jumped right out of that booth praising God! She said that all of her pain was gone and I could visibly see that the swelling had gone down in her face! She was so full of joy. I told her that her faith in the healing power of The Lord causes Him to pour out His healing touch on her in abundance.

She was then able to chat more with me and without pain. When Ava left, I noticed that an hour of time had transpired. The Lord reminded me that He is the Great Redeemer. He can redeem anything! I felt Him encouraging me not to worry about the time. He was more than able to take care of it all. His word says in Matthew 6:33 that if we put His kingdom first, He will take care of everything else, so why do we worry??

As the day wore on, I found myself writing all the way up to the closing time of the diner. That night, the diner closed later than normal because a large family had come in to order dinner and dessert just before the kitchen closed, so they had to stay open longer. That meant that I could stay longer, too. Yes, you guessed it.

The diner stayed open exactly one hour longer than usual! The Lord had redeemed the time for me.

When we choose to obey God's still, small, first voice, *we never lose out!* Obeying God is always better than sacrificing anything on our part. Seeing someone be healed and walk away without excruciating pain is so precious and so worth it all. As I packed up my things to go home that night, I praised The Lord for showing me once again that His ways are so much higher than ours!

Crazy Eights: Part One

One of the things I enjoy about walking in the prophetic realms is that it is so personal to the people that the Holy Spirit wants to minister to. When the Holy Spirit has something to say to us, He will often use specific words, colors, numbers, places, vehicles, etc. People who routinely experience the prophetic in their lives each have their own prophetic language through which the Spirit conveys His messages to an individual. In my life, I have noticed that the number God likes to speak to me through is often the number eight. This has been happening to me ever since I turned eight years of age. Biblically speaking, the number eight means 'new beginning', 'regeneration', or 'resurrection'.

Why does eight mean these things? In Scripture, we find these things associated with the number eight: David was the eighth son of Jesse and ushered in a new beginning for the nation of Israel; circumcision was always done on the eighth day after a baby boy was born and was connected to the concept of a new creation; besides Jesus and the saints, Scripture mentions eight individual resurrections (3 in the Old Testament, 3 in the Gospels, and 2 in Acts). God speaks so clearly to us through His Word, which must always be our plumb line for understanding Him.

Having said that, I want to share with you what happened at a Christmas party I once attended in the House of Lords at Westminster Palace in London. God is so good and kind. He is also full of fun! He loves to bless His children.

On this occasion, I was attending the party with several friends. Everyone was enjoying themselves in the Lord's Dining Room at Parliament and the evening would soon be coming to a close. Earlier that night, the attendees had been encouraged to purchase raffle tickets for a charity. Now it was time to hand out the prizes attached to the tickets. As soon as that was announced, I felt a prompting in my spirit that said I was going to win the grand prize of the evening. I leaned over and said this to my friend, Justin. He just looked at me like I was crazy. There were hundreds of people in the room and he had a hard time believing I was going to win the big prize.

What Justin didn't know was that I had been given a green raffle ticket with the number 8 on it. My ears are always pierced to hear from The Lord when I see the number 8 appear in my life.

As the secretary for the host of the evening stood on the podium to announce the winning numbers, several people came forward to collect their prizes, which were all sealed in unmarked envelopes to choose from. Soon the secretary called out: 'Green Eight!' I just winked at my friend Justin and went forward in my green ball gown to collect my prize.

There were five brown, unmarked envelopes on the table by the secretary. She told me to choose one. I asked the Holy Spirit and He showed me which one to take. I handed it to the secretary and as she opened the envelope, she told the entire room that I'd won the Grand Prize, which was a 500 pound four-course dinner for two on the Thames River in a glass boat with live music. I glanced at my friend Justin and his mouth was wide open in shock! It seemed only fair to take him on the dinner cruise!

Once again, the Holy Spirit made me laugh and giggle. The Holy Spirit knew all along what was going to happen! We serve an all-knowing God. Nothing is a surprise to Him. Absolutely nothing. If we listen to Him and get an understanding of how He wants to speak to each one of us, oh the fun we can have in life! There is never a dull moment when walking with The Lord.

Justin ate his words that night and we both had a fabulous evening on the Thames River a couple of months later. Incidentally, he decided to take our course on how to hear God's voice as a lifestyle: Led By The Spirit.

Crazy Eights: Part 2

For many years since I moved to the UK, I have had several friends come over from the States to visit. No one has been more times than my friend, Cinzia. Both of us are single professionals who enjoy many of the same things and pastimes. Somethings we both love are travel and supporting the arts. Whenever Cinzia comes to the UK, we almost always try to take in the delights of the City of London. This is another fun story about how God uses the number eight in my travels.

One of those visits found us in London for the express purpose of celebrating a major birthday milestone for Cinzia. Her birthday is Christmas Eve, so it's always part of the holidays. I really wanted to make it memorable for her. We began the day by having tea in a famous tea room where Cinzia received a special birthday serenade and a cake with her name on it from the chef. She cried with great emotion because she felt so special.

Whenever I am with this particular friend, both of us sense the hand of The Lord giving us His favor in our travels. Like so many other times before, Cinzia and I were asked by the doorman at the hotel if he could give us both a kiss on the cheek. He said that we both looked radiant. We knew it was the joy of The Lord, but in a world where darkness is the norm, two women alone and full of joy is often a rarity.

From there, we went to hear a special guitar player at Fortnum and Mason's department store. There, we had a birthday toast of a glass of champagne. I asked if they had some strawberries to go with it and although they didn't, the people who served our champagne went and got us a bowl of strawberries to eat with our drinks. Cinzia was having a fabulous birthday.

Both of us like going to the theatre to see plays, so with this birthday celebration, I had gotten tickets for us to see 'Fiddler on the Roof' at the famous Savoy Hotel in the Strand. The production was marvelous! Seeing this wonderful Jewish story only served to remind us both of how good our God is. Jews and Christians alike serve the One True God. We are so blessed to know Him!

We came out of the play rejoicing over this fact. Cinzia had one incredible birthday in the Big City. Now it was time for us to return to my home on the south coast. We knew we'd probably catch the last train to our destination from London.

We came out of the show and caught a cab back to London Victoria station and found out that our route home was really going to be a long one by way of Brighton. It meant that we'd probably be getting home close to 2 a.m. We'd had such a perfect day and now I was wondering how we'd get home from the station. It would be way too late to call my faithful assistant to come and collect us from the station and drive us home. It was time for a miracle! Cinzia and I prayed and asked The Lord for a solution to our wee problem.

Well, we had a lovely journey home on the train, and as we left Brighton, I began to praise The Lord for the solution to our need for a cab to be there when we got to Chichester, my train station. I knew full well that the cabs don't run that time of night because all of the pubs are closed by that time. It was clear that only The Lord could help us.

It seemed that we were the only ones in our train car by the time the train got to Chichester. We got off the train and, lo and behold, there was only one bright red cab there!! It was full of Christmas lights and little bouncing snowmen on the dashboard and in the back window, too! Cinzia and I started laughing and praising The Lord.

As we got close to the cab, Cinzia said, 'Did you notice what was on the door, Charlynne?' I could plainly see the number 888-888 on the cab's door. It was the number to call City Taxi Service in Chichester. We really began to laugh then because God always speaks to me through the number '8'. The Holy Spirit often uses that number in prophetic things that happen to me. For Cinzia, it is often the number five.

On top of that, the cab driver was especially jovial and kind to us. He was very bubbly in personality and full of Christmas cheer. This was really wild, seeing as it was after 2am in the morning! Cinzia and I both wondered if our driver was really an angel sent by the Hosts of Heaven to take us home! The trip from the station to my front door was about 20 minutes, and our driver was full of joy the entire trip. Cinzia and I kept giggling. We felt that it was The Lord all the way.

We thanked our driver and he pulled away from the curb and we fell into my home, laughing. What a day we'd had, from start to finish --The Lord was with us! Yes, God does care about birthdays. Absolutely. No doubt about it.

Suffer The Little Children

In the early days of my ministry in the UK, I was not a UK resident yet and would come over for two or three-month stints of time. During those occasions, I would often stay with my godson's family in their medieval stable that had been turned into a cozy, one-bedroom flat for me. I had my own entrance, bath, and kitchen, but would often be invited over to eat with the family in their house.

One such evening, my friend's husband was away in Asia on business, so it was just she and I having dinner with her three young sons who were aged 10, 8, and 4. We were enjoying our meal and hearing all that had happened with the boys at school that day.

When the discussion turned to what we'd been doing that day, my friend shared that she and her close friend had asked to receive their personal prayer languages or the gift of speaking in tongues. I had prayed with her and her friend earlier that day and both women received the baptism of the Holy Spirit with the evidence of tongues! What a joyous occasion!

The boys were all ears and all three said that they wanted to receive what their mom and her friend had received. My friend looked at me and asked if it was possible for her sons to speak in tongues. I said, 'Of course.'

Her sons were so thrilled and immediately cleared the table for us and went upstairs to brush their teeth and put their pajamas on. Then they joined us in the lounge, by the fireplace, and sat on their bean bags.

As the mother watched, her sons sat in front of me, waiting for what would happen next. I explained to them what we were going to do and that it is The Lord God Who gives the gift, but that my role as a minister is to pray with them and agree with them that they would receive their individual prayer languages. I asked who wanted to be prayed for first. Immediately, my godson, Geoff, the 4 year-old, raised his hand and said he wanted to go first. I told them that the language would come out of them like 'rivers of living water' according to the Bible. I asked Geoff if I could put my hand on his belly. I also told him to open his hands because he was about to get a gift from The Lord.

Before I could even touch him, something amazing happened -- his prayer language began to come out of his mouth!! There he was in his pj's and his Superman cape, speaking in tongues. His mother began to cry with joy.

Before I could even begin to pray for the others, my Godson Geoff told his 8-year-old brother to open his hands to receive his gift from God! That brother spoke in tongues, with the youngest praying for him! The oldest also received his language that night. My friend was really crying now and she wanted to call her husband in China to tell him the happy news.

Their story doesn't end there. The next morning, my friend woke up to discover that the middle son had a horrible ear ache and was in a lot of pain. All three sons were sitting on her bed that morning before getting dressed for school, so she asked them what they should do about the middle son's ears. Her baby boy, Geoff, said he had an idea. He said, 'I know what we can do, Mummy. We can pray for his ear with our new prayer languages!' She told Geoff that was a brilliant idea and they all did as he suggested, with Geoff laying hands on his older brother. His ear was instantly healed! Geoff went on to say that using his new prayer language was clearly the answer to all hurts that might happen on the playground from now on! My friend and I just laughed as she retold the morning's events to me over a cup of tea later.

Children are so priceless in their pure faith in God! No wonder Jesus had all the time in the world for them! We must, too. He said that the Kingdom of Heaven belongs to such people (Matthew 19:14). Oh God, may we all be child-like in our faith!

Adventures At Ashburnham

In the last 10 years, my team and I have had the privilege of ministering and teaching at Ashburnham Christian Trust in East Sussex. It was three years ago that I became a trustee for this grand piece of property. Prior to that, I regularly taught many different courses there, led retreats, and prophesied with my team over many, many individuals, couples, and Christian leaders. Many people who have gone to Ashburnham over the last 50 years will say that it is a special place where the presence of God is keenly felt. I most certainly agree. I'd like to take a moment to share some of our favorite testimonies of miracles we as a team have witnessed there.

As was the custom for our ministry before I became a trustee of Ashburnham, I was often asked to do a week of teaching for a special group of day courses I had customized for that conference center. Through this offering of courses to the public, people from various backgrounds would come from all over the UK. The team and I always enjoyed ministering in this way because it was different every time and we always met new people in every course.

During one such week of day courses, there was a particularly strong touch of The Lord throughout the courses. On one of my teaching days, I heard the Holy Spirit ask me to stop and close my notes to go and lay hands on the sick in the room. He told me that He'd show me who to pray for. With about 30 people in the room, I closed my notes and went over to an Indian woman who had to be carried everywhere because she was paralyzed on one side of her body. Her name was Sira. I told her about my prompting from the Holy Spirit and asked her if it was okay for me to pray for her with the laying on of hands.

As it turned out, Sira was Catholic. She told me that she was happy for me to pray for her. She had a stroke several years prior to our meeting and had been unable to work for all of those years. She was on disability and had been for ages. I got out my anointing oil, and with her permission, used it as I laid hands on her. I asked Jesus to heal her and take away her paralysis. He did! It was instant! She had full use of her limbs on both sides of her body for the first time in years! Sira was crying with joy and told me that she couldn't wait to call her priest with the news! Everyone in the room was so happy for her! The air was electric with our praises to The Lord. I wondered what He was going to do next during that week of courses. There was more of the miraculous where that came from.

Freedom From Torment: Part One

Things were going very well during that week of courses at Ashburnham. Once God began to move in His Mighty Holy Spirit amongst us, I had a real expectancy in my spirit for something else in the supernatural. Our classes were quite full that week and we had about 30 people in each of our day courses. People had come from near and far to grow in their faith. When people are eager to learn in a class, it really spurs me on as a teacher. Needless to say, I was full of joy for their hunger and thirst for more of Jesus.

One afternoon, I was in the middle of teaching about all the ways that God speaks to us. No one was restless or fidgety in this group. All ears were open and hanging on my every word.

As I let a pregnant pause for thought descend upon the group, one of the female students cried out. Her name was Liv, and from within the group silence, she cried out, 'He's tormenting me, Charlynne!'

Immediately, I asked the Holy Spirit what her cry was all about. He told me that she was being oppressed by a demon and that I must bring The Lord's deliverance to her. I looked at my watch and the concerned faces of my other students and calmly said to Liv, 'I know, Sweetheart. We are going to take care of that in a moment.' I spoke to the rest of the class and said that it was time for our normal afternoon tea break in the atrium, outside of our class room. The class was only too happy to leave the room and take that break after hearing Liv's cry for help!

My team and I escorted Liv to the adjoining room and promptly closed the doors to minister to her. My associates, Lesley and Caroline, were assisting my on that course and they both came over to me and whispered that they had both seen Liv cutting her wrists to the point that they were bleeding. They went on to say that they had watched her suck the blood from her bleeding wrists during class. Yes, this young girl needed true deliverance that only Jesus Christ can bring.

We got Liv to sit down in a chair in front of the three of us. We asked Liv if she wanted to be set free from the demon that was tormenting her. She nodded her head and said, 'Yes!' We began to pray in the Spirit and I opened my mouth to rebuke that tormenting spirit and I sent it into the abyss to be judged at the footstool of Jesus. The atmosphere in the room changed and there was peace! Liv's countenance changed instantly. I asked her what she was hearing. Liv said that she heard this phrase, 'I am your Advocate.' She said she kept hearing that over and over again. I asked her Who it was talking to her. She began to beam with a huge grin on her face and said, 'Jesus!' My colleagues and I said, 'Amen, Liv, Amen!'

Liv said she no longer had the desire to harm herself or drink her own blood. Praise God! With great calm and joy, she asked me if I would like her to get a cup of tea for me. She never harmed herself again and was totally free! Hallelujah!

When I think of her freedom story, I am reminded of the countless people that Jesus delivered of demonic possession and oppression during his time on this earth. There is no other name higher in the universe than the name of Jesus Christ of Nazareth!!

"...Where the Spirit of The Lord is, there is freedom."

2 Corinthians 3:17

If you have not done it lately, I encourage you to stop and take a moment to breathe in Jesus and thank Him from the bottom of your heart for the immense freedom that you and I and all who know Him have because of what He has done for us! Meditate on this right where you are and take time to say, 'Thank You, Lord!' Words seem so inadequate when you think about the width and depth of what that means for you and me. We are so blessed as the sons and daughters of the Living God!

You and I carry so much power on the inside of us. It is the power of the Holy Spirit living in us that allows us to move so mightily in the supernatural realms. Imagine for a moment what our world would be like if every Christian man, woman, and child walked in the authority of the Spirit's power within us. The world and atmosphere around us would be so different!

Being the temple of the Holy Spirit means that you and I can plug into that wonder-working power whenever we are pressed into service to meet the countless needs of the people around us. When we let the world around us see Christ in us and experience Him through the power of the Holy Spirit, we release the Kingdom of Heaven on the earth for all the world to see. We become atmospheric changers!

Freedom From Torment: Part Two

I wholeheartedly believe that the Lord loves to move on holy ground. Ashburnham Place is such a place. I know that many people over the years have been set free and welcomed into new freedom in Christ on this Christian Property. Here is another testimony of deliverance.

In the early years of my move to the UK, I went to a leader's meeting in London where a famous prophetic team was going to minister to all in attendance. When we broke up into small groups for the team to prophesy over all who wanted prophetic encouragement, I received a word from the team that said that I was going to come into a season of hearing from old friends all over the planet. I received that word and felt it was of the Lord and recorded it into my prophetic words journal at home, not knowing how very true that word was.

One day, I was sitting in my office and I opened an email message from an old friend, Tara, that I had gone to college with. She brought me up to speed on all that had transpired in the 20 plus years since I'd last seen her. It was a very hard testimony and my heart ached for her as I read all that had happened to her over the years since we'd graduated. As I kept on reading and came to the last paragraph of her email, Tara told me that she had been praying and asking the Lord what to do at this point in her life. She said she felt a prompting from the Lord to find me and ask if she could come and see me.

I wrote her back and told her that I was now living in the UK, was in full-time ministry there, and that she was more than welcome to come and see me. Tara was so excited and said that she'd love to come see me right away for ministry. I told her that I was doing a lot of traveling on the road and doing some teaching at Ashburnham. She asked if she could come along and I said yes, and that we could book her in as a conference participant.

Lesley and I picked Tara up at the airport and drove to the conference center. Everything was going very well and the weather was sunny and marvelous. On the second night, however, things began to change in the Spirit.

At about 3am in the morning, I heard Tara scream out for me from her bedroom. She seemed to be in great distress. I put my robe and slippers on and immediately knocked on Lesley's door and said that Tara was in need. As Lesley got up, she saw, in the spirit, a big python-like snake coming through her window! Putting on her robe, she rebuked the evil spirit she had seen and came out of her room. I knew that the enemy was attacking.

Together we knocked on Tara's door and when she opened her door, I looked in her face and could tell that she was in desperate need of deliverance. This is why the Lord had brought her to the UK. She said I was the only person she knew who could help her.

Once inside of Tara's room, Lesley and I began to pray in tongues and take authority over Tara's room in the name of the Lord Jesus.

As we had walked into the room, Tara began vomiting up a green substance that was not of this earth. She was choking and vomiting all at once. I laid hands on her back and commanded the enemy to come out of her and never come back in the name of Jesus. The green substance stopped coming out of Tara and she wasn't choking anymore. She was at peace!

She came out of the bathroom and gave me a long hug. Now tears of joy began to flood her face and she began to praise the Lord. Lesley and I stayed with her until the sun came up and we sang some songs of praise to the Lord and laughed because we knew the Presence of the Living God had caused the enemy to run once again. Hallelujah, and all glory to the Lord of Lords and King of Kings! It is such a joy and a thrill to serve Him and watch Him set others free!! I never tire of witnessing His hand at work. Tara left the UK later the next week, totally free of all that had gripped her for so long and is living well and prospering today. Mission accomplished!

"For He has rescued us from the dominion of darkness and brought us into the Kingdom of the Son He loves, in whom we have redemption, the forgiveness of sins."

Colossians 1:13

Got Protein?

One of the things that we must have as we travel is good food. In the hustle and bustle of activity, when you are on the road and away from home, you need sustenance to keep you fueled and ready to go. On one of my trips away from home, I was doing some Christian teaching and had just finished my course. Lesley, my faithful traveling companion, was driving and we were pulling away from the conference center we'd been at in the early morning. No one was around to give us breakfast so I thought we could just get something as we drove along.

Lesley told me that because we were out in the middle of nowhere, the likelihood of us finding a breakfast place that was open was unlikely. She said, 'This is not America, Char.'

I had some medicine I needed to take and I knew that it would help if I could take it with protein so I wouldn't be queasy later.

While I agreed with her, I was hopeful that God might feel like changing the situation on our behalf.

Within about five minutes of leaving the conference center, we drove through a little village. In the village was a big restaurant that looked quite nice. It had a large parking lot next to it and there was a sandwich board out on the sidewalk advertising what was on offer for lunch and dinner.

I asked Lesley if she could pull into the parking lot so I could take a closer look. Lesley reminded me that the board on the sidewalk said lunch and dinner, not breakfast. I still asked her to stop, so we pulled into the parking lot.

I hopped out of our minivan to read the proper menu under glass there. As I was reading the full menu, a woman came out of the side door of the restaurant and asked if she could help me.

I asked, 'You only do lunch and dinner?'
She answered, 'Whadd'ya need?'
I replied, 'Protein!'
She asked, 'Will eggs and bacon do?'
To which I replied, 'For me and my friend?'
She said, 'Of course ya can.'

Lesley was shocked. In that little discourse, I'd gotten a fine restaurant owner who doesn't do breakfast for anyone to open up for us and prepare a made-to-order protein-filled breakfast! Lesley got out of the van and I grabbed my handbag. We went inside that lovely establishment, having no idea what The Lord had in store for us all!

We walked into the most amazing place. About 600 years ago, that property had been an inn for smugglers. Now, it was a lavish restaurant serving cocktails, lunch, and dinner, and now breakfast in one supernatural moment. The owner was the woman who'd invited us in, and her name was Wendy.

Wendy ushered us into the main dining room which was across from a very cozy bar. We walked into a large dining room that was carpeted from wall to wall. There was the largest fire place nook that I have ever seen in restaurant! Wendy had gone to the trouble of starting a most inviting fire that was now blazing just for us. No one was there because they did not serve breakfast to anyone. It was definitely a place where reservations were required and yet we had been invited in without any! (I hope you are now beginning to understand why I chose to call this book *No Appointments Necessary*.)

Wendy sat us down at a table, complete with a fine linen tablecloth and fresh roses from her garden in a vase. There was a huge basket overflowing with freshly baked bread that had been toasted just for us and a carafe of rich cream for the freshly brewed South American coffee that was very enticing for our nostrils. Lesley and I were so amazed by this coffee Wendy gave us in bottomless cupfuls. Wendy would only tell us that it was a secret special blend. To this day, I believe it to be the best cup of coffee I have ever had in my life. Once we were seated, Wendy asked us how we both liked our eggs. Lesley said over-easy and I asked for my eggs to be fried hard. Wendy said, 'In other words, you want them murdered,' and off she went to give our order to her husband, who was the chef.

As we waited, Lesley and I kept pinching ourselves because of the opulent treat that God had undoubtedly held waiting just for us to step into! We knew, without a doubt, that The Lord was behind all of this and it thrilled us. Our next thought was what He might want us to pour out as a blessing for this dear woman who had taken us in. I began to study her, outwardly first, and then by the Spirit of God.

Here's what I saw; I saw a woman who had a no-nonsense countenance. She had many wrinkles and the look of someone who had been deeply scarred emotionally. She didn't smile at all and yet I knew that somehow we'd found favor with her. As she served us our huge plates brimming with lots of eggs, thick cuts of bacon, and the most amazing sausages ever, I noticed that her hands were gnarled and twisted. Wendy also suffered from a clubbed foot. She quickly put Lesley's plate down and then made a point to let me know that mine was taking a wee bit longer because my eggs needed to be 'murdered'. A few moments later, my plate came out with my well-done eggs and all the trimmings. It is absolutely the best British cooked breakfast that Lesley or I have ever eaten!

While we ate, we mused over the apparent hurts and needs in Wendy's life. I knew that our coming to her fine restaurant was clearly about anything but my medical need for protein! I could feel God's compassion and love for her so strongly. We'd been sent on a mission for Wendy. I pondered these things in my heart as I ate the sumptuous meal set before us and began to pray for Wendy and the leading of the Holy Spirit to hear from Him when and how to minister to her and those ailing hands of hers.

After we'd drank nearly two pots of that amazing coffee, I asked the Holy Spirit what He wanted me to say and do next. Here's what He asked me to say to Wendy:

'Wendy, might it be possible for us to book you for another eight weeks of private breakfasts at the same day and time each week? We may have one or two others with us but couldn't tell you until the day how many will be with us.'

Wendy thought and said what became her pat answer to anything I asked of her, 'Course ya can.'

Lesley and I walked out to the minivan that first week with glee and a real bounce in our step. It was like we'd just parted the veil of some magical place. Lesley said to me, 'I want you to know that that sort of thing just does *not* happen in the UK. God is clearly all over this situation and it is not over yet. We have eight more weeks of this incredible adventure!'

I totally agreed with her and was tingling with excitement over all that God had done and was about to do in our midst. It would make doing that particular course very exciting indeed. We drove home anticipating the unexpected for the weeks ahead.

In that course, a student named Jared said that he was in the middle of leasing a property near Bath, England where he could envision me teaching. Each night after class, we'd talk and talk about all the possibilities for me in Bath at his property that he was turning into a small conference center. He told us that he wanted to offer his guests great breakfasts and teaching. We couldn't resist sharing with him about our new friend, Wendy, and her fabulous breakfasts at the old smuggler's inn nearby. He was salivating as we told him about the amazing food and asked if she might let him join us the next time. We made a plan and decided to have him join us.

The next morning, the three of us drove off to Wendy's magical breakfast emporium. Lesley and I were in the minivan and Jared drove in and parked his silver Mercedes Benz. Wendy had a Mercedes too and he parked right next to hers. As we got out of the van, Wendy came out and asked us who belonged to the Mercedes. I told her my friend and student Jared. She said, 'Oh well, that's all right then.' She welcomed Jared into her place.

Jared was just as impressed as we were. He was blown away by the look of it all and the excellent way in which we were served. He took one whiff of Wendy's secret blend of coffee and couldn't believe that she let us have bottomless cups of the stuff with a big pot of real cream. No one does this in the UK! I told him that it was nothing but the supernatural favor of God at work. Our breakfasts with Wendy were getting bigger and bigger each time she served us!

There were nine breakfasts in all that Lesley and I had with students and members of our team. Before our last breakfast, The Lord impressed upon me His deep desire to see Wendy's gnarled hands and feet healed. I felt His love and compassion for her and had been praying about what to do on His behalf. I had one chance to get it right and didn't want to make any mistakes with Wendy.

Our second to the last time at Wendy's wonderful establishment was the moment I sensed the leading of the Holy Spirit to ask Wendy to sit down and speak to me about the issues of her heart. She began to tell Lesley and I some stories about her impoverished upbringing in Ireland and how she and her family were despised by the priests in the Catholic Church there. The straw that broke the camel's back for her, with regard to faith, was the day that she and her family were walking to mass and the car driven by the priest sped past her and her family, kicking up a ton of cold, wet mud on them all! The priest never slowed down and Wendy decided then and there that she would never go to church again.

We listened intently as she told us this horrible story with a lifetime's worth of pain. The Lord asked me to ask her forgiveness as a member of Christian leadership. I said yes to His request and told Wendy that I did empathize with her old wound. I asked her if she would accept my standing in proxy as a church leader and asking for her forgiveness for what had happened all those years ago. Her hard, stony face and heart softened and one solitary tear slid down her wrinkled face. Amazing. The Holy Spirit was clearly at work! Hallelujah! I proceeded to ask Wendy if I could pray for her hands and feet to be healed. She quietly nodded her head 'Yes'. I told her that Scripture says church leaders are meant to pray for the sick and anoint them with oil. I greased my fingers with the anointing oil and began to pray for Wendy's knotted hands and her clubbed foot. The Lord had also impressed upon us the need to bless Wendy with a special gift from us. She was so overjoyed that day and hugged and kissed me and Lesley! She had never expected to receive prayer and a special 'kiss' like that from The Lord God Himself. The three of us were grinning from ear to ear because The Lord was clearly in our midst.

On our last breakfast at Wendy's, we'd gotten permission from her to have our core team members join us. What a feast she prepared for us all! The men were astounded and we all got up and had our picture taken in front of Wendy's enormous fire place that had given us so much joy on those frosty winter mornings. It was the end of a very special moment in time for all who had experienced it with us. We were so blessed!

You may be wondering if Wendy ever received healing for her hands and clubbed foot. Well, of course she did! A year later, we dropped in to see her and she came running down the steps to hug and kiss us with such joy. She was proud to show us her healed hands and the absence of her clubbed foot! God is so faithful!! Once again, we were shown that the absence of bitterness brings healing. I wish for everyone to experience what happened to Wendy once she was able to give her bitterness to Jesus and make room for forgiveness. The spirit of offense can be so debilitating once it is picked up! None of us can afford the fruit of it. The Bible tells us that if we confess our faults to each other, we can be healed (James 5:16). Isn't God good and merciful to us?

Tortoise and the Hare

My teammates and I have learned over the years that one of the traits we must possess as prophetic voices is the ability to be flexible in all situations, especially whenever we are on the road and ministering together. We never know what unexpected circumstances we may find ourselves in. Jackie Jacobsen, the founder of the Led By The Spirit School, has always told me to 'expect the unexpected.' This story gives validity to this statement.

A few years ago, I was invited to speak at a women's conference on the coast of Cornwall. The fact that it was a conference for only for women makes what I am about to share quite interesting.

We'd come to the time when the host of the conference had set aside time for my team and I to minister prophetically to any and all of the women who wanted to receive prophetic ministry. There were about 300 women there, so Lesley and Caroline and I were quite busy that weekend.

Everything was going well, and we were nearing the end of our time of ministry, when we got an 'unexpected' request. One of the attendees of the conference who was local was so blessed by the word that she had received during her ministry time with us that she went home to share the experience with her husband. The upshot of her testimony was that she asked her husband to come back to the conference with her to receive ministry! The next thing we know, our conference host is asking us if it's all right for this lady to bring her husband in for a prophetic word. We never turn anyone away who wants ministry, but we honestly were not expecting a man to ask for ministry during a women's conference---especially a man who we were told did *not* believe in the prophetic at all.

If body language is 80% of our communication, then this man's body language said it all. He was not excited to be sitting in front of us at all! He was a good case in point that we cannot prophesy by the sight of our eyes, because what our eyes were seeing in him was not encouraging to us at all. Praise God we have been trained to walk by faith and not sight.

We welcomed the man and his wife to our circle. We introduced ourselves to him by our first names and then explained what would happen next. He sat quietly waiting and we prayed against any spirits of doubt, fear, or unbelief that might be trying to operate there. Caroline and Lesley shared what they sensed was on God's heart for the man. He sat quietly with his wife sat beside him.

The whole time that Lesley and Caroline were giving the words and pictures they had for this man, I was somewhat perplexed at what I was seeing in the eye of my spirit. What I was seeing was very unscriptural and I was struggling with the prospect of giving it to this man. The image I kept getting was of the story of the famous Aesop's fable, 'The Tortoise and the Hare'. There was absolutely nothing Biblical about this picture at all! Yet the image kept coming back to my spirit. I kept asking the Holy Spirit about it. Finally, I heard The Lord say, 'Go ahead and give him the word and picture you are seeing. It's all right.' So that still, small, first Voice I know had spoken. Now it was time for me to obey The Voice, despite what my flesh was feeling.

I opened my mouth and began to share with the doubting Thomas in front of me that I was seeing Aesop's fable of the Tortoise and the Hare played out before my eyes. As I said that, the man's wife gave a sharp, excited scream and clapped her hand over her mouth as soon as she cried out. With one hand over her mouth, she took her other hand and slapped her husband on his thigh. I looked at him and his jaw dropped wide open. I continued speaking until the Holy Spirit bid me to stop and I handed him a cassette tape of all that we'd shared. Then we prayed a seal over his words.

As he took the tape out of my hand, he shared with us that he was a pastor and that he really didn't believe that the Gifts of the Spirit were for today. He said his jaw dropped because what I'd shared was exactly what he'd written just moments before for his next sermon. He was in shock that a total stranger could know with such shocking detail what he'd just typed at his computer within that hour! Only he and his wife knew what was in that sermon. Now he knew that God did too.

I told him that all the glory goes to The Lord in every prophetic moment that is true or comes to pass because we know nothing but the Holy Spirit and Lord of Heaven and Earth knows *everything* about us. He stood in awe of the God we all serve. The man had received a specific word of knowledge that showed him without a shadow of a doubt that God in heaven knows and sees his every thought and movement. Needless to say, the man became a believer that day that all nine Gifts of the Spirit are absolutely for yesterday and today. He also learned that anyone can learn how to hear God's voice for themselves and in ministry to others. He and his wife walked away blessed out of their socks!

Ministering to the body of Christ is so much fun! We just have to be ready and willing vessels for the Holy Spirit to move through to experience the joy of our salvation. All three of us were truly blessed to be a blessing to the people at that conference—male and female!

My Shack Experience

For the last seven years, Lesley and I have been experiencing some incredible angelic encounters when traveling together. I want to share here the experience that we believe opened the door to all the experiences with angels that we have witnessed together on the road.

When the best-selling book, *The Shack,* came out, Jackie Jacobsen sent me a copy to read and I gave it to Lesley to read first. She did and then gave it to me to read. Both of us were so affected by it that we could hardly wait to talk about it. We planned to meet for dinner on a weekend that she and I were going away for a ministry road trip.

She picked me up and we soon found ourselves stopping for a bite to eat at a lovely Indian restaurant in the town where I lived. Lesley and I seemed to be bursting at the seams to share with each other what our insights were regarding *The Shack.* Lesley began first sharing what really affected her as she read the book and then I shared as well and both of us knew that we would be changed forever. We could've stayed in the restaurant for many hours but we knew we had to hit the road and begin our journey back to the south coast. We paid the bill and got into Lesley's mini-van.

The journey to her village went very fast because we continued to talk on and on about what the Lord had shown us in this fascinating book. The air was electric with anticipation for what the Lord was speaking to us and we were both so excited.

By the time we came to Lesley's village, it was dark. Lesley decided to let her husband, John, know that we were almost home but that we wanted to go and park by the ocean to continue our chat for a few more minutes. John was fine with that and said he'd put the kettle on for us. On we went to the sea to see if the moon's light was dancing on the waves.

The town of Selsey is right on the southern-most coast of the UK. As you drive along the High Street and go all the way to the very end, you find yourself at the sea. On a clear day, you can see all the way across the water to the Isle of Wight.

On this special night, we drove to the end of the High Street like we'd done many times before and turned into the car park. We found it completely empty. There was no one there, not even a lone dog walker.

Lesley parked the car and the sea was in front of us. The moon was big and bright. The cascading moonlight was so white and beautiful against the dark waves. Praise and worship on the CD player continued at a low volume, and Lesley and I were amazed by what our eyes were seeing.

To the right of the driver side door of her car was the most gigantic whirlpool we'd ever seen! It seemed to be the size of a huge city block and, my oh my, was it churning round and round. I asked Lesley if that was normal for that part of the coast. She sat amazed and said that in her 35 years living in that area, she'd never seen anything like that. We could see the whirlpool in its entirety because of the light of the moon. It was such a display of power!

About this time the street light at the entrance to the car park switched off. It was getting late and so it got very dark where we were parked. The CD that was playing stopped too at that moment and we were totally unprepared for what happened next.

As we sat in silence and total blackness where we were parked, we saw three fast bursts of the most blinding white light ever! It was so bright that it enveloped the entire van. Lesley and I both hit our heads on the windows of the car because we were trying to see if something had landed on top of us!

Lesley screamed, 'What was that?!!'

I shouted back, 'The clash of angelic swords!!' All I kept thinking was that it was frightening and so like the old flash bulbs the press would use when taking photos of big events and old movie stars. Our eyes had such a time adjusting to the severe lights.

The next thing out of Lesley's mouth after the first flash was 'Hit the deck!!' There were three flashes in all and we heard nothing and saw nothing and no one around us. There were no planes or helicopters overhead either. If we'd been anyone else, we might have thought we were about to be apprehended by a UFO but we knew in our spirits that this was absolutely *not* the case.

As we sat there looking around us and wondering what would happen next, we sat in silence for a few more minutes and then Lesley turned the car on, put it in reverse, and flew out of that car park. We knew that we had just witnessed a supernatural experience. God had allowed us to see what we saw because we had been lifting up His name for several hours beforehand.

When we got to Lesley's house, our eyes were as big as saucers and her husband and older son wondered what in the world had happened to us. We recounted to them what I have written here and when we looked at the front cover of the book we'd been discussing, we realized that what we'd seen by the sea looked exactly like the bright light on the cover of the book!

Lesley's son said he wanted to know if there was any verse in the Bible that could confirm what we'd seen at the sea. We pondered these things in our hearts for the next couple of days and were so excited about it all.

Two days later, I found myself preparing to go on yet another trip with Lesley. Before I left my house to catch a train, I saw that my mentor and friend, Morris Ruddick, had sent me a new prophetic message from his ministry. It was a word about 'swirls' in the Spirit. It really caught my eye, and because of time, I printed it out and quickly threw it in to my handbag as the cab came to take me to the train. Lesley was picking me up at another station and then we'd journey on together.

To my astonishment, I sat on the train and read the prophetic message that Morris had just penned. In that message, there was the full explanation of what Lesley and I had just experienced by the sea! He talked of swirls in the spiritual realm that bring about the convergence of angelic presence and whirlpools! He referenced a verse from Ecclesiastes 1:6. This is what it says:

"The wind goes toward the south, and turns around to the north; the wind whirls about continually, and comes again on its circuit."

This was astounding to me because this is exactly the direction of the whirlpool that we'd seen on that incredible night. As soon as my train pulled into the station, I came out and read the 'swirls' message from Morris. She agreed with me that it did confirm what we'd experienced earlier that week. We shared the message with her son who had asked for a scriptural reference for what we'd seen.

What Lesley and I found out from our experience is that when we as God's children speak of Him and bring glory, honor, and praise to Him through our speech, He and all the minions in heaven above who serve Him are stirred and led to show up in our midst! What a glorious experience! How it inspires me to speak of Him anytime that I can because of this truth. In Psalm 22:3, we are told that God inhabits the praises of His people. We are so blessed to serve the only wise God Who is the Master and Creator of the universe.

What also comes to mind every time that I think of this experience we had is the fact that our Heavenly Father is The Father of Lights (James 1:17). His light is so bright that in a day to come, there will be no need for the sun or the moon because His light will be all that we need to see by! The New Jerusalem will be filled with the glory or 'the shekinah of the Lord'.

"The city had no need of the sun or of the moon to shine in it, for the glory of God illuminated it. The Lamb is its light."

Revelation 21:23

The glory of God cannot be overcome by darkness. That is so very comforting to us who know Him and call Him Lord (John 1:5). Hold onto this truth knowing that you and I are the children of light (1 Thessalonians 5:5) because of all He has done for us.

A Pound To My Name

About three years ago, I woke up and checked my bank accounts online to see what bills could be paid and to pay for a train ticket online for my next speaking engagement out of town. To my shock, I had exactly £1.29 to my name! Three days after that, I was to have my train ticket and be prepared to tell the pastor of the church that had booked me what time my train was due. One problem—I had no dosh to even buy a train ticket to go and speak anywhere and there was no money coming that I could see anytime soon.

As a seasoned overseas missionary, I know that worry and fretting never helps anyone in need. We must take all of our petitions and requests to the Lord in prayer, so I did. And when I did that, the Lord came back ever so sweetly, but firmly, and said, 'I will take care of you. Do not tell anyone that you have no money for your bills right now or the train fare you need this week. No one must know of your need except me. I am Jehovah Jireh, the One Who provides for you, and Your Husband. Trust me, Charlynne.'

I don't know about you, but when the Lord speaks to me with such conviction and intensity about a situation, I listen and do my very best to obey His instructions. Although my flesh and mind were screaming at me to ask for financial help, I did not. My mind knew that there would be direct debits for household bills coming to my bank account soon, yet there was no money to cover it in the natural. Living by faith had never been so fun!

I left my prayer request with my Lord and Savior and prepared my notes for the class I was teaching in my village. No one knew what I was trusting the Lord for. Not even my trusted associate, Lesley, who travels everywhere with me. I told no one of my situation or need.

That night in class, it was a full house of folks hungry to learn about being more like Jesus. It was a course on humility that I was teaching. We normally break halfway through the evening, and this night was no different. As students made their way to the coffee and tea bar, one older lady called Angelica from our ministry team came forward to talk to me.

Angelica and I have been friends for many years and I know her to be an extremely prophetic person. She is such an asset to our team and not a stranger to anything in the supernatural realm. Over the last seven years, we have enjoyed hearing about her many experiences with the Lion of Judah. Jesus appears to her in the form of a Lion that leads her through many different adventures in faith during her quiet time with Him. Occasionally, she receives a message from Him that she feels she must share with me or our entire prophetic team. This night in class was one of those occasions for sharing.

Angelica made her way up to my lectern and spoke to me as only she can. She said that the Lion was standing right next to me during class while I was teaching. I said that was fabulous and I asked where He was now. She proceeded to tell me that He was standing next to me at that very moment! I felt the hairs prick up on the back of my neck and asked her what He was doing. She went on to say that He was roaring over me! I asked for more explanation and she told me that the Lion was roaring grace and favor over me! That was indeed what I needed in that very moment. I thanked her for sharing that word and picture of encouragement with me, and I heard the Lord encourage me to still remain quiet about my predicament.

After the break, I began teaching the rest of that night's class and felt much encouraged. I shared with Lesley what Angelica had shared and she smiled as she drove me back to my house. As we drove up to my house, Lesley handed me a white envelope. She said that a couple in the class had asked her to give it to me. I thanked her and went into my house.

As I unpacked my teacher's bag and took off my coat, I opened the envelope. Inside was a cheque from the couple for £500! Talk about being overwhelmed. I could not stop praising the Lord and promptly sat down to write the gracious couple a thank-you note. God's timing is amazing! While I was very happy to receive the generous financial gift, in the UK it takes about five business days for cheques to clear. That meant that I was still up a creek where my bank account was concerned. Direct debits were due to come out of that account at any moment and the cheque I'd just received wouldn't have cleared in time to cover any of what was due. I deposited the cheque into my bank account; continued to praise the Lord, and thanked Him once more for hearing my petition and working behind the scenes on my situation.

A couple of days later, I received the phone call from the pastor of the church that had booked me to come and preach. She was calling to find out if I'd booked my train ticket to come to them. Inside, I heard the Holy Spirit tell me to hold steady. I was still not permitted to say anything to anyone about my financial need at that moment.

When the pastor asked if I had my ticket yet, I said an arrow prayer up to the Lord; 'How do I respond to her question, Lord, and still not break my silence about my situation??' The Lord said to tell her that I had not bought a train ticket yet, so I did. To my surprise, the pastor was elated that I hadn't bought a ticket! She went on to say that a lady in another town really wanted to speak to me and had heard I was coming to their church to speak. This lady told the pastor that she'd love to come and bring me to their church! I nearly dropped the phone when she told me this. There was *no* doubt in my mind that the Lord God above was sitting right in the middle of this grand scheme of things. I chuckled to myself all night and shook my head every time that phone call came to mind.

I packed my bag to go away for the weekend and speak at the church. The lady who'd asked to bring me came and we had a good time chatting along the way to the village where I was speaking. I didn't have to pay one dime for that journey! God was on the move for sure.

I always enjoy spending time in this particular village. I personally know several in that congregation and have taught classes for them there as well. They are not strangers to me. I always have great times of fellowship with them.

Sunday came and I shared the message with the congregation and gave an altar call for salvation and prayer. Several couples came down to the altar for prayer. I prayed for them all. The last couple to pray with me had experienced some challenging times in the early days of their recent marriage and I had prayed with them and made some suggestions of things that might encourage them in their journey toward marital bliss. That morning, they came to the altar to give God all the praise and the glory for what He'd done to repair their marriage. It was a time of joy for them and I was so glad to hear of it. We prayed and hugged one another and they went on their merry way.

The church treasurer came and asked me to sign off in their ledger that they'd given me a love gift. Now, this was a small street church with very few people in the congregation. Their normal love gift was £100 and I knew that. I never squabble over what churches can afford; I just trust the Lord with all that comes in. This Sunday was different though—the church treasurer gave me a cheque for double the normal amount! Once again, the Lord was at work and I was so grateful. That really encouraged me.

The pastors took me to a lovely lunch by the water nearby and then the kind lady who drove me to the church generously took me back to my home. When I got home, I unpacked my things and found a thank you note from the last couple I'd prayed for who'd shared the praise report about their marriage. In their note, they thanked me for encouraging them along the way as they dealt with their early marriage woes. What fell out of that card made me burst into tears of joy! I held in my hand a cheque from them for £1,200! This is quite surprising from a newly married couple in a church of about 20 people that normally apologizes for only being able to afford a love gift of £100!

For a recap, in less than five days, the Lord had miraculously brought £1,900 into my lap. From £1.29 to £1,900 in five days is pretty good, wouldn't you say? The Lord kept reminding me that if I do His will, whatever needs present themselves to me are His bill. His will. His bill. I could only smile with joy. Once again He had creatively reminded me that He is My Eternal Husband and is more than capable of taking care of all, not some, but *all* of my needs. I can't tell you how comforting that is for this single, missionary chick!

"For your Maker is your Husband, The Lord of Hosts is His name; And your Redeemer is the Holy One of Israel; He is called the God of the whole earth."

Isaiah 54:5

Walking The Beat

I'm going into my fourth year living in the town of Selsey in West Sussex, and like every town or city in the UK, there are law enforcement professionals who are charged with keeping the peace and keeping everyone safe. When I moved to Selsey, I felt the leading of the Lord to seek out these officers who walk our streets and keep us safe.

After prayer one morning, the Lord prompted me to leave my house and go on a prayer walk. As I rounded the corner from my cul-de-sac, I could see two community officers patrolling their beat. Once they crossed the street, they'd be exactly where I was on the corner.

We greeted each other and I asked if I might walk a bit with them. They teased me about my 'lovely Sussex accent' and asked where I was from in the States and what I was doing in Selsey. I simply told them that God had called me to their country when I was 21 and that I was an ordained minister of the Gospel of Jesus Christ.

We continued walking and discussed the main needs of our town. I asked if the officers would agree to email me the three main concerns for our town on a regular basis. They said they'd love to do that and we parted ways.

Later on that summer, I flew home to the States for a break back home in Colorado and an opportunity to update my ministry partners on what God was doing in and through my ministry in the UK. It is always a joy to share what the Lord is doing overseas. Nothing I report can happen without the team effort that makes this ministry successful. It is the Lord+Charlynne+The Ministry Team+All of our US and UK partners that make it all possible. Teamwork is everything.

On this trip home, I was asked to share at the home of the missions house group in my US home church. During my chat, a young man snuck in a few minutes after I'd started. He sat down quietly and took out a notebook to write in. Unbeknownst to me, he was getting a serious download from the Holy Spirit for me.

After I finished sharing and folks began chatting amongst themselves and collecting their things to leave for home, this young man came up to me and gave me what he'd been writing while I was speaking. It looked like it was about two pages of a prophetic word, single-spaced. I thanked him for writing it all down for me and asked what his name was. He told me he was called Kirby. I asked Kirby to write his name and the day's date for me on the page. He did all of that and also added his phone number. Kirby handed the papers back to me, thanked me for sharing, and left quietly.

Others came up to me to say goodbye and I stayed up for a few more hours chatting with my host family before heading off to bed. When I closed the door, I heard the Holy Spirit prompt me to read and digest what Kirby had heard for me.

I opened up the pages once more and sat down on my bed to read what he'd received. I was so encouraged to see that he'd heard things that are definitely a part of my 'prophetic language' by which the Lord often speaks to me. While my spirit agreed with what Kirby had scribed for me, one paragraph in particular stood out to me. It said that God was about to open up a door for me with folks in law enforcement. I could hardly believe my eyes because Kirby couldn't possibly know that just before I came back to the States, I'd had a favorable encounter with the officers in my town! I read the rest of that prophetic word and then I prayed over it and put it into my prophetic journal.

Three weeks after that incident with Kirby, I flew back to my UK home. I had barely finished unpacking my suitcases when there was a knock on my front door. There standing in front of me were the same officers who had allowed me to walk the beat with them before I flew to the States.

I jokingly asked if I was in trouble and they said that I wasn't in trouble but they were! I invited them in. There they stood, in my lounge, in their uniforms. One of the officers asked me if I'd be interested in becoming the police chaplain of our town! Inside me, I heard the Holy Spirit tell me that this was the fulfillment of what Kirby had heard for me regarding working with law enforcement. The Holy Spirit told me to say *yes*. When I asked where this was coming from on their part, the officer said that they had chosen me because of the discussion I'd had with them on the beat. You could have knocked me over with a feather! I asked what I needed to do next and the officer told me that they just needed to get the green light from their supervisor and it would be official.

As soon as the officers left, the Lord prompted me to call Kirby in the States that day. I decided to call him after he got home from work. When I called him, he picked up the phone and I told him all that had happened since I read the prophetic word he received for me. He was truly blown away and so glad that I had called him with that word of encouragement from across the pond. It made his year!

After that, I received a call from the officer saying I'd been given the green light and my first official police assignment. Emails came with the main police concerns of the town for me to pray about.

Currently, the community officers are trying to get me a meeting with the police commissioner. Again, the officers are moving this forward. I know that beyond that, the Lord is at work in all of this.

As I think on this testimony, I am reminded how very important it is to thank faithful, hearing people in the prophetic when their words are sound and come into being. If we don't take the time to tell prophetic people when their words come to pass, how will they know that they are, in fact, hearing from the Lord? Secondly, I am reminded how important it is for each of us to pray over prophetic words that resonate with our spirits. We can choose words of life or death with whatever we say. It is so important that we speak words of life over those 'fresh testimonies of Jesus' (Revelation 19:10) that bear witness with our spirits, no matter who the vessel of delivery is, and no matter how old or young they are. Whenever we do, we must be expectant for what God has in store for us.

Immigration Instigation

One of the most amazing times in my life as a missionary occurred from 2008-2011 when the UK's immigration laws began the most drastic of changes in the nation's history. During that time, American Christian ministers underwent many challenging trials along the road to receiving work permits and residency in the UK.

During this time, I was one of those ministers facing possible deportation if the authorities were not happy with my paperwork. I absolutely needed the supernatural hand of the Lord and His wisdom and discernment to get me through the maze of red tape and documentation necessary to live out the calling He gave me to steward in His name. I also had to trust Him for an incredible amount of money for each stage of the game. Thousands of pounds were needed for me to stay in the UK as a working minister of the Gospel of Jesus Christ each year since I'd left the US in 2004. What was needed now was a whole new ball game compared to what I'd needed before. My UK team and I had no earthly idea what that would look like, but God was with me the entire time. I'd like to share some of the truly miraculous things that happened during those years before I received the right to stay in the UK without a work visa.

In the spring of 2008, severe persecution of American Christians began at all UK airports and immigration entry points. Hundreds of American believers were deported and not permitted to enter the UK. Some of the headlines in the UK papers reported American believers as saying that the 'UK Is A Godless Nation.' It was not an easy time for US ministers here.

I had come back through UK Immigration just before the new rules began to be enforced, and even then, I was told that the UK didn't need any more Christian missionaries. Despite this attitude by the border officials that I'd encountered, I was determined to stay and carry out my calling regardless of what was happening around me. When I asked the Lord what I should do during this time, He told me to do a liquid fast and paper the walls of my office and bedroom with the Word of God about my situation.

The first financial miracle during this time came from a couple in a neighboring county. They said that the Lord told them to gift me £1,000! This super generous gift came right on time. I asked the Lord what to do with this specific amount. He told me to ask the couple if they knew of any immigration lawyers. God told me I'd need one right away. The couple didn't just know an immigration lawyer—they knew a *Christian* immigration lawyer. Hallelujah! His fee was £400 per hour! That meant I had just enough for two billable hours of his time. Yikes, and praise God for the dosh to cover his fees and my serious questions.

The lawyer asked to come and meet with me and decided to make a decision on whether or not he'd take me on as a client once he'd read my book, *True Grid*. He later called to say that he was absolutely sure that my calling to the UK was true. He decided to take me on as a client.

Once my lawyer started working with me and hearing about all of the new rules regarding immigration for ministers, he couldn't believe how I was being treated by the system and said that God had told him that I was *not* to be charged after the first two hours! Once again, the Lord was sending goodness and mercy to me. I thanked the lawyer and waited to see what he thought we should do next.

The authorities had my passport, and my debit card had been erroneously double-charged for the necessary amount for immigration permit fees. I was in serious financial need and had absolutely *no* money in my account. I kept fasting and praying and trusting God to hear my cry and to move on my behalf against the obvious forces of darkness that were at work in my situation. Each day, the UK government kept saying that if I didn't comply with their demands I could face deportation or imprisonment. I was between a rock and a hard place with no passport or money. All I had was Jesus and His precious book of promises to read from each day.

One morning, I woke up and heard the Lord say to me that I should go on a prayer walk around the duck pond in my neighborhood. Lesley had come to pray with me and we walked around the pond together. It felt good to get out of the house and literally stop and smell the roses! I walked for about an hour and finally made my way back home. When I opened the door, I found that a fat, white envelope had been dropped through my mail slot. I picked up the envelope and closed the door. When I looked at the front of the envelope, all I saw were these words: 'To Char, With Love xx.'

With that, my spirits began to lift. I opened the envelope and could feel the tears begin to fall as my eyes beheld a fat stack of fresh, crisp twenty pound notes!! There was about £1,000 in my hands. Lesley and I praised the Lord together for His great kindness. To this day, I have no idea who gave that huge gift. Only God knows. One thing I do know is that whoever gave that money has great rewards waiting for them in Heaven! That was not the first or the last time that money was placed into my hands that way during that time. Each gift received was just as precious to me as the one before. My cup continued to run over.

One funny thing happened when I went to see my doctor for my normal annual check-up. She was a kind Christian doctor and she was pleased to see that I'd dropped some weight. She had no idea that I was fasting for the Lord. When she asked me how I'd lost the weight, I told her I'd lost it through the Immigration Weight Loss Plan. She actually thought it was a new book that was out and asked how she could get a copy! I had to chuckle to myself over this. Sometimes real life is stranger than fiction.

As the red tape in the system got tougher and tougher to sort out, my lawyer told me that he thought it would be best for me to write a letter to someone who was a high-ranking UK government official. He'd read in my book that I'd written to the American President for a job and got the job I wanted, so he thought why not try the same thing in the UK? He felt it was our only hope at that moment to see justice in my situation.

I prayed like I had in the States when I felt led to go and work in my nation's capital. I asked the Lord who I should write to about my immigration woes. He told me to write to the Cabinet Minister of the entire UK. The Lord told me exactly what to write. In the same week that the Cabinet Minister got my letter, I received a phone call from his office saying that he knew absolutely nothing about the new immigration rules and that he was sorry to hear about what I was experiencing. He also said that he was going to put his entire office on my case! I was elated with this response and knew that God was bringing justice to my cause.

Every step of the way, I saw miracles, but what happened next blew even my lawyer's mind. The Cabinet Minister called the head of the entire UK Border Agency, and through a series of emails and phone calls, got my whole case turned around!

Soon after that, my passport was returned to me. The next day, Her Majesty's Treasury hand-delivered a cheque for the full amount of the money that had been erroneously taken from my bank account! The cheque didn't even go through the normal computer system but was written out by hand! I called my immigration lawyer and he told me that he'd never seen a difficult case handled so swiftly in all of his career! He said he was going to catch a train and come and see me right away and told me to be sure to make a copy of the cheque before I deposited it in the bank because it was such a rare occurrence.

When I looked through my passport, I realized that I now had the new credentials required for ministers of religion to live and work in the UK. As it turned out, I became the first minister of religion in the whole world to receive the new credentials under the new laws that were in place. My story soon spread all over the world. People began to call me to find out what I'd done to be allowed to work and live in the UK without hindrance. Charlynne couldn't do a thing---*Jesus* did it all. There is no doubt in my mind or spirit about it.

Next, I was invited to meet the Cabinet Minister face-to-face at a dinner where one of the Queen's chefs served us a pheasant dinner. I was asked to have a VIP tour of Westminster Palace with a champagne toast with the Cabinet Minister's staff. The Cabinet Minister wanted to see my new credentials and asked if anyone was bothering me about my immigration status. I told him that everything I needed had been returned to me, including the missing funds. I thanked him for all he'd done on my behalf. It was such an incredible moment in my life. If I didn't know it before, I certainly knew now that the battle I'd been in was clearly the Lord's!

When the dust settled, I threw a huge 'Thank You, Lord' Party to give praise and honor to the Lord for all He'd done to make my ability to stay in the UK a reality. The entire process was such a miracle! It was also allowed for my own spiritual growth. Like Joseph's time in the dungeons of Egypt and then his successes in the palace, I had literally gone along in this season in a similar way, with the possibility of imprisonment, that ended up with me being welcomed into Westminster Palace with a champagne toast in my honor! Only the Lord God could cause such an amazing turn of events to take place. At the end of the day, all I'd lost was 30 pounds of flesh that I hardly needed! God is *so* very, very funny!

One of the verses that I'd repeated and declared over and over during my times of great duress in those years was:

"Strength and honor are (my) clothing; (I) shall rejoice in a time to come."
Proverbs 31:25

Rejoice I most certainly did, and shall continue to do until Jesus returns. Through this trial, I learned about praying through spiritual warfare and governmental principalities. I also learned the discipline of fasting for prolonged periods of time and the undying power of God's Word when your back is up against the wall. The weapons of our warfare are mighty for the pulling down of all strongholds (2 Corinthians 10:4-5).

Nothing is more trustworthy than the pure Word of God when applied to the trials and tribulations of our lives. The longer I live, the more I am beginning to see what the Apostle Paul meant when he said that our momentary, light afflictions are working for us a far more exceeding and eternal weight of glory (2 Corinthians 4:17). In other words, our troubles, when drenched with the Word of God, strengthen us and give us the ability to walk as overcomers through anything. It is all because of Him—Christ in us the hope of glory!

I don't know about you, but nothing revives my spirit like a pure dose of God's Word when I am in need. Whenever I read God's promises to me, I am reminded that He must be my center every day and every night. His living Word is my life line.

This testimony of God's power at work on my behalf is proof that this verse is absolutely true for all of us:

"For I am persuaded that neither death nor life, nor angels nor principalities nor powers, nor things present nor things to come, nor height or depth, nor any other created thing, shall be able to separate us from the love of God which is in Christ Jesus our Lord."

Romans 8:38-39

This triumph in God was the gateway for my becoming a resident of the United Kingdom. I will never need to pay for a visa to live or work in the UK ever again. Hallelujah!

Salvation Station

While it is routine for me to use all sorts of transportation as a full-time missionary, the mode that I most often use is the mini-van that belongs to my associate and trustee, Lesley. When cars are working hard for us, we love them, but when they break down, we have found that our inconvenience often becomes an open door for the Lord to move in the miraculous.

One evening, Lesley and I had driven two hours away from where we live on the South coast to a destination east of us. We were teaching the congregation of a Baptist church how to hear God's voice as a lifestyle and we were all having a great time in the Lord. The class began at 7:30 p.m. and finished at 10 p.m. each Wednesday night. We arrived at our class venue just fine, but about 30 minutes into our home journey, the van broke down. This happened just as we were nearing a roundabout that had an Esso petrol station on it.

We praised the Lord for this because we were in a very remote place, late at night where gas station are few and far between.

Lesley pulled into the station and used her mobile to call for a tow truck. She found out that the earliest that we could get a tow back to her garage was about two hours! Next, she called her husband to say what was happening and ask if he could meet us at their garage when we got there. It looked like we wouldn't be getting home until the wee small hours of the morning.

Lesley and I didn't panic, but began to pray and ask the Lord what adventure He had for us. We wondered amongst ourselves if God would open a door for us to share the Gospel with our tow truck driver that was on the way? Only God knew. We had no earthly idea what the Lord had on tap for us that night. We couldn't have come up with what actually did happen in a million years!

I sat in the car, praying and pondering the happenings of class that night, while Lesley chatted with her husband and the tow truck driver on her phone inside the gas station. The next thing I heard was Lesley tapping on the glass of the passenger window. She said, 'I think we have a situation. The man on the register, in the station, is demanding that you come in and speak with him.'

Her words pulled me out of my ponderings and abruptly brought me to attention. Was this the adventure that God has for us that night? It certainly sounded like it. I undid my seatbelt and walked with Lesley back into the station. No other cars had pulled in when we did, so there were only Lesley, the gas station attendant who had beckoned me to come in, myself, and the Living God, who's presence never leaves us.

The man who stood before us was of Arabic descent. He came from behind the register and I smiled and asked how I could be of assistance. The minute he heard my American accent, his facial features changed altogether. He didn't seem to have any problem with Lesley but he definitely had an issue with my being American.

He seemed quite angry as he said, 'You are American!' as if it was the most despicable nationality on the planet. I told him that I was American. He then went on to ask me if I cared to guess what nation he represented. I told him that I thought he was of Arabic descent. He nodded yes and went on to tell me that he was a Syrian Muslim and that, as such, the people of his nation hate America. He then went on to say that he could kill me, and that Americans are infidels.

This was undoubtedly 'the situation' that Lesley had alluded to when she came to get me outside. We definitely *did* have a situation—a situation where we needed the Lord's wisdom, discernment, and presence to show up in a huge way! Lesley stood behind me, praying in tongues, and I shot up an arrow prayer at that moment, asking for the Lord to give me His words in this threatening moment. Saying the wrong thing at that moment could cost both Lesley and I dearly.

The man waited a moment to see what I would say, and I was silent. He asked me what I was doing out that time of night without a man (Apparently, for a woman to be alone without a man late at night in the Muslim world was seen to be quite unlawful.). I told him that I was teaching a class in that area and that I was a minister of the Gospel of Jesus Christ. He was astounded by this, because I was a woman, traveling alone with another woman.

The interrogation continued. He asked what I was teaching. I told him that I was teaching people how to hear God's voice as a lifestyle. Now it was my turn to be astounded. The man asked me if I was teaching from the Bible in Greek and Hebrew. I told him that I was. I could see the muscles in his face calming down. The Holy Spirit was on the scene! Hooray!

Next, the man asked how often I would be in the area teaching the course. I told him that I had nine more Wednesdays to be in that area. It was time for me to be in shock and awe over the movement of the Holy Spirit because the next thing the man asked me is if I would consider coming to that station for the next nine Wednesdays to *teach him*! I said I'd be delighted to come and introduce him to how we are designed to hear the still, small voice of the One, True, Living God. I looked at Lesley and she nodded her head in agreement that, yes, we would come back each Wednesday, no matter how late it was, to share the Gospel with this man who was clearly in need of a Savior.

In the weeks that followed, we shared many things with the man whom I will call Jack. Jack asked me why I hadn't flinched when he threatened me on that first night. I told him that the difference between us at that moment was that I knew where I was going, if I died then and there. But Jack didn't have peace or rest in his life or in what his beliefs held for him. I assured him that what was waiting for me and anyone who gave his life to Christ was absolutely more than a paradise with 72 virgins! That discussion compelled Jack to ask more and more questions about the differences between our beliefs and how God can move in a very volatile family situation.

To teach Jack about Jesus, I bought him a Bible and gave him a concordance so he could learn how to do Word studies on his own. In the year that we ended up teaching in that area, Jack gave his heart to Jesus!! As a result, he stayed with his wife and the mother of his three children, even though he previously wanted a divorce. With our encouragement, Jack also agreed to go home to Syria and make amends for the years of anger between him and his family members there. While in Syria, Jack discovered he had Jewish relatives, too. He decided that he would go and meet the family he never knew in Tel Aviv. When Jack came back safely to the UK, just before the Syrian crisis began, he emerged as a brand new man of forgiveness and love! Jack's new guilty pleasure became watching sermons on Christian TV from well-known American pastors! Talk about a complete transformation! *Only the Lord Jesus can do this.*

When you think you have someone in your life who seems impossible to save, remember this story. This testimony shows us that no one is too difficult for the Lord to save! No one. This verse cements this truth:

> *"Is not My Word like a fire? says the Lord, And like a hammer that breaks the rock in pieces?"*
>
> Jeremiah 23:29

Once Jack became a Christian, he refused to let us buy any drinks or snacks for our sessions at the gas station. Early in his conversion experience, he began to offer us the best hot chocolate that we have ever had. He told us that he took no credit for how it came out and immediately dubbed his concoction as *Holy Spirit Hot Chocolate.* Anything good that he gave us had to be from the Lord, he said. That became our drink of choice whenever we pulled into the station. What a precious brother we had received into the family of God!

Now, whenever Lesley and I pull into an Esso On-The-Run gas station, we look at each other and chuckle. Twice now, we have had the grand gift of leading men of opposing faiths to Jesus at a gas station by the same name. We are now wondering and waiting for the

Lord to use us again, if He so desires, at Esso On-The-Run Number Three! I can hardly wait. Will it happen again? Only the Lord knows.

Because of this testimony, I look at every inconvenience in the flesh as a possible portal for the supernatural realm to come down from Heaven and touch down here on earth. We must always remember that we are *not* human beings having a spiritual experience, but the polar opposite. *We are spiritual beings having a human experience!*

The old Petra song says it best: 'We are strangers. We are aliens. We are not of this world.'

How do we know we are not of this world? Jesus adamantly tells us this truth in a prayer that He prayed to God The Father as recorded in the Gospel of John:

"I have given them Your Word; and the world has hated them because they are not of the world, just as I am not of the world. I do not pray that You should take them out of the world, but that You should keep them from the evil one. They are not of the world, just as I am not of the world."

John 17:14-16

Aren't you grateful for all that the Lord has already done and is eternally doing for us? His matchless love for you and me can dispel the darkness and any evil forces we may encounter in this life. His love poured out of us for Jack, and we, as Christians, can give love on command in any situation, anytime and anywhere. Where there is no love, there is a vacuum screaming to be filled with the rich, warm, supernatural Presence of our Living God.

Travel Thoughts

1. What's the funniest thing that ever happened to you on a trip?

_____
_____
_____

2. Have you ever been on a trip where you were the minority? What happened?

_____
_____
_____

3. Have you ever shared your faith with a stranger, while traveling? If so, what was the outcome?

_____

_____

_____

Charlynne M. Boddie

3

SUPERNATURAL IN SCOTLAND

"It is only when you are under pressure, when forced to choose one way or another, that your true character is demonstrated."
Brian Tracy

"You shall know the truth and the truth shall set you free."
John 8:32

"Dig the well before you are thirsty."
Chinese Proverb

"Courage is not limited to the battlefield. The real tests of courage are much quieter. They are the inner tests, like enduring pain when the room is empty or standing alone when you're misunderstood."
Charles Swindoll

Elvis Lives: Part 1

You may be wondering why in the world this first testimony refers to the late King of Rock 'n' Roll, Elvis Presley. It may sound strange, but while I have been in the UK and elsewhere, there have been some uncanny instances where mentions of him seemed to have a connection to something or someone the Lord wanted me to pay attention to. In the beginning of this book, I said that some of the content might make you laugh out loud or at least smile. Perhaps you will do that as you read this section. Let me share my first UK story that mentions this star from yesteryear.

In the beginning of my ministry in the UK, I had an assistant, Ariel, who was half English and half Scottish. At that time, I had written a few letters to a famous missionary to Mozambique called Heidi Baker who was coming to Scotland. Ariel and I were excited about the prospect of going to Scotland to hear her speak and perhaps meet her. Ariel went about looking into flights and how to book in on the conference.

As it turned out, the conference was totally booked! In the natural sense of things, it looked like we were not going to be able to attend, but we asked the Lord what He thought about it all and we got a 'green light' in our spirits. We booked a flight and went up to Prestwick Airport, near Glasgow. Our wild adventure was about to begin...

The first 'sighting' of Elvis was near our gate. It was about 5am in the morning and we were catching the red-eye flight to Scotland. We got some hot drinks and croissants to munch on while we waited and I got up to find a restroom. On the way to the restroom, I couldn't believe what my eyes beheld! Blocking my path was a plethora of men in all shapes, sizes, and nationalities sporting Elvis apparel in sequins, gold fabric, and high collars! They even wore his trademark sunglasses and sideburns! I had obviously bumped into an Elvis convention. What a bizarre things to see at that time of the morning! It made me laugh.

Next, it was Ariel's turn to go to the restroom. They were still there in the hall. She couldn't believe her eyes, either. We both wondered what the Lord had for us on this wild trip. If nothing happens in a believer's life by accident, then what could bizarre sighting possibly mean??

We weren't meant to find this fact out until later. Ariel came back from the restroom and we marveled at the oddity of what we'd seen at such an early time in the morning, and then focused on praying for our adventure in Scotland. Soon they called for us to rise and get onto the plane.

It was not a long flight because we were going from England to Scotland, not even an hour. Imagine our surprise when we landed and were walking down the concourse to baggage claim—there on the walls of the concourse were large photos of men dressed like

Elvis!! It was unbelievable! Ariel and I just laughed out loud. We really couldn't believe it. It made absolutely no sense to either of us. It was clearly something that we'd have to tuck away into our minds and hearts until further notice.

Before I tell you what I believe God was doing by allowing us to see all of those Elvis images, let me say that it is really good for us to look for God in every part of our lives. Those things we understand and those things we don't understand can both show us a part of His plan in the workings of our lives. We must remember that His ways are higher than ours.

In keeping with this line of thought, I decided to ponder these images of Elvis in my heart and pull them out at a later date. In the 10 plus years that I have lived and worked in the UK, I have had several Elvis occurrences.

The next time that I found myself looking into Elvis in the UK was soon after I'd spoken to a group in London, several years after that trip to Scotland. The Great City of London is a truly incredible place. There is a myriad of things to see and do. To me, it is the European spin on New York City. It is very expensive, yet I praise God for showing me, a single, missionary chick, how to have fun in London on a shoestring budget. It's a must if you have champagne tastes but a beer budget.

Ariel was no longer my personal assistant. Lesley was my traveling associate at this time and she and I were not wanting to take the train home yet. I suggested that we go to the grand Savoy Hotel in the Strand section of London, just off of the famous Trafalgar Square. I knew that if we went to the American Bar in the hotel, we could listen to some really great jazz for free if we went in before 6 p.m; there was no cover charge then. Off to the Savoy we went.

It really is a beautiful hotel, and at that time, it was full of art deco glory. We took a cab to the entrance and went through the huge revolving door to the lobby. We turned left and went up the stairs to the entrance to the American Bar that had hosted many, many American and British celebs in its illustrious history. As we waited to be seated, we could hear that someone who knew his way around a piano was definitely tickling the ivories. We had come to the right place.

It was a Friday night and so there were various groups of men and women scattered around this intimate setting. Lesley and I sat up against the wall right next to a rather boisterous group of ladies who were celebrating something and singing with the man at the shiny, black baby grand piano in the middle of the floor. He seemed to be enjoying their gaiety as much as they were enjoying his singing and musicianship.

We discovered quickly that it is a tradition there to make requests of the piano man. If he knew the song, he'd sing it and even welcomed the guests to join in. The ladies next to us were really having fun and asked us to join in with them. I love singing, and what they were singing were all old standards, so I joined in. Lesley thought this was hilarious, and a great time was had by all.

After about an hour or so, the ladies, who'd just left work, decided to go home. It was still too early for us to go, so we stayed a little while longer. At the break for the pianist, he came over to meet us. We found out his name was Janzen and that he had a real affinity for all things and people American. He was quite humble and extremely gifted. I told him how much I enjoyed his talents and he said that he'd come back and chat with us after the next break, which he did.

I did some singing with him on my own on some of the songs and Janzen said at his next break that I should come sing every Friday! I told him I'd love to do that, but that because of my work, that probably wouldn't work. That comment prompted him to ask what my work was. I told him that I was called by God at age 21 to be an evangelist based in the UK. This really intrigued him.

Janzen immediately asked if I'd seen any miracles in the UK since I'd moved here. I told him that I had seen lots of miracles. He asked if I'd seen any angels. I told him yes on that question, too. His eyes got as big as saucers and he suddenly remembered that he had to go back to his piano. The long and short of it is that he gave me his cell phone number and asked if we could do lunch so that he could find out more about my walk with God.

Soon after this chat with Janzen, Lesley and I decided we'd better be making our way back to London Victoria Train Station to go home. All the way back, we chatted excitedly about our encounter with one of the top entertainers in London. I knew that God wanted me to share His light and love with Janzen. I prayed that Janzen would call me so that we could pick up where we'd left off in our discussion about Jesus.

Sure enough, Janzen did call and we booked a date to meet in The Strand on one of his days off. We were to chat and then do lunch with his lovely wife, Lucinda, who was a celebrity cook-book editor. I was really excited to share more Gospel truths with Janzen and meet his wife.

Janzen met me at Charing Cross Station and we walked to an Italian restaurant. There, we chatted about his music dreams and career hopes. I asked him where I could get an album of his music and if he had a website. He had no album or website yet. This astounded me because he was so gifted. I gave some strong entertainment encouragement from the Lord on this. His artist's spirit drank it all in with joy. He told me that he wanted me to meet his manager. He asked me for more testimonies about God's hand in my life and was really thrilled to hear more. Soon, his wife, Lucinda, appeared and the three of us had a fabulous lunch together. I got a sense that this was the beginning of a great relationship. Jared said he had no sisters and asked if I'd be his adopted sister. I said, yes I would.

Are there any connections to Elvis in Janzen's story? Yes! As it turns out, during that first lunch with Janzen, I asked him what had inspired him to become a musician. I almost fell out of my chair when he said *Elvis*! Apparently, his mother used to watch Elvis movies all the time and play his music to Janzen when he was a little boy. He told me his earliest music memories involved Elvis and America. Janzen also told me that he'd been to Graceland, Elvis' Estate near Memphis, Tennessee, several times. Janzen was clearly more than a huge fan of Elvis. Janzen was an Elvis encyclopedia!

In this newfound friendship with Janzen, I discovered the mystery of why I saw so many Elvis images in Scotland. Janzen unlocked the mystery for me. He said that I had seen the images of Elvis in the Prestwick Airport concourse because Scotland was the only place in the entire United Kingdom that Elvis had ever walked! In fact, Janzen said that that airport we had landed at was the only place Elvis' foot had ever been in the UK. Elvis was on his way to Germany and got off of the plane just to buy a packet of potato chips. I had never heard that story and it definitely filled in the blanks for me about the connection between Elvis and Scotland.

Again, I remind you that God moves in mysterious ways in our lives. If we will make it a habit to look for God in *every* part of our lives, we will see Him at work. God loves fun stuff, and the wild and wonderful things in life, too. He takes great delight and makes loads of detailed arrangements to orchestrate seasons and times for you and I to experience what are commonly known as serendipitous moments. God above is the Master Mind behind all such occurrences in our lives. From the time that I was a little girl and was given my first journal, I have endeavored to record every single serendipity that God has shown to me in my own life. It is one of my favorite things about knowing and walking with God. It is also why I believe it is absolutely *impossible* for the Christian life to be boring or uneventful. *Our incredible, matchless God is in every detail of our lives!*

"O Lord, You have searched me and known me. You know my sitting down and my rising up; You understand my thoughts afar off. You comprehend my path and my lying down, and are acquainted with all my ways. For there is not a word on my tongue, But behold, O Lord, You know it altogether. You have hedged me behind and before, and laid Your hand upon me. Such knowledge is too wonderful for me; It is high, I cannot attain it."

Psalm 139:1-6

Was that it for me and my Elvis sightings? No way! In another section of this book, there are the details of yet another sighting. You must keep reading to discover where and how it happened. Oh, the suspense!

A Professor Finds His Tongue

On my very first trip to Scotland, I went with a speech therapist called Andrea who was married to a Scottish doctor. This couple had many close Scottish friends in their lives and the therapist felt especially close to me because she said that my ministry reminded her of a painting she owned that was in storage in Scotland. The painting was called: 'Purpose and Vision'. Those are two of my favorite words. As a result of the connection between my ministry and her painting, the therapist promised that she'd take me to Scotland to meet a select group of her friends there in Glasgow.

Andrea made good on her word and bought two tickets for us to go to Scotland. We were going to stay with a couple who were old friends of her and her husband. I was looking forward to what God would do. Her friends were believers. Andrea had told her friends that I was part Scottish, so they had all sorts of fun things planned for me.

Once we got to Scotland, we found out that the first thing Andrea's friends had planned for me was a drinks party with other friends in Glasgow. About 20 others turned up to meet and fellowship with us. It was really fun for me and challenging to hear all the Scottish accents in one room at one time!

I felt the Holy Spirit speaking to me about one gentleman in particular that night. He was a Ph.D. in engineering at the university. He was called Angus. I sensed right away that he was warm and full of life. Angus had been told by Andrea that I taught Biblical studies and led a UK prophetic school. My connection to the Holy Spirit interested Angus a great deal. He had many questions for me about the Holy Spirit. In talking to him, I realized that he had a real hunger and thirst for more of the Holy Spirit. He attended an Anglican church in Glasgow and said he wanted his vicar to meet me so that I could speak there. That was certainly more than I'd expected on a first-time trip to Scotland, but said that I'd be delighted to speak on Scottish soil. Angus was married to a headmistress at a school and said he hoped that I'd be able to meet his wife on my next trip to Scotland. The evening ended well and I felt encouraged by the conversations I'd had during the cocktail party.

Andrea's friends were all so warm and down to earth. I liked them all and enjoyed visiting downtown Glasgow and other sights nearby. Unbeknownst to me, there was to be another social evening at my host's house. This time, they had decided to go all out and purchase *haggis* for me to eat with a group of friends. It is a famous Scottish delicacy that folks either hate or like. I had no idea which side of the coin I was on because I'd never had it before. It was a first for me, and though I'd heard of it, I'd never eaten haggis before.

What is haggis, you ask? Haggis is meat offal in ground or minced form, mixed with oats and spices. That mixture is then placed into a sheep stomach, sewn up, and cooked. When the haggis is ready, the sheep stomach is slit open and the contents are eaten and served with turnips and mashed potatoes.

Andrea's friends went to the top butcher in all of Glasgow to get the best haggis in town for me to try. I felt very special. Once all the guests had arrived for my special introductory feast to haggis, they brought it out on a platter. The hostess served it to me first, with all of the trappings. With all eyes on me, no one said a word. Everyone was poised to see what my first mouthful would be like.

What they didn't know is that my father ate lots of game, and as a result, I grew up eating all manner of things—from snapper turtle to giant conch snails and frog legs, too. I was not scared one bit to try haggis. I scooped up a mouthful of the hallowed concoction and down the hatch it went. Guess what? I loved it! When I gave everyone a thumbs up, they all cheered and raised a glass to me with a toast. It was such great fun! The rest of my time with Andrea and friends went very well, and we soon traveled back down South to Sussex, where we both lived.

Now, back to the inquisitive professor. He was true to his word, and as a result of his kind words to his vicar, a few months later, I was invited back to Scotland with my trusty assistant, Ariel, for a visit to his church to speak for a ladies' coffee morning. I said yes, of course, so off we went to Scotland.

While Ariel and I were very excited to be officially asked to minister there, we had a bit of a hiccup. We needed wheels to get around from place to place for the time that we felt we should be there. We decided to fly up to Ariel's mum's house and borrow her car. Ariel's mum was an elegant lady who jokingly dubbed me and Ariel *'Thelma and Louise'* once we spent the night with her and took her car off to Glasgow. It made us laugh and feel like we were up to some serious mischief!

Once we arrived in Glasgow, Angus and his wife offered to put us up for a couple of nights. We were glad to receive their kind hospitality. Laura, Angus's wife, was a serious, no-nonsense headmistress who didn't seem to know quite what to make of us ladies. She was polite, but not as warm and gregarious as her other half. We tried hard not to be too noisy while we were in their home. Angus was no help because he was so excited that some Spirit-filled ladies had arrived.

Angus showed us to our rooms and let us get settled. Dinner would be a wee bit later, so the food was cooking and Laura excused herself to run some errands. There was electricity in the air as she showed us where the tea and coffee supplies were and said when she'd be back. I must admit that her air of authority made Ariel and I feel a bit like reprimanded children--and Angus with us. I just knew, as did Ariel, that the Lord was definitely about to do something in our midst. As soon as the front door banged shut, Angus pounced on us and escorted us to the front lounge. With tea and coffee mugs in hand, we followed him right in. Excitement was in the air

We three began to pray, and it was clear that Angus wanted to receive his prayer language. We prayed and asked for permission to lay our hands on his shoulders in agreement. He said that was fine with him, so we did. I explained what we were going to do and that the Lord was the Giver of the gift—Ariel and I were just standing in agreement with what the Lord clearly held on reserve for Angus in Heaven. To say that Angus was in high anticipation of what was coming down from Heaven would be a gross understatement!

I anointed Angus's ears, eyes, and mouth to be able to fully receive all that God had on tap for him in that moment. I asked him to open his arms and hands in preparedness to physically receive his personal prayer language. He, being a willing vessel, did just that. He was so expectant! And I know how much God is moved by a willing, hungry, empty vessel.

In moments, Angus received what he so wanted! He was laughing with great jubilation and it was all so contagious! Ariel and I couldn't help but join in. His tongue began to escape from his belly and soon he was speaking in tongues with great freedom and fluency! We actually felt a rush of wind come into that closed lounge! It was glorious! I told him that he could speak, sing, and pray in many different ways with his newfound prayer language. He was *so* very excited and grateful to the Lord for bestowing such a great gift to him.

After all of the excitement, we all decided that we could use another hot drink, so Angus led the way back to the big kitchen at the other end of the hall. We sat there with our steaming hot mugs of drinks and kept on giggling with each other. He was positively gleaming with joy. Yes, the uncontainable joy of the Lord! Hallelujah!

We must have been in the kitchen, laughing and giggling with glee like schoolkids for about 15 minutes, when we heard the key turning in the front door look and footsteps coming down the hall. To Laura, it looked like we'd sat there in the same places for the better part of the last two hours! She shook her head in disbelief that we'd not moved since she left. The three of us had a hang-dog look like all that she'd said was true. Angus knew his wife was not quite ready for that type of experience, but, man oh man, had he been waiting for such a day as this! He wanted to hold onto his secret for a little while.

The next day was the ladies' coffee morning, and all went well. I had a feeling that that was not going to be the last time that Ariel and I would be in Glasgow. We had sown some seed on that trip that was bound to produce a harvest that had to be reaped!

On the flight back home, all that Ariel and I could think of was the joy that Angus had because God had placed the evidence of the same Spirit that raised Christ from the dead on the inside of him. There truly is *nothing* like being with God's people *and* experiencing the awe-inspiring wonder of the One, True, Living God, up close and personal!

> *"When the Day of Pentecost had fully come, they were all with one accord in one place. And suddenly there came a sound from heaven, as of a rushing, mighty wind, and it filled the whole house where they were sitting. Then there appeared to them divided tongues, as of fire, and one sat upon each of them. And they were all filled with the Holy Spirit and began to speak with other tongues, as the Spirit gave them utterance."*
>
> Acts 2:1-4

Angus had an encounter with the Holy Spirit that no one could take from him. He now had an experiential knowledge of the Living God. As you may have guessed, Angus was changed forever and was never the same again!

Marathon Ministry

Just as I'd sensed would happen, Ariel got a call from Glasgow from the leaders at the church that Angus and Laura attended. They wondered if I might like to come with my team and minister at their first-ever ladies conference! Of course, I said that I'd be delighted to come and bring some encouragement to the folks of that congregation again. There was just one catch: I would not be allowed to preach in the church itself *or* prophesy there.

Heavenly protocol demands that leaders respect the guidelines of the churches you minister in. We are to exhibit humility wherever we go. So, I told the leaders that what they had asked of me would be followed. No problem. Let the Lord's will be done and not mine.

So the date was set and we began to prepare for this auspicious occasion. While the men of the church had always gone away on a retreat, this was a true first for the women of that church. They were all so excited to attend. My prayer was that the Lord would show up in all of His glory for these hungry ladies.

On that retreat, we invited the Holy Spirit to come and sit amongst us for the next three days. We shared with these hungry souls how many ways the Lord can speak to us, and numerous ways to hear Him speak back to us. They drank up every word we had for them. We had several moments of blessed quiet and stillness, too. We taught them how to hear in stillness and peace. The Lord's presence was keenly felt by all. It was a very precious weekend.

When the ladies retreat was over, we all went back to the church for a Sunday evening service. The church was large and heaving with people. Just before the service, the worship leader asked if I might come and pray with them before the service. I agreed to do it and went into an ante-room to pray. In the middle of the worship team's prayer, I heard a loud rap on the door.

Outside the door was the priest. He was beckoning me to come outside. I wondered what this could mean, but quietly excused myself, as the others watched and wondered. As I closed the door behind me, the priest asked if he could have a word with me. I stood with him at the back of the church. He leaned close to my ear and whispered these words to me, 'Would you please prophesy over me?' I stood in amazement at his request, but nodded my head and graciously said yes, I'd be honored to prophesy over him.

Now, I'm not going to lie and say here that I was not absolutely gob-smacked that the very person who'd told me I was not allowed under any terms to prophesy in that church had just asked me to do the forbidden thing right then and there! No pressure, right?!

You and I know the Lord *loves* such moments. In moments like these, the Comforter, Our Great Teacher, the Holy Spirit comes in as gentle as a dove and gently nudges even the most closed of hearts to His still, small, first Voice of Love. I know that that is what had just happened to the priest who was now standing in front of me.

Because the Holy Spirit causes us to love on command—His command—I was more than able to pour out a blessing on the man in front of me. I humbly asked the Holy Spirit what His heart was for this man, his son, the priest. I opened my mouth and the Lord filled it with His words for this man. The door opened where the worship team had been praying and I knew it was time for the service to begin. The priest left my side, and my team and I took our seats at the very back of the church in the last row (I remind you, that women were not allowed to speak or prophesy in that pulpit.).

What happened next was the second surprise of the night—the worship team began and the Holy Spirit descended upon that service! People began to dance in the aisle! The priest was in shock and clearly didn't know what to do. It was his turn to truly be amazed. This had *never* happened in that church before. The Lord was on the move and He was not even done yet. He was just getting started. What happened after that astonished me again.

When everyone was able to finally sit down and catch their breath, the priest stood up to go to the pulpit. Angus kept turning around from his seat near the front and grinning at me and Ariel. It was hilarious! He was beside himself with more joy!

The priest stood in the pulpit and said that through a series of odd 'nudgings' from the Holy Spirit, he must give his pulpit over to a friend of God and not himself. He looked right at me and beckoned me up to the front of the church to deliver the sermon! Now folks, when I go to speak at denominational churches, I absolutely do *not* go up to the pulpit in blue jeans, fleece jackets, and sneakers, but that was what I was wearing because I'd already been told that I'd *not* be speaking. The tables had just been turned on me *and* the priest! Although I didn't feel prepared, the Holy Spirit is never caught off guard.

As I walked up the aisle from the very back of that large church, I prayed in the Spirit and asked the Spirit for His heart for this congregation that sat in front of me. He told me these words: 'Tell them about the Audience of One.' I said yes to Him in my spirit and agreed to obey His will and not mine. I delivered a message about the fact that nothing in our lives is more important than all of us getting our identity and validation from the Audience of One, the One, True, Living God, and not the validation of man. That subject matter was a first for me and every word that came out of me that night was from the Holy Spirit. I can take no credit for any of it.

After the service, the priest came up to the pulpit again and brought the fourth surprise. He gave me and my team permission to prophesy over any and every one that would want a word of encouragement that night! The entire church was in total shock and awe at what the Lord was doing in their midst, all in one service!

There were around 800 people there and only eight folks from my team. We quickly got ourselves situated in four private rooms in teams of two each to minister to all 800 people. The team was trained and ready to serve on the Lord's command. All of us served that night until 2 a.m. in the morning, when the last person left the church.

As we all came out of our rooms and wandered into the very quiet sanctuary, there stood the priest! He had asked all of the area fish and chip shops to stay open for us, and some of the pizza shops, too! There in the side chapel of the church was the biggest late-night feast, with dessert and drinks, too, that our eyes had ever seen in a church! I could hardly believe my eyes. It was really amazing what he'd prepared and done for me and the team.

He told us to all sit down at the tables that had been laid out for us, he prayed over our food, and we ate and drank and fellowshipped amongst each other and with the priest. As we finished our meal and thanked him and prepared to go to our hotel to sleep before going home, the priest told me that he'd never seen such a humble display of service in all of his years as a priest! He said it was his pleasure to lay on the feast for such a precious team of saints. I told him it was our duty to serve wherever and whenever the Lord has need of us. It was a night that will never be forgotten there. The entire congregation had experienced the risen Lord! His tangible Presence was keenly felt that night. So many of the words that were spoken on that supernatural night have already come to pass. To God be all the glory, honor, and praise, forever and ever and ever!

As we drove back to Sussex, I kept thinking over and over again that nothing and no one is too difficult for the Lord to deal with. Our God can and will do anything necessary to make His Presence known--His Shekinah glory on the earth. He is Sovereign and Almighty.

"And I heard , as it were, the voice of a great multitude, as the sound of many waters and as the sound of mighty thunderings, saying, "Alleluia! For the Lord God Omnipotent reigns!"

Revelation 19:6

Charlynne M. Boddie

Secrets and Submarines

It wasn't long before I was asked to lead another ladies conference. Just like before, the date was set and we began to put the word out and see who would like to go on our team for yet another adventure with the Holy Spirit. I had a real expectation in my spirit for what the Lord would do this time around, as did team. He'd already blown our socks off on the last trip and we all wondered what was next.

This time, the guidelines from the host church leadership team were different because it was an Assemblies of God church. They believed in all of the gifts, so I didn't have the same restrictions as before. We arrived at the same retreat center and got settled in to have a really fun vision weekend. However, the spiritual environment on this trip felt entirely different. I could feel opposition in my spirit and immediately told my team to begin to pray about it. My core team and I sensed a strong Jezebel spirit(an extremely strong and particularly evil, controlling spirit) in our midst and it needed to be exposed and sent packing.

Almost as soon as I began to speak, I sensed a mocking spirit in the back of the room. So at the first break, the core team and I began to bind what was present and clearly *not* of the Lord. When it was time to come back to teaching and the break was over, the most extraordinary thing happened! Three women got up and left. Get this—the three women were both of the pastors' wives who were hosting me *and* the worship leader!! These three women were not hosting me but hosting the Jezebel spirit!! Our prayers had intimidated them and they couldn't stay one more minute at the retreat center! They had to go, and go they did--immediately! Halleluiah!

My teammates looked at me with a knowing look. Our prayers had been answered and now it was time to get on with some serious Kingdom business! I could instantly sense a lift in the Spirit. The air was cleared and the enemy routed away from God's plans and strategies. I sensed the Holy Spirit saying that I should ask the ladies there who wanted to receive their prayer language.

Now, I must share something with you, dear Reader, this retreat was quite full and had every sort of background imaginable represented there— both high and low socioeconomic backgrounds.

Even before we said the first 'Amen', there was opposition. The opposition was not just from the presence of a Jezebel spirit but a strong spirit of prejudice as well.

In fact, certain women had even gone to the trouble to ask if I would consider holding a separate meeting in Scotland for high society and highly ladies only! They told me that they were concerned that people who were less than desirable might attend the event. I knew that this grieved the Holy Spirit to no end. I lovingly but firmly told the caller that *everyone* is welcome at the table of Jesus and that I would *not* be holding a separate retreat for high society ladies on that trip. The caller hung up the phone, very dismayed to say the least. I began to pray against the spirit that had prompted that less than charitable call. As I hung up the phone, I was reminded that our Lord had said something quite telling about the rich and well-to-do:

"Then Jesus said to His disciples, 'Assuredly I say to you that it is hard for a rich man to enter the Kingdom of Heaven. And again I say to you, it is easier for a camel to go through the eye of a needle than for a rich man to enter the Kingdom of God."

Matthew 19: 23-24

I prayed for the heart of the lady who had rung me and asked the Lord to change her mind and heart. I firmly believed that the Lord had something for that lady and her friends who wanted to hear what I had to share but wanted it their way. I knew that only the Lord can change the heart of a man or woman. I couldn't do it, so I petitioned the Lord to move on the hearts of that group of women.

"....God is greater than our heart. And knows all things."

1 John 3:20

God did another miracle in our midst. There were late-comers to our event. As the women oppressed with Jezebel left us, the wealthy women descended upon us! The Lord God had changed their hearts and minds, as only He can do! I just knew we were in for a grand meeting! The unity that must be present in order for the anointing of the Holy Spirit to come and abide in such a place was evident. We could sense His presence. It was heavy and delightful.

As I asked for those to stand up who wanted to receive the evidence of the baptism of the Holy Spirit and their prayer languages, 15 ladies stood up. I explained that we were opening ourselves up to receive exactly what the early church received in Acts 2 and that rivers of living water were going to come forth from inside of them, where the Holy Spirit lives. Their faces were radiant!

"They looked to Him and were radiant, and their faces were not ashamed."
Psalm 34:5

In that moment, those ladies discovered that when we look to the Lord, He rushes to fill us with Himself. Yes, each of them received exactly what they asked for! It was truly like a domino effect. As the first lady was prayed for, the anointing and power of the Holy Spirit shot through each woman right away. There was such joy in that place when that happened! All of us were so encouraged and excited in our spirits, but there was more where all of that had come from.

Then the Holy Spirit prompted us to lay hands on those who were sick or infirm. A lady who had not been able to walk much or dance before the Lord in over 15 years came forward. That same Spirit that raised Christ from the dead flowed through her damaged limbs and she began to walk and run around the room with incredible joy!

Next, the young male wait-staff of the conference center came forth, they wanted to get in on all of the action. Even though this was a ladies' conference, the young men wanted a touch from the Lord! This time, the Holy Spirit prompted me to hear what was ailing one of the servers and then ask one of his friends to lay hands on him. It was time for impartation. That means it was time for me to pass the anointing in me to him.

The server said that he had injured his back severely earlier that week and was in mega pain. I asked the injured server to slowly get down on the floor and lie down on his stomach. I then told his friend to ask him if it would be all right for him to gently lay hands on his injured back. The server said yes, that would be fine. I asked his friend to hold out his right hand and let me pour some anointing oil on his fingers. I walked him through the laying on of hands and a healing prayer, which he repeated after me. The injured server hopped up, totally healed and praising God!! With that visible proof of the Lord in our midst, high praise for the King of Kings erupted from the ladies who witnessed this miracle. Man oh man, were those servers revived in the Lord. They were the conduit for a miracle and not just the speaker. The servers found out that the Lord is the Lord of multiplication!!

God says that His power is held in earthen vessels. Guess what? Those earthen vessels He is speaking about are *you* and *me*! What an incredible thing for God to have made possible in the people He's made. The catch to this power or the treasure within us is that it was never meant to just remain inside of us. It is meant to be shared with the world that is in darkness around us. We must pour out His power on all of mankind in these dark days! We hold a Light inside of us that cannot be contained! Let it out whenever you can. For we never know who or what is waiting for us on the other side of that kind of action.

"But we have this treasure in earthen vessels, that the excellence of the power may be of God and not of us."

2 Corinthians 4:7

During that miraculous retreat, I was struck with awe by what the Lord showed me one morning as I stood in my pajamas, looking out of the upstairs window in the retreat center. The center was right on the sea and it was very early in the morning, with lots of fog rolling in. As I stood there sipping a comforting cup of tea, I saw something dark and ominous rise out of the fog! It really shook me and got my attention.

What in the world were my eyes beholding?! Was it a whale or something else? Soon the dark mass fully emerged and I realized that I was looking at a ginormous nuclear submarine! Wow. It was incredible in its massive length. I was reminded that where we were situated was very close to a British naval base. This mammoth vessel was on its way home from a tour of some sort.

As I continued to watch and ponder the movements of this great piece of armament, I heard the Lord say, "What is hidden will be revealed, Charlynne. What is hidden will be revealed. That is what I have done in this place before your very eyes. What the enemy of your soul tried to keep hidden, I have revealed it and mine is the glory!" I shook my head in total agreement and an inner joy because the Lord had completely foiled the plan of the enemy in our midst! He is so very worthy of *all* praise!

> *"I will give you the treasures of darkness and hidden riches of secret places. That you may know that I, the Lord, Who call you by your name, Am the God of Israel."*
>
> Isaiah 45:3

The retreat was nothing but a great success for the Lord and His Kingdom. We had given His best to the ladies in attendance and those who served us on-site. Everyone leaving was full of joy and expectancy for what the Lord had in store for us all, but there was more!

My team and I were packing our cars to head back down south, and the director of the center came up to me and began to prophesy a word over me about my gifts and calling. I was so blessed by what he shared and felt a real agreement in my spirit over the prophetic words that were spoken. My cup was absolutely running over at this point! God gives to His children in such abundance! I and my teammates went home so full and more than excited about the promise of our next spiritual adventure in Jesus! We were created to live like this every day. Daniel, God's prophetic governmental leader in Persia, knew this truth:

> *"...but the people who know their God shall be strong, and carry out great exploits."*
>
> Daniel 11:32

There truly is nothing as encouraging for us as the Word of God coming to pass in our lives. Whatever *He* says will come to pass. What a comfort! When the words of man are fleeting and full of holes, we can rest assured that the Word of God is our unshakeable and firm foundation.

Travel Thoughts

1. What uniquely specific things always happen to you when you travel? Describe them here:

   _____
   _____
   _____

2. Have you ever received a special revelation from God while traveling? Describe what He revealed to you here:

   _____
   _____
   _____

3. While traveling, have you ever had to go out of your comfort zone in some way? How?

   _____
   _____
   _____

Charlynne M. Boddie

4

GOD IN GREECE

"In a moment of decision the best thing you can do is the right thing. The worst thing you can do is nothing."
Theodore Roosevelt

"Behind me is infinite power. Before me is endless possibility. Around me is boundless opportunity. Why should I fear?"
Stella Stuart

"Faith is taking the first step even when you don't see the staircase."
Martin Luther King Jr.

"A person's mind stretched to a new idea never goes back to its original dimensions."
Oliver Wendell Holmes

"Progress always involves risks. You can't steal second base and keep your foot on first."
Frederick B. Wilcox

A Mediterranean Introduction

I do hope that you are enjoying these travels around the world with Jesus as much as I am as I write them down. It brings me great joy to share with you what our God has done in my life and the lives of so many others. Each word I type puts me right back in the supernatural zone of life in the Spirit. Once you taste of it, you never go back!

Now, I ask you to turn your attention to the beautiful nation of Greece. It is so full of history and mysteries of both the ancient and Biblical worlds. I was privileged to live there one summer in 1999. Before I go there, I must tell you that none of what I'm about to share would have been possible were it not for the input of my first real Bible teacher in grade school, Mr. Antonio Mendrinos. If that name sounds Greek to you, well, it's because it is! While my classmates and I were meant to call him 'Mr. Mendrinos', I never did. To me, my Bible teacher was always 'Uncle Tony'.

I met Uncle Tony at a school called Jesus Center, in Denver, Colorado. While the school itself no longer exists, the memories my sister and I had there most certainly do. For me, it is where I began to memorize Scripture as not just a part of my schooling but my life. I found the teachers to be loving and more than teachers. They were my friends and took a keen interest in the expansion of my mind and God-designed destiny. It was a private Christian school that had a heart. They knew my Mom couldn't afford the full tuition for us so they made a way for us to go there when there seemed to be no way. God bless them all for what they did for the education that my sister and I received while on their roll books!

Bible scholars anywhere will tell you that to have a real depth of understanding for the Word of God, one must look closely at the original Greek and Hebrew manuscripts. How wonderful to have had a Bible teacher who is 100% Greek! He is and was such a treasure to me and my learning process. I have to say that Uncle Tony helped me get my first glimpse of what being a person of excellence was all about. For when other students were happy to turn in mediocre work, Uncle Tony would give back my homework assignments that were less than my true capabilities and make me do it all over! As a child, I scowled over these moments inwardly, but as an adult, I smile with respect and admiration for the way that God used him in my life to become a seeker and person of excellence. The Apostle Paul said it like this:

"When I was a child, I spoke as a child, I understood as a child, I thought as a child; but when I became a man, I put away childish things."

1 Corinthians 13:11

Uncle Tony taught me Bible, Civics, and World History. I loved it all, and all three subjects were, unbeknownst to me, the basis for what would shape my career in government and ministry when I was done with school. One day, when I was at school, I walked up to Uncle Tony to hand in something that we were meant to turn in during class. It was the end of the day and there was some time for him to have a quick chat with me. This is the line He spoke that I never forgot —the one that would be forever etched on the blackboard of my mind: "Charlynne, promise me that as soon as you possibly can, you will leave America to broaden your horizons and see the world." My first feeling was that I was bewildered by such a statement, yet I felt compelled in my inner being to make a promise to him that I would someday do what he'd asked.

Fast-forward with me to 1999. Uncle Tony no longer lived in America with his American wife. They had felt the leading of the Lord to return to Greece and be full-time missionaries. Uncle Tony's wife had trained to be a librarian and worked at the American university in Athens. Uncle Tony began a Christian bookstore called The Upper Room. Together, they had seven children. Even though they had a large family, Uncle Tony always stayed in touch with me over the years and would call about once a year or try to visit me and my family if he came to Denver.

In the early summer of 1999, I received a phone call from Uncle Tony. The call started off with chit chat and then he dropped the bomb: "Charlynne, I feel that you must come to Athens to help me open up my second bookstore." Wow. That came out of nowhere! I was not expecting that, and asked when. He said, "This summer." Again, I was gob-smacked but excited in my spirit, all at once. I told him that because I'd just left my government job the year before, it would have to be the Lord that made a way for this to happen because of the change in my finances. He asked if that was not a problem, would I come? I said *yes*!

As soon as I got off the phone, I berated myself for saying yes so quickly. I immediately began to shoot some arrow prayers up to the Lord on this request that seemed to come down right out of the ether! What was I thinking?! The thing was, I hadn't thought at all. I believe my spirit overrode my mind and spoke over my flesh and soul!

The next two people I spoke to were my sister and a young friend who worked in the IT world. Both of them told me that they felt led to buy half of the ticket I'd need to go to Greece! I couldn't believe my ears! As soon as I prayed about this new development, I knew that I had to call Uncle Tony right away.

When I called Uncle Tony, he was so excited and eager to choose a date for my arrival. I asked him if I could bring a friend with me who wanted to go on a mission trip, and he said that that was great. The dates were chosen and the tickets were bought and my first adventure with Jesus outside of the UK was underway!

Because there was always a tug on my heart regarding the UK, I asked a close single gal pal there if she might be willing to put me and my friend up for a night before our flight to Athens. She was glad to do it. I began to pack and prepare spiritually and mentally for a very hot summer trip to the Mediterranean.

Petra at Lakavitos

Soon it was time for Tony to pick up his teens from the open air concert and he parked the car in the huge lot next to the amphitheater. There were hundreds of cars and lots of bright lights and the rock sounds of what I knew to be the band Petra. I had always loved them and it was quite surreal to see them on foreign soil.

We walked through the entrance and looked down on the stage and the throngs of young people and their parents milling around. It was happy pandemonium and full of the buzz of excitement that comes with the Presence of the Lord. Tony looked around for his teens and I felt the quickening of the Holy Spirit inside of me. This quickening told me that I was to move forward, through the crowd, and ask to speak to the drummer. I sensed the Holy Spirit telling me to give Him a word in due season, or a prophetic word of encouragement.

The band members were chatting with teens and signing autographs. One of them looked down on me from the stage and heard my request to speak to the drummer and went to get him. Tthe drummer came over to me and sat on the edge of the stage while I gave him his word from the Lord. I was totally unprepared for what happened next. He was so overcome with joy for what I'd shared with him that he jumped off the stage and picked me up and swung me around! He was laughing and crying at the same time. When he finally put me down on the ground, he asked what my name was and I told him that my friends call me *'Charlie'*. This information really made him grin then. Apparently, his sister, who he dearly loves, is also called Charlie! Here was miracle number three! Golly, we'd just arrived in Greece and the Lord was already moving in such a powerful way. To say that I was really excited was a gross understatement. I went to bed that night tingling all over with a great spirit of expectancy!

A Word in Due Season

That week, Tony took us to see his shops and what he needed us to do to help him get the second store open. He also introduced us to his trusty shop assistant who was about my age and very kind. Our new duties entailed helping them to inventory books for the second store that had arrived and were stacked on pallets, ready to be placed on shelves.

It was very hot outside every day, so we found ourselves sitting in the square in front of the bookstore at break times each day, sipping cold drinks at tables with umbrellas. In the square, we met all sorts of people from all over the world who came to check out the new bookstore and me and my friend.

One day in the square, an African woman came to visit the bookstore. She was a believer who I later found out was definitely sent that day by the Holy Spirit. She asked if I'd pray with her about some things in her life and I said I'd be happy to do that with her. It was particularly quiet, so we did it there and then. The Lord often uses me in the prophetic gift of giving words of knowledge and He did the same on that day. This really blessed this woman. As a result, she told me that she believed that I had a word for her roommate who was a nurse there in Athens. She really felt that we needed to meet up. I told her that my first duty was to Tony and getting the bookstore ready, but if the Lord allowed my path to cross with her roommate's, then I'd certainly be happy to pray over her. I never saw that African woman again, but I'm sure I will some day in Heaven. What is important to note is that that meeting with her was *not* by chance but by divine appointment.

You may be wondering what happened after that. Did God open a door for me to meet up with the African lady's roomie? Look at what God did much later in my Greek Odyssey. Towards the end of my time in Greece, Tony told me about another Christian concert that would be happening in Athens. It was a concert with the world famous Integrity Music worship leader, Ron Kenoly. I thought that was fabulous! Then Tony told me that he was going to have a book table there and would I like to go with him to the concert? That was an offer I couldn't refuse. Ron had come to our church and I knew that his music director was friends with my adopted brother. It was going to be a great event!

Divine Positioning

Soon, it was time for Tony and I to go to the venue for the big concert with Ron Kenoly. (I must tell you that by this time in my Greek adventure, I was alone in the flat. The friend I'd come to Greece with was now gone.) It was a large venue, but not outdoors like Lakavitos. There must have been about 10,000 Christians gathered there. The air was electric with anticipation for the Presence of the Lord that was about to descend upon that place. Tony set up his table and I stood with him at the back and later sat down as we were told to take our seats.

What magnificent praise was lifted up to the Lord that night! It was glorious! Everyone's hearts were lifted by each word and each sound heard.

When it was over, people stood around with joyful faces, chatting to each other, and Tony began to sell products off his table. Many came to buy the latest CD from Ron Kenoly's collection. All of asudden, the crowd in front of me parted and there was Ron Kenoly and his music director standing right in front of me! It felt like God had placed a spotlight on me because the next thing I know, Ron asked me who I was. I told him my name, then told Ron's music director who my adopted brother was. He immediately asked how he was doing and to tell him hello. Ron asked if I would go to dinner with him and his wife and the couple who had opened the concert for them. I asked Tony if that was okay and he said absolutely. I grabbed my handbag and went to dinner somewhere on the coast of Greece with Ron and his wife. We all had a wonderful time talking about the Lord and what He was doing in the arts and entertainment world. Once again, I had been divinely placed into a special appointment by the Lord.

When they dropped me off in the wee hours of the morning at my flat, once again I went to bed on a high, chewing over all that had been discussed. What a night!

The Lord was not finished, though. Someone was throwing a dinner party for Ron and his team in Athens later that week and they had rung to see if I could come! I thought that would be fun and said I'd be delighted to attend. The worship leaders I'd met with the Kenolys earlier in the week came to pick me up and take me to the dinner party. It was at a very large house with a rooftop patio. The meal and the discussions with believers there from all over the world let me have a taste of what it must be like to attend an event put on by the United Nations! Heaven was going to be like this too, I thought.

Sometime during that evening, I found myself sitting on a couch near the sliding door to the rooftop patio. There was great Christian music playing in the background and loads of conversations happening all around me. A pretty young woman came over to me, smiled and introduced herself as Lani. When I told her my name, her eyes lit up! She asked me if I'd prayed prophetically over an African woman in the square near The Upper Room Bookstore one day in Athens. When I told her that I had, she told me that *she was the roommate of that African woman!!* You could've knocked me over with a feather! It was amazing. God had done it again! She didn't tell me what her need was, and to be honest, I didn't want to know so that when I did pray prophetically over her, she would hear from the Holy Spirit and not from my flesh. We decided to find a time that would work with her schedule to meet at the bookstore and pray in the square. As you can probably guess, I wasn't going to get much sleep that night. either. God just kept on blessing my socks off!

The day and time came for me to meet with Lani. It was yet another hot, sunny day and when it was time for me to take a break from the bookstore, she was sitting there in the square at a table under an umbrella. We went to the Albanian snack store nearby and got some ice-cream then got ready to pray. I asked the Holy Spirit to show me His heart for this dear sister in the Lord and I waited for Him to speak. When He did, she cried tears of joy for the word He'd spoken through me. It was just what her spirit needed and she asked me how I'd known what I'd shared with her. I told her that Charlynne in and of herself knows nothing, but the Holy Spirit knows all things. Yes, He even knows the innermost secrets of the heart. She went away truly blessed, and so did I!

"And thus the secrets of his heart are revealed; and so, falling down on his face, he will worship God and report that God is truly among you."

I Corinthians 14:25

Supernatural Mystery Tour

Uncle Tony always gave me break time during the work days at the bookstore. One day, however, he told me that he was giving me an entire day off to do whatever I wanted to do on my own. He was not going to open the store on that day. So I went back to my flat, in Viktoria Square, and had a relaxing evening pondering what the Lord may want me to do on the following day.

I woke up the next morning and had my quiet time with the Lord. During my time of stillness, I heard the Lord tell me to get dressed and go to the train station around the corner from my flat and get on a train. I asked the Lord where I was going. He told me to just go and trust Him. Can you say 'adventure'? I knew that this was going to be fun. yet I will not lie to you, I obeyed with some trepidation. It is one thing to read about Abraham doing the same sort of thing in the Bible but to find yourself in the same shoes, in a foreign country, is something entirely different!

As a little girl, I remember Uncle Tony teaching me and my classmates a fair bit of Greek words-- Biblical Greek. Being on a moving train where everything is in the spoken Greek language is quite unsettling when you are an American woman on your own. In my flesh I felt like I was all alone on this adventure, but in my spirit, I knew that I was absolutely *not* alone.

"...for He Himself has said, 'I will never leave you nor forsake you.' So we may boldly say: 'The Lord is My Helper, I will not fear. What can man do to me?'"

Hebrews 13:5

As the train chugged along down the track, we stopped at several different stations and I kept on speaking to My Comforter, the Holy Spirit, all the way. I kept on asking Him, 'Is this where You want me to get off, Lord?' And the Spirit kept on saying, 'Trust Me'. I took that to mean, 'No, not yet.' As people got on and got off, I remained in my seat.

Soon it was quite obvious that we had left the great City of Athens and were now traveling through the countryside. I believe we were going way north of Athens along the coast. Try as I might to look at the station signs and translate the Greek alphabet into English, I had no earthly idea where I was!

When I had been riding along on the train for well over an hour, I heard the still, small, first Voice of the Lord, the Shepherd's Voice say, 'Now you must get off at the next stop, Charlynne.' I thought to myself, 'Okay, Lord, but then what?' The Spirit responded to me with, 'When you get off the train, look for the red car.' This blew me away. 'Really, Lord?!' I thought to myself.

My relationship with the Lord has taught me, since I was a child, that this spiritual truth first spoken by the Prophet/Judge Samuel is absolutely right:

> *"Has the Lord as great delight in burnt offerings and sacrifices, as in obeying the voice of the Lord? Behold, to obey is better than sacrifice, and to heed than the fat of rams."*
>
> 1 Samuel 15:22

Scripture shows us time and time again that it is not good to disobey the Voice of the Lord. I certainly couldn't do that when I knew that I was hearing Him very clearly.

> *"Your ears shall hear a word behind you, saying, 'This is the way, walk in it,' whenever you turn to the right hand or whenever you turn to the left."*
>
> Isaiah 30:21

In keeping with what I'd heard the Spirit say, I grabbed my handbag and got off the train. The train moved on down the track and there I stood, pondering when to take my next step. The Spirit had told me to look for a red car. I looked to my left and then to my right. Lo and behold! There was a red, four-door car sitting there at the station.

I wondered what to do and I sensed the Spirit leading me to go right on up to the car. I could see that a man was sitting at the wheel. As I approached the driver, he turned to me and said, 'Are you the American?' To which I said, 'Yes.' The driver quickly said, 'Get in!' It may sound crazy, but the Holy Spirit prompted me to do just what the driver said!

Did I know this man? No. Had I ever been to this place before? No. Did I even know where I was? No. Did I know where he was taking me? No. How in the world could I be in this situation?! The Holy Spirit had led me, of that, I was absolutely sure.

It is important to note here that whenever we hear the still, small, first Voice of the Holy Spirit, other voices come and try to talk us out of whatever the Holy Spirit has told us to do or say. They are the voice of our soulish reasoning and the voice of our senses, or our flesh. Both of these voices fight for our attention all the time. Yet, we as believers have the authority over both of these voices that often lead us into deception, if we give ear to them and follow their leading.

"For the weapons of our warfare are not carnal but mighty in God for pulling down strongholds, casting down arguments and every high thing that exalts itself against the knowledge of God, bringing every thought into captivity to the obedience of Christ and being ready to punish all disobedience when your obedience is fulfilled."

2 Corinthians 10:4-5

Whenever you and I choose, as an act of our will, to consistently follow the leading of God's Voice of Wisdom, then you can guarantee that you will walk in divine wisdom at every turn and receive blessings and favor from the Lord as a result of your obedience to Him. This is what is known as the Spirit-led life and is the reason why the Christian life is a far from boring existence! Adventures of the supernatural kind await every believer who chooses to obey the leading of the Holy Spirit.

The voice of soulish reasoning was telling me that what I'd agreed to was not wise, and the voice of my flesh was asking me, 'What if this man is an ax murderer?' The root of both voices was fear, not the fear of the Lord, which is the beginning of wisdom. What the other voices said to me actually brought confirmation that what I'd heard first was the Voice of the Lord. Halleluiah!

The driver and I sped along down the road and soon turned into a Greek village that, to this very day, I have no idea what it was called. It was not a very big town at all and we soon stopped in front of a one-level cottage. No sooner had we stopped at the cottage when the front door flew open and there before me stood a large woman whom I later found out was Katerina.

Katerina was as warm in personality as she was loud. She stood in the doorway, telling me these words, 'Come on! Come on in! We've been waiting for you!'

Had I met her before? No. My mind was reeling. Clearly the Lord was at work here. Instantly, my mind went to the book of Acts. There is a place in Acts where the Holy Spirit told Paul and Silas *not* to go preach the word in Asia. As a result, they ended up in Troas for the night. During that night, we read that Paul had a vision:

"And a vision appeared to Paul in the night. A man of Macedonia stood and pleaded with him, saying, 'Come over to Macedonia and help us.' Now after he had seen the vision, immediately we sought to go to Macedonia, concluding that the Lord had called us to preach the gospel to them."

Acts 16:9-10

Had Katerina seen me in a vision? The answer is *yes!* When I walked through her door, there was a quickening of the Holy Spirit inside my belly. I knew that I knew that I was right, smack dab in the middle of a most exciting supernatural adventure! Katerina was a woman of strong faith and she had cried out to the Lord for someone from America to *'come and help them'* in her village! That someone was me! Man oh man, was I excited! God had gone ahead of me and told them *that this day was the day an American evangelist would come to them!* They had put their faith into action and placed a car and driver at the nearest station in divine expectation that I'd show up!! Halleluiah!

Katerina showed me where her restroom was and then she went into the kitchen to check on the dinner she was preparing for lots of people. When I met her a few moments later in the kitchen, she began to tell me that they'd been waiting for me to appear. She was *so* overjoyed! Her face was beaming. She told me that after dinner, she had arranged for *the entire village to come for healing prayer!* This was absolutely the Lord's doing and His party, for sure. In my mind, I was just praying that I would say and do only what the Holy Spirit led me to say and do. I had no thought whatsoever what time it was or where I was.

Something else that comes to mind as I write this is that when we are in the company of the family of God, there is no such thing as being a stranger! I was struck with the deep, wide love of God that exuded from this woman whom I'd never met in all of my life! It was a spirit-to-spirit connection that bonded us instantly. She gave me the details of what was on her heart for the people of her village and we were off and running into the plans of God.

Soon, dinner was ready and the guests Katerina had invited began to appear. I was introduced to several friends of hers and we had a lovely meal and time of fellowship in the Lord. I knew that Heaven was going to be just like this!

When dinner was over, a long line of villagers appeared who needed prayer for all sorts of things. As a rule of thumb, I always traveled with anointing oil in my handbag. I was so glad that I had it with me. It is something that every evangelist ought to have on hand in their 'go-kit' for any journey.

"So they went out and preached that people should repent. And they cast out many demons, and anointed with oil many who were sick, and healed them."
Mark 6:12-13

The Lord filled me with His compassion for all the people who kept on coming and coming. My heart ached with love for them all. Their needs pulled on my giftings and caused the anointed, healing touch of the Lord to flow from me. The Lord loved on them and touched them through my hands. I felt humbled by it all. This part of my God-designed, Greek Odyssey was so much more than I expected!

Once I'd prayed for the last villager, I realized that it was about 3 a.m. in the morning! There was no way that I would be catching a train back to Athens, so Katerina took me to a bedroom and gave me one of her own nightshirts to sleep in. I had nothing with me but my handbag and an airline toothbrush. Again, I was reminded of how the Lord sent out his men to minister in the highways and byways of the

Holy Land. If traveling in the service of the Lord with next to nothing was good enough for them, then, by all means, let me have the same deal as them! I at least had a handbag!

"And He called the 12 to Himself, and began to send them out two by two, and gave them power over unclean spirits. He commanded them to take nothing for the journey except a staff---no bag, no bread, no copper in their money belts---but to wear sandals, and not to put on two tunics."

Mark 6:7-9

When I woke up the next morning, Katerina told me that we had to go to another village and pray for more people. The entire adventure was prepared for me! All I needed to do was say and do whatever the Spirit of the Living God led me to say and do. It was marvelous! Each moment, I felt like I had been transported back in time to the book of Acts! To be quite honest, I didn't want it to end.

I got into her car and we went to another village and the same thing happened again and again! People seemed to be pouring out of every nook and cranny at each place we went. This went on for three days, and it occurred to me that perhaps I should call Uncle Tony.

I told Katerina what I was sensing in my spirit and she asked information for the number for a bookstore in Athens called The Upper Room. Instantly she began to speak in perfect Greek to Tony. She introduced herself and began to tell him of all the supernatural exploits that had happened while I'd been in her home. He was excited and told her that he suspected that I'd been caught away by the Holy Spirit and didn't seem to be bothered about my absence in the least! This truly amazed me, but then I knew Uncle Tony was a man of God who also heard His voice. I spoke to Tony and told him I was fine and thrilled to have had this wonderful adventure in the Spirit. He told me what station to get off at and said that my newfound American friends at the American University were somewhat worried about my absence and had asked if they could host me for a bit to hear what God had done. Tony gladly let me have the rest of that week off.

I hugged Katerina and thanked her profusely for the 'great ride' in the Spirit and we both agreed that if we never saw each other again in this life, we would certainly meet again in Heaven! She put me on the train and that chapter of the Greek Odyssey closed.

Sometime later, I got off the train and my American friends, the Saxtons, picked me up and seemed quite relieved to see me! Tony had assured them I was all right, but I believe that they wanted to see me for themselves. The first thing they asked was if I wanted to go home and get some fresh clothes from my flat before they whisked me away to their lovely home. I believe a new adventure was about to begin.

Monk Magnet

The friend that had been with me for the first 10 days of the trip had left me with a huge bag of candy to give to the children of a Greek orphanage that was run by a friend of mine named Christodoulos. In Greek, that name literally means 'slave of Christ'. He was a believer in the Greek Orthodox Church who had taken the vows to be a monk. I met and befriended him in America. It was there that I had told him that if I ever found myself in Greece, I'd like to visit the orphanage that he ran. He is the first of many such monks who have crossed my path and befriended me—hence, my UK nickname of 'Monk Magnet'.

My trip was coming to a close and I knew that I had a couple of weeks left and that I didn't want to leave without getting the candy to the children at the orphanage. I had a real mission on my hands where this was concerned. It had been months since I'd last seen Christodoulos. I knew what Greek island the orphanage was located on, but I had no way of getting in touch with my friend, the monk. Monks are known for living in hard-to-get-to places without many amenities. It was going to be a real task and I knew that my not being fluent in Greek would be unhelpful in this quest. I prayed about it. God had a plan—of that I was sure.

After praying and pondering this quest in my heart, the Lord spoke to me about a very real possibility. He asked me to speak to the Saxtons and ask if I might borrow their son, Jake, and his best friend, Avi, to take me on yet another Greek adventure. They thought that was a wonderful idea because both boys were fluent in the language and would relish a quest like this. What boy wouldn't? Didn't all men everywhere crave adventures? Well, we'd find out.

I told Uncle Tony about my new mission. He was shocked to find out that I'd befriended a Greek Orthodox monk in the States and that I wanted to seek him out and the orphanage, too. I told him that I didn't want to tell my friend that we hadn't made the delivery of the candy to the children. Tony told me that we needed to get plane tickets to Rhodos. That was where the orphanage was reported to be.

Jake and Avi were so excited! Rhodos was known to be a great place to visit and take in some sun. The guys had, of course, gone ahead of me and scoped out the best beaches there and other important logistics. Haha! They assured me that in the midst of them trying to give me a run for my money on my tan, they would absolutely help me find the monastery and the orphanage!

So we packed and got dropped off at the airport to take the puddle jumper flight to the Island of Rhodes, or Rhodos. There are so many different Greek islands, but this was a very pretty place. The guys were really amazing. The first thing they were tasked with doing once we landed was getting us a car to use while on the island. We had maps and bottles of water, plus our bags, as we began our island adventure.

The guys told me that their research had shown that there were three beaches worth checking out, so we did. It was wonderful because it seemed like we had the beaches to ourselves. They were clean and full of dunes and sea grass. Such tranquility! We were all in heaven and decided to chill out for the first day.

On the morrow, we woke up and got our bearings so that we could make our way to a church to start sleuthing for the quest we were on. In the first place we came to where we could see a large Greek Orthodox church, we parked our car and got out. We could see that there was a service going on as we walked up to the front entrance. There were nuns at the entrance, ready to greet us.

Jake and Avi spoke in perfect Greek to the sister who now stood in front of us, wondering how she could assist us. They told her about my quest and she listened to them, then looked at me and nodded with a smile. She spoke to the guys about the man she called 'the American monk'. Although he was 100% Greek, he was a Greek American and that is how the locals distinguished between him and other monks in the islands. Because of his accent, everyone knew him and he was apparently very much loved. The information that she gave us really encouraged me and I knew that we were on the right trail. The Lord had clearly gone before us! Hooray!

I am a real 'foodie'. Well, my nose was speaking to me at that moment and what I smelled was interesting. It was a mixture of incense from the mass that was undoubtedly taking place inside the church and the comforting smell of freshly baked bread. Sure enough, the nun spoke to Jake and Avi and asked if we could wait for a moment. The guys said yes, not knowing what the nun was going to do next.

She went to the nearby convent and came back, beaming, with a big loaf of fresh bread for us! She had cut it into pieces and put it into a wooden bowl, offering it to us. The amazing smell was enticing, but eating it was even better! Whoever said it is important to stop and smell the roses was so right! We can rush, rush, rush in our lives or we can choose, as an act of our wills, to stop from time to time and enjoy moments like these that God so lovingly prepares for us to drink in or eat up, as this case most assuredly turned out to be.

We gobbled up the warm bread and thanked the sister profusely for her kindness and the information she gave that pointed us in the right direction of the monastery and orphanage. What a fortuitous moment that was!

Next, we thought it would be a good idea to find our next place to stop for the night, closer to our destination. We found a great B & B set up on a hill. It had a quaint little courtyard that was full of beautiful lemon trees that were heavily laden with the most perfect lemons and oranges you'd ever want to see. The owner was very friendly and we were so glad that we had chosen that place.

My two trusty tour guides and interpreters were eager to try out the next beach on their list—we all were, to be honest. It was so hot and we knew that we were on the right trail, so we took a happy break to put on our swim suits and drop ourselves into the cool refreshment of the sea. My entire time in Greece, we had temperatures that stayed in the upper 90s and 100s in Fahrenheit, so I welcomed every opportunity to get into the Mediterranean water. It was on this trip that the guys discovered that ,yes, Black people's skin does peel in intense sunlight. I'd never had a freckle in my life, but I got several that summer.

The next day, we set off again with eagle eyes on the island map and a spring in our step, feeling like we were very close to our final destination. We drove and drove along some windy and curvy mountainous roads, wondering if we were ever going to get there. All of the sudden, we found ourselves in a very wooded place with a large building in a clearing. It was the monastery that we'd been searching for! We consulted our notes and all that the islanders had told us we'd see at the property. Yes, that was the place that we'd been searching for, but there was only one glitch. There didn't seem to be anyone there!! I am not sure if they were all on a field trip that day or what, but there was nothing but silence. So we waited there for about 30 minutes, in the hopes that someone might come back or show up. No one came.

While I was sad that we had missed everyone, I refused to be discouraged! I took out a notepad and wrote out a note to Christodoulos and the children telling them that the candy on their doorstep had been brought by an American lady who was a Christian, just for them. I prayed that the Lord would open up a way for me to connect with the monk at a later date.

All was not lost, though. We completed the mission with flying colors and were so glad that we were able to make the candy drop, too. That being done, it meant that there was still one more beach for the guys and me to check out. And so we did. It was glorious, just like the other two! We were hardly surprised. The votes were in. Rhodos was a splendid place to have a short adventure. No doubt about it.

We finished frolicking in the sea and went back to our lovely B & B on the hill, only to find that the owner was there with a great going-away present for us all! He had spent the afternoon picking oranges and lemons that he had put into small, brown paper bags for us to take home with us! That was the icing on a very nice cake that had been baked for us on this mission. God's goodness and mercy had followed us wherever we'd gone.

"Surely goodness and mercy shall follow me all the days of my life; and I will dwell in the house of the Lord forever."

Psalm 23:6

We left that lovely place feeling refreshed and very satisfied in our monastic quest. Even though things had not quite turned out the way we'd hoped, we could still see that the Lord had blessed us anyway. We were glad in our spirits and praised the Lord as we boarded the plane bound for Athens.

Travel Thoughts

1. Have you ever felt compelled to give a prophetic word to a stranger on a trip? If so, what happened?

   _____

   _____

   _____

2. Ever been on a scavenger hunt? Where was it and what was the strangest object you had to find?

   _____

   _____

   _____

3. Has God ever asked you to go somewhere without giving you all of the details? If so, where did you go and what did you do there?

   _____

   _____

   _____

5

INTERVENTION IN ITALY

"Sometimes our candle goes out, but it is blown into flame by an encounter with another human being."
Albert Schweitzer

"To get the full value of joy, you must have someone to divide it with."
Mark Twain

"When you do the things you have to do when you have to do them, the day will come when you can do the things you want to do when you want to do them."
Zig Ziglar

"It's our attitude in life that determines life's attitude toward us."
Earl Nightingale

"The key is not to prioritize what's on the schedule, but to schedule your priorities."
Stephen Covey

"People say that what we're all seeking is the meaning of life...I think that what we're really seeking is the experience of being alive."
Rudyard Kipling

"Be content with what you have; rejoice in the way things are. When you realize there is nothing lacking, the whole world belongs to you."
Lao-Tzu

I have long dreamt of going to the beautiful country of Italy. As a child, I wondered if the famous Leaning Tower of Pisa really did lean. I wondered what it would be like to sit in a gondola on the Grand Canal of Venice. As a serious foodie, I longed to try real hand-made pastas from every region and the Italian version of ice-cream called gelato.

Living in the United Kingdom, and therefore, very close to Italy, only sweetened the pot of my dreams. I knew that my dreams were in reach as soon as I moved to the UK. The question was not if I was going to Italy, but when.

Angel on Arrival

About 10 years ago, I met a very adventurous woman who had recently turned 40. She talked of how she'd made a plan to celebrate her 40th birthday with a group of lady friends on the south coast of Italy on an Italian farm that hosts tourists. This is called an *agriturismo* in Italian. She said that she and her friends had thoroughly enjoyed themselves in chalets by the sea and that there were plenty of attractions where they'd stayed. When I asked her for the information for the place she'd been, she gladly gave me the contact details for the owner of the farm. I wasn't 40 yet, but I purposed in my heart to go there myself with some of my close friends to mark that milestone year in my life.

A couple of years down the road, I invited one of my closest friends, Maire, to come and stay for a few weeks in the UK. She was chewing on the prospect of working with me in ministry and wanted to see what it was like to live as I do here. Lesley wanted to host her in her home and I thought that it would be nice for the three of us to have an Italian adventure to celebrate my 40th birthday.

Although my birthday is in late November, I decided to celebrate the occasion by going to the Italian farm for a whole week in July. I knew it would be seriously hot in the Mediterranean, but ideal for swimming at the beach and packing light. We saved our pennies and emailed the farm to make our booking. Maire and I would share a chalet there and Lesley would have a chalet all on her own.

We were so very excited! The Lord had made a way for yet another dream of my heart to come true. I was so grateful and wondered what He had in store for us all on this adventure. I'd always pondered what turning 40 would be like for me spiritually because I knew that 40 was always a milestone number with God: It rained 40 days and 40 nights when God destroyed the earth in the days of Noah (Genesis 7:4), Isaac married Rebekah when he was 40 (Genesis 25:20), Esau married when he was 40 (Genesis 26:34), The children of Israel walked in the wilderness for 40 years and their clothes and shoes never wore out (Numbers 32:13), Jesus fasted 40 days and 40 nights when He was led by the Spirit into the wilderness to be tempted of the devil (Matthew 4:2). Yes, the number 40 is of great significance to God.

The day came for us to take ourselves to the airport. We boarded an Easyjet flight to Naples, Italy. None of us had ever been there, so it was a first for us all around. To say I was tad bit excited was an understatement!

We landed and got our bags off of the carousel and then began to look for a bus that would take us into the city center so that we could take the necessary train to Sorrento, where we would then make our way to the farm by taxi. I am not fluent in Italian and neither were Maire or Lesley. We needed the Lord to make a way for us.

"For you shall not go out with haste, nor go by flight; for the Lord will go before you, and the God of Israel will be your rear guard."

Isaiah 52:12

Italians can talk very fast, so understanding whether we were on the right bus or not was quite a feat! We did our best to choose what we thought was the right bus and then got off where they told us to in the middle of Naples. By this time, it was very dark outside and I knew we needed to get to the train station safely. We had to trust the Lord. I knew we needed a miracle.

Lesley and Maire wondered where to go next and just as I turned around to see if there were any signs that might point us toward the train terminal, a man appeared out of nowhere! He motioned to me that I should follow him. Lesley and Maire wondered if it was safe to do so. Again, none of us could speak Italian, so this was risky for us to follow someone we didn't know in a rather seedy part of town at night, in a foreign country! I had peace, and so we followed the man that had appeared to us in the darkness.

He led us down several streets and a couple of alleys. The ladies began to wonder where he was taking us. I must admit that I did, too. Soon, I could see a building ahead that was lit up and seemed to be the terminal that we were in search of. What a relief!

As we got to the entrance to the train terminal, I realized that our guide in the dark was gone!! The man who had silently led us from the middle of Naples to the train station was gone. As quickly as he'd turned up, he disappeared, seemingly before our very eyes. We praised God and were so grateful for what was clearly an angel whom He had sent to aid us in our hour of need. God is so kind!

We went to a ticket counter and told the attendant that we needed three tickets to Sorrento. He told us what platform to go to and we boarded the train. It was a while before we got off the train, but when we did, a taxi was there to take us the rest of the way to the farm where we'd be staying.

Our hosts were the farmer, Gino, and his Irish girlfriend, Marie. Marie was waiting up for us and showed us to our chalets and where the main clubhouse was for the guests to eat their meals and gather in. She told us when breakfast was and said she would see us in the morning and that Gino was the cook.

It felt great to finally be where we were supposed to be. We were quite tired after our flight to Naples, our angelic adventure, and the train and taxi to our final destination. Sleep came swiftly. Our Italian adventure had begun!

You Smell Fantastique!

Things looked so different when we'd arrived in the night! The daylight brought us all such delight as Maire and I opened our eyes to the reality of where we were and all the sounds, sights, and smells around us. It really was glorious! Our tummies were rumbling and we wondered what Gino was cooking for us. We got dressed and went to the clubhouse for breakfast.

Lesley was already dressed and waiting for us at a table on the deck, right by the water. Wow! What a beautiful sight to dine by. The sea was right at our feet and the table was set for three. Gino was there to bring us juice and coffee with scrumptious lemon bread that he made himself from a family recipe that had no doubt been handed down from generation to generation. There were cheeses and meats, too. And it was already warm. We had the deck all to ourselves. We were not sure if there were other guests there or if we were the only ones on site that day, but we were jumping to see the area and take a peek at the pretty city of nearby Sorrento.

Marie greeted us as she was preparing to clean chalets and gave us the information we needed to catch a bus into the city. We grabbed our cameras, sunglasses, sunscreen, hats, and comfy walking shoes for a day on the town.

We climbed the long drive up to the main road to catch a bus and marveled at the olive and lemon groves of the farm. We saw a large antique olive press on the deck where we ate our breakfast and relished the idea of eating some local produce from the farm, drizzled with extra virgin olive oil. What a treat that would be! Our eyes really popped when we saw the size of the lemons. I wondered if they were some strange Mediterranean fruit that was unknown to me. The lemons there are the size of American footballs! I couldn't believe that the branches could hold them. We saw a crate of them that had been picked and placed into a small green farm truck outside the clubhouse. The smell of them was intoxicating and I knew that these must be what the Italians of this region used to make the famous Italian liquer called *limoncello*.

Once we got to the top of the drive, we had a very long wait for a bus but it finally did come, and then we got off to catch another bus to the city centre of Sorrento. The views from the bus as we drove along the hilly coastline were mesmerizing, to say the least. From our perspective, we could see the most inviting ocean-blue hue of the water. It was as vibrant as the blue-green of a peacock's feathers. That's what came to mind.

When our second bus let us off in the center of Sorrento, our eyes saw so many things that drew our attention. The three of us decided to take a stroll down an alley that seemed to be the place of many artisans. Most women love shoes and so we went to see the cobbler there. He was busy making sandals out of the fine Italian leather that they are famous for. It was fun watching him and seeing how he did it. There was every color of leather imaginable. He turned to me and asked if I wanted him to make me a pair of flat sandals. I have long feet and wondered if he could do it. He said he was happy to measure my feet and do it. I had sandals made while I waited. That was the first treat of that day for me personally.

Wherever we went, we were called *bella Americana,* or beautiful American. God's favor followed us wherever we went and the people seemed truly happy to see us and do business with us. Our cameras were clicking all of the time. We began to discuss amongst ourselves the prospect of catching a boat to the Isle of Capri and another prospect further down the coast to scout out the pretty coastal towns of Positano and Amalfi. We went to the boat docks and got some literature on these excursions so we knew the cost and timings. It was definitely something we wanted to do later in our week.

After a great day exploring Sorrento and eating lots of great food, we made our way back to the farm and chilled out on the deck to watch the sun go down on the horizon of the sea. What a beautiful sunset! It was wonderful to relax and just be for a moment and drink in all that was around us and where we'd been that day.

Gino and Marie asked us if we'd enjoyed our day and how things went. We told them we really did have fun. They were glad and asked if we'd like for them to make us dinner the next day. Gino had planned to visit the local fish market and asked me if he could make something special for us. I told him that I'd like to have some swordfish. He said that he could get that for me and would make me a lovely dish from that. I could hardly wait. Maire ordered something and Lesley said she'd do dinner there with us the next night, but that she was not fond of fish. Whatever we were going to eat, I had a feeling it was going to be fabulous! Italy is a land of great cuisine. It doesn't matter what region you are in. It is impossible to starve there!

Since the farm was located right on the Mediterranean, we had the advantage of a very short walk to a bathing area and small village with shops and restaurants right off the cliff path below our chalets. It was ideal really. So the next day, Lesley and Maire decided that they wanted to go to the beach and cool off. It was extremely hot, so they were ready to take a dip into the cool waters of the sea. I went with them for a while but then I wanted to be quiet for a moment on my own. So I told my friends that I wanted to journal on the deck in the hammock for a bit. They said they wanted to stay in the water longer, so I agreed to see them later at the clubhouse.

I put my beach things away, took a shower, then grabbed my journal and a pen. I locked the chalet and set off down the path toward the clubhouse. As I walked along, I saw a man coming towards me. He was obviously one of the new guests that had arrived. I smiled and he nodded as he went past but then he turned right around and said this to me: "*Cherie*, you smell *fantastique*!!" What a thing to say, I thought, and later I wondered if God would say that I smelled great to Him. For I knew that He'd once said that of a very Godly man called Cornelius in the Book of Acts long ago.

"...Your prayers and your offerings have come up to the Lord as a sweet aroma."

Acts 10: 4

When I heard the man's statement, I turned around and thanked him for the compliment. His accent told me he was a Frenchman. He introduced himself to me as Sebastian and proceeded to ask me what fragrance I was wearing. I told him that it was not perfume at all but a shower spray. He asked if he could get it in Italy. At that time, it was only available for purchase in the States. He recognized my accent and asked what I was doing in Italy.

I told him that my friends and I were celebrating my birthday. At that moment, an older woman he introduced as his mother appeared. He introduced me to her and then asked if I would join him and his mother for a refreshing drink at the clubhouse. I said that would be nice. Right then, I got that familiar sensation in my stomach that always tells me that the Holy Spirit is about to do or say something through me.

As Sebastian's mother sat down next to me, she spoke to me in perfect English with a French accent, asking me where I lived. I told her I was from Colorado but now living in the UK. She pounced on me then, with great excitement in her eyes, and asked why I lived in the UK. I explained to her that I had a call of God on my life. I was sitting between her and Sebastian, and she instantly told him to pay attention to what I was saying. The next words out of her mouth were electric: "Have you ever experienced a miracle of God?"

Well, how could I let that question go unanswered? By this time, other members of their family arrived, were introduced to me, and pulled up a chairs, and *suddenly* there were 12 of us in all – including the teens and adults in their extended family. My birthday trip had become an Italian/French missions trip! God has a deep and wide sense of humor. No doubt about it.

Gino and Marie brought lots of cold drinks and Sebastian asked that we be brought the famous limoncello. It came ice cold in small liquor glasses. With a captive audience, I began to share several healing miracles from my time in the UK. The entire French family was enraptured with awe and had many questions about God's miracles today. Sebastian's mother clapped her hands with joy and the teens sat in amazement at all I shared. What a special moment!

As I had a break in sharing testimonies and answering the family's questions, Maire and Lesley appeared. Sebastian got up and added two more chairs to our number and asked if they would like something to drink! Lesley and Maire were astonished to find me in the midst of a large French family, sharing the exploits of our wonder-working God. What a day that was!

Once they got their drinks and were introduced all around the circle of Sebastian's family, we chatted some more about the Lord. As the family rose to go and get ready for dinner in town, they hugged and kissed me twice on the cheek as if they'd known me for years! They thanked me for sharing the wonders of the living God with them and asked Marie to give me their email address. Amazing! I truly believe that there are no strangers in the body of Christ—only brothers and sisters we have not met yet. Sebastian's mother was one switched-on granny! It was such a joy to meet them all.

We knew that we'd have a great meal that night with the food prepared by Chef Gino and we had a lot to discuss over dinner. My swordfish, freshly caught that day, melted in my mouth. Gino had grilled it to perfection and put it on a bed of greens, then drizzled the fillet with his own olive oil and served it with fresh lemons from his own trees. It was simple and so delicious! We went to bed with happy tummies and excitement in our spirits because of what had happened that day. We decided to go on boat trips for the next couple of days.

Amalfi Surprise

On our first boat trip, we went to the Isle of Capri. The weather was perfect and we found favor with a driver who promised to take us to all of the sights on the island, complete with lots of Roman ruins. It was really lovely. We had his service for the whole day at a bargain basement rate. Yes, the Lord was going before us wherever we went and we were grateful.

The second day of boating was equally as wonderful, though very different from the first day's excursions on Capri. On the second day, we were on a big sightseeing boat that would stop at Positano and Amalfi. We decided to get off at Amalfi and see the church there because it was the legendary burial place of the bones of one of the 12 apostles and meant to be a lovely town to explore.

The three of us walked through the alleys and cobblestone streets to the main church square. Lesley decided to rest in a cafe on the square while Maire and I went into the church. It was very beautiful inside and full of history. We thought the literature of the church was very evangelical in its presentation and that cheered us.

When we came out, we went to have some refreshment with Lesley in the cafe on the square, decided to wander some more together, and to pick up some postcards and other souvenirs as we walked. I liked that it was not crowded at all but easy to get around.

As we made our way back towards the water, we knew that it would soon be time to catch the last boat back to Sorrento. We went to the beachfront and soon meandered back towards the docks for the tour boats. We had some time, so Lesley and Maire decided to wander to the end of the pier. I chose to stay at the beginning of the pier and look out to sea.

I had bought a very large, wide-brimmed red straw hat on the Isle of Capri the day before and was wearing it in Amalfi. It was a beautiful sunset and I was enjoying being on my own, alone with my thoughts of the sights and sounds of the day, when all of a sudden, a man below me on the boat launch, called up to me: *"Bella,* that is a very beautiful hat you are wearing."

His statement brought me out of my silence and I looked down at him and thanked him for the compliment. He commented on the fact that I was obviously an American and he wondered what I was doing there. I told him that I was celebrating my birthday. He asked where I lived in America and I told him I was from Colorado but living in the UK. Like everyone else, he asked why I was in the UK. I told him that I had a call of God on my life and that I was a minister of Jesus Christ.

As he continued to tie up several speedboats of various sizes, he stopped and looked up at and said: "I think God is against me."

I continued to look down at him and said that I totally disagreed with him. He beckoned me to walk down the stone staircase near my side and explain to him what I meant by that statement. Before I walked down the stairs, I looked towards the end of the pier to see that my friends were still down at the very end looking out to sea. Our boat had not come in yet and I just waited to see what the Holy Spirit was saying. The Lord said I could go down the steps to speak to this man.

He introduced himself as Vincenzo and gestured to the man sitting nearby, stating that he was his father. Before I could answer Vincenzo, his father got up off his chair and came over to me, assisted by his cane. The statement of Vincenzo's father let me know that the Lord was absolutely in this situation that had opened up before me. This is what his father said to me: *"Bella,* I saw you talking to my son and as you walked down the steps, I heard God tell me that you are a woman who hears the voice of God. Is this true, *Bella?* Do you hear the voice of God? Do you?"

I felt the familiar tingle of the Holy Spirit's Presence down my spine as the old man spoke to me and I told them that I most certainly do hear the voice of God. Vincenzo asked me to explain why I believed that God was for him and not against him. I shared the Gospel with Vincenzo, while his father sat in agreement, nodding his silver head. I answered several questions for Vincenzo about the Lord and encouraged him to read the Bible for himself and ask the Lord to be his partner in life. Vincenzo said that he would consider what I'd said, and I declared that I needed to catch a boat back to Sorrento with my friends.

Praise God that I said that, because Vincenzo and his father said that we were on the wrong pier and that we had just enough time to catch the last boat back at another pier, if we hurried. Before I went back up the steps, Vincenzo ran to his office and brought me his card and said that if I was ever in Amalfi again, he would be happy to taxi me anywhere I needed to go via his fleet of boats. I thanked him and he and his father kissed me on both cheeks as I left.

When I got to the top of the steps, Maire and Lesley were there, once again looking at me with surprise, wondering what I had been doing chatting with the men on the dock below. Maire asked if I knew them, and I said no, it was my first time in Italy, just like them, but that God clearly had some assignments for me there. They smiled and shook their heads in wonder. I told them we needed to hurry to catch the last boat that we could see was ours at a nearby pier. We ran and successfully caught it. Halleluiah!

On the way back to Sorrento, we chatted about what had transpired between Vincenzo, his father, and me. God can open any window, anywhere, anytime to reach anyone! He never ceases to astound me with His ways! They really are *so* much higher than ours—and aren't we glad? We are so blessed to know Him.

"For a day in Your (the Lord's) courts is better than a thousand (elsewhere). I would rather be a doorkeeper in the house of my God than dwell in the tents of wickedness."

Psalm 84:10

I love this little Italian story because it reminds us that if we will just choose to put the Kingdom of God first, making all things on His heart a priority to us, He will take care of everything concerning us in this life and the next. It is a simple truth and yet, so hard sometimes for us to obey the leading of His still, small, first voice. But, man oh man, when we do, the rewards are truly out of this world!

"But seek first the Kingdom of God and His righteousness, and all these things shall be added to you."

Matthew 6:33

The Lynne and Lang Tour: Teaching In Tuscany

I've just shared some stories from my first trip to Italy. Now, I'd like to share some stories from my second Italian adventure. The year was 2008 and I went with my dear friend, Cinzia (That is the Italian name for Cynthia.). I had told her about my first trip and she had expressed an interest to go with me for something different. Once again we saved our pennies and prayed about where to go and how. It was time to do some research on tours.

I found out that there were several companies that offered great tour packages for various amounts of money and lengths of time. We found a steal of a deal that would give us great value for our money over almost two weeks of time! We'd be crazy not to take this offer and the price was so right.

I must say that whenever I am with Cinzia, we both feel the favor of God in a rather unique way. Incredible doors open for us when we are together and we know that God is in our midst, blessing the way ahead for us. Cinzia had come to see me every year since I moved to the UK for about five years at that point in time, so she was used to and loved the ways of European people. She was as excited as I was to make the trip to Italy. Both of us are serious foodies and we decided to do a proper road tour of Italy from the north to the south.

What a joy to travel with a sister in Christ who has a sense of fun and adventure! Let me say here that the gift of friendship is something that we must always make the time to invest in. If this is an area in your life that needs some attention, take the time to reach out and touch someone. Friends are an elixir to your physical, emotional, and spiritual well-being. I really believe this quote:

"There are not many things in life so beautiful as friendship, and not many things more uncommon."

Unknown

Lesley had driven Cinzia and me to the white cliffs of Dover to board a tour bus that would be driven onto a large ferry boat to France, on the continent of Europe. There were a whole lot of people that we'd never met before in our lives that would be traveling with us. Most of them were couples and we wondered if any were Christians.

We loaded our suitcases and got onto the bus and chose seats for the two of us. The air was abuzz with the voices of others all around us. Soon it was time for the bus to drive up to the numbered lane that would lead us to the our ferry to France.

Before I go any further, let me explain to you why this section is called 'The Lynne and Lang Tour'. Early in this adventure, I noticed something wild about our names. In the Asian world, there is something called the yin and the yang. If you take the last syllable of my first name, which is 'Lynne', and the only syllable of Cynthia's last name, which is Lang, you have a fun spin on that Asian term. I also noticed something else that goes with yin and yang. The symbol for yin and yang is a circle cut in two with a black teardrop shape and a white teardrop shape that fit together like puzzle pieces. In Chinese philosophy, the phrase is used to explain that opposites can be complementary rather than opposing forces. In fact, the belief goes on to say that opposites can be not only complementary, but also interconnected. The funny thing about that is that I am black and Cynthia is white! God put us together as friends, like two well-placed puzzle pieces. We laughed and laughed when we saw the similarity between us in this way.

Back to the beginning of our Italian adventure...

It was amazing to see the size of these large cross channel ferries that carry cars, trucks, and buses to the other side! They are like mini-cruise ships because they have malls, restaurants, and all sorts of amusements on them. There are even gigantic lounge chairs that can actually hold two people in the reclining position. We could relax a bit during the crossing but would have to get back onto the bus once we came into the port of Calais, France. That was where our bus would leave the ferry and begin the journey to Italy via different countries.

Cinzia and I thoroughly enjoyed our many stops at various rest stops along the way in Belgium, Germany, and Austria. We noticed that we were the only Americans on the entire tour, so we stood out like sore thumbs because of our accents. We found many reasons to giggle and laugh at our blunders along the way because of all of the differences in cultures we discovered along the way.

In the beginning of our tour, we found ourselves in Switzerland, where we would be stopping for the night. I was glad to see words on signs in the German language which were familiar to me because I took German in high school and had tried to keep speaking it over the years. Cinzia was German and she was excited to be there, too.

Even though we were traveling in April, the scenery was dappled with snow in the mountains. We had stopped at a lovely little village and our hotel looked like a very quaint chalet. Our room was spacious and very comfortable and cozy. We were told that once we got our room assignment, we should settle in and come downstairs for dinner.

Cinzia and I were about to make our first blunder and didn't even know it. We had freshened up a little bit before dinner and chosen a booth. Where we sat, there didn't seem to be anyone in our group and we kept looking at our watches wondering where everyone else was. Soon, the Swiss server came to us. She didn't look very happy and I could tell by what she was saying that we were sitting in the wrong part of the restaurant. As we rounded the corner, we discovered our entire group sitting together! *We* were the odd ones out, not our fellow tour-mates! Talk about embarrassing.

We quickly sat down at a table with others from the bus and began to make introductions. We ended up sitting among some of the ladies who were single like us but traveling with friends. They were friendly and we had a good time chatting and eating.

Soon, it was time to go up to bed because we were going to have an early start the next day, making our way south to our many Italian destinations. We ate a continental breakfast of breads, cheeses, and various meats. It was different from what we'd eat in the States, but delicious all the same. Then, it was time to board the bus and leave our Swiss chalet.

The next time that we stopped, we found ourselves in Tuscany. Hooray! What a thrill to be in a place that I'd seen in films my whole life but wanted to go to for what seemed like forever. The landscape was just as I'd imagined it. So many little villages.

Soon. we stopped at a rather large hotel and out we all popped. When we got to the check-in desk, our tour guide, Giorgio, gave out our room assignments. We went upstairs to a very large room and flopped out on our twin beds. Cinzia and I both pinched ourselves. We were finally in Italy! *Viva Italia!*

Our question about whether we were traveling with other Christians was answered that night. When we came down for dinner, we decided to eat at a table with an older couple that was in our group. They welcomed us and introduced themselves. Dick was a doctor and his wife, Denise was a nurse. They told us that they'd just retired and decided to go to Africa to be a missionary doctor and nurse! Wow. We had found fellow Christians! God is so good.

We congratulated them on their decision to follow the Lord's desire for them. That comment prompted them to ask us about our own walks with God. They wanted to know how we'd found out about that particular tour. So I shared with them that I was called to the UK and that Cinzia was a dear friend who often visited me. Dick asked me what sort of Bible teacher I was. When I told him that I taught people how to hear the still, small, first voice of the Holy Spirit as a lifestyle, he was fascinated.

Our dinners came and then it was time for coffee and dessert. Through it all, we had a delightful time in Jesus, chatting with our newfound friends. Being in the presence of God's people while we are here on earth is but a glimpse of what our lives will be like when we are all living in Heaven in eternity! Over coffee, Dick began to ask me more and more about how to hear God's voice. I continued to share with him and Denise. Little did I know, but this was going to be something Dick continued to discuss with me throughout our trip. What fun to know that there are no accidents in our lives when we choose to walk in obedience to God's still, small, first voice! Our innocent Italian tour had become a classroom for two medical missionaries to Africa! Proof once again that our God is very, very practical.

That night, Cinzia and I went to bed smiling at the ways of God. He had left us two gems called Dick and Denise to meet along the way and we were so blessed! Before we went to sleep, we prayed that the Lord would further encourage Dick and Denise in their mission and walk with Him.

Bell-ringing Blunder

Somewhere along the way in our nearly two-week excursion in Italy, we found ourselves in a sweet little hotel near Rome. We were going to be there for two days, so we got our room assignment and waited in line for the tiny elevator that would take us upstairs to our room. I think it is always a good idea to find things to laugh at when traveling. You are out of your comfort zone and things are definitely not going to be like they are wherever you are from, so it behooves one to make the most of whatever happens.

The first thing in this sweet little hotel that we had to laugh at was the size of the elevator. Only 2 people at a time could get into it. To some, this was *not* funny. To us, it really was. When it was our turn to finally get into the elevator, or lift, as they are often called in Europe, it was the tightest squeeze ever! We both barely fit inside of it and the only way we could do it was if Cinzia would straddle herself across the top of her luggage, like she was riding a horse! I had to breathe in so the doors would shut on both us and our bulging bags in that very tight space. By the time we got to our floor, we were laughing hysterically like schoolgirls who had passed a funny note to each other behind the teacher's back! When the door to the lift opened, we popped out, like a cork on a wine bottle. Tears were streaming down our faces because of the fits of laughter we had.

Our laughter had just begun. We found our room and almost immediately, Cinzia asked if I minded that she wanted to take a shower before dinner. I told her to go right ahead. As she undressed, put a towel around herself, and wrapped up her hair, I decided to stretch out on my twin bed and write a bit in my travel journal. Cinzia closed the bathroom door and pulled the cord that would normally turn on the electricity for the shower, but nothing happened. She really wanted a shower and nothing was happening. So, she pulled the cord again. I was on the other side of the door writing away, totally oblivious to her mishap. I heard water running and thought nothing of it.

While she was in the bathroom, I kept on hearing the most annoying buzzing sound every few seconds. It kept on happening over and over again! The sound seemed to be coming from the hallway outside our door. Finally, I got up off of the bed and opened our door to take a look outside. I wondered if it was a faulty fire alarm or something. It was that loud. No one dressed like emergency personnel came up the staircase or off of the elevator in either direction, so I closed the door and went back to my journal.

Soon, Cinzia came out of the bathroom and shared with me her problem with the shower. Both of us wondered why the cord to start the shower wasn't working, but were not going to let it ruin our evening either.

We saw that we had shuttered windows that operated like big metal blinds, yet we couldn't get those to work for us either! Our room seemed to be full of blunders! Again, we smiled and got ready for dinner instead.

Since we weren't carrying our luggage with us, we decided to skip going down in the lift and went down the stairs. Dinner was great. We were thoroughly enjoying all of the different foods from the various regions we were traveling through, and we generally liked our fellow travelers. When it was time to go back to our rooms again, we walked up the stairs.

As we got ready for bed, we heard that same aggravating bell tone that I'd heard when Cinzia was trying to get her shower earlier. Again, it seemed to be coming from the hall. This time, I opened the door and there was a hotel staff person outside one of our tour mates' door asking if everything was all right. I also noticed that there was a light on over their door that was flashing on and off – like an alarm of some sort. Then it dawned on me, the bell that was ringing was coming from the cord in the bathroom that each of our rooms had. The hotel staff person told me that it was an emergency cord for elderly people to pull if they fell or tripped on wet tiles in the bathroom! When I heard that, I laughed and laughed and shut the door.

When I told Cinzia what the cord was for and that each time someone pulled it, the staff thought someone had fallen in the shower, Cinzia fell on her bed laughing her head off; again, we laughed and laughed. All night long, we heard the bell ringing over and over again. Apparently, not everyone in our tour knew what those bathroom cords were all about! We couldn't stop laughing. Was it the incessant bell ringing or the extra glass of Prosecco we'd had with our dinner? We'll never know...

"A merry heart does good, like medicine, but a broken spirit dries the bones."
Proverbs 17:22

Dancing In The Street

It was our first time in Rome and we really wanted to take in the sights and smells of this romantic city. In honor of the occasion, we decided to wear skirts and sandals. We knew that we were going to see some famous churches and other famous sights on a very hot, sunny day, so skirts were also going to be cooler.

We went into a cathedral in a not-so-touristy part of Rome that had some quiet streets. We got off of the bus with our group and explored the grounds of the church, inside and outside. It was quite refreshing to walk in the cool interior on such a hot day. Both of us liked art and we were drinking in everything that we saw.

Soon, we found a door that went outside to a small courtyard that had lots of ancient ruins from the glories of the Roman Empire and we decided to take pictures of each other there. We knew that our bus was parked on the avenue in front of the cathedral, so we decided to take a leisurely stroll back to the bus along the avenue.

Straight ahead of us, we could see a cafe to our left. There were several guys there watching us as we approached. There was a huge 'ghetto blaster' stereo unit in their midst that they were listening to. As we got closer to them, they heard our accents and asked us to wait. They were so excited and kept on screaming, '*Bella Americanas, Bella Americanas!*' One of them kept rummaging through his CD collection and finally held up something he obviously wanted us to hear. He popped it into the giant CD player and sat back in his chair with his friends, grinning from ear to ear as the song began to play. It was "Born in the USA" by the very popular rock and roller Bruce Springsteen! They were so excited that they'd found that song for us! Again, we laughed and laughed and told them '*Grazie mille! Grazie mille!*' Thanks a million, in English.

As the guys in the cafe allowed the song to play, Cinzia and I twirled in our skirts to the beat and bowed and curtsied to the guys in the cafe before we boarded our bus that was parked a few feet away. What a joy to be in a place where the people are so happy and find ways to enjoy every bit of life, as it comes to them! That was an Italian moment that we'd never forget. The happy Italian believes these things to be true:

> "*A merry heart makes a cheerful countenance, but by sorrow of the heart the spirit is broken.*"
>
> Proverbs 15:13

> "*All the days of the afflicted are evil, but he who is of a merry heart has a continual feast.*"
>
> Proverbs 15:15

All along the way, the Lord was giving us reasons to not just smile but to laugh out loud often. We were having an absolute blast and, yes, a feast of joy. Both of us had chosen to enjoy everything that the Lord brought our way on this incredible journey. Each day, we woke up to new possibilities and we joined our wills with His plan for us and delighted in it all. We were gracious wherever we went and the Lord gave us favor.

> "*A gracious woman retains honor...*"
>
> Proverbs 11:16

Being gracious to others around us is a choice. It costs nothing, but when you are, the rewards are out of this world. Each time that Cinzia and I travel anywhere together, God moves on the hearts of the people around us and blessings flow. We share the love of God and whoever is on the receiving end blesses us back. Don't get me wrong, that is not why we do it. The blessings are a happy result of delighting in the things of God. When you give of yourself to others, God cannot help but bless you in return.

"Delight yourself also in the Lord, and He shall give you the desires of your heart."

Psalm 37:4

"Give, and it will be given to you: good measure, pressed down, shaken together, and running over will be put into your bosom. For with the same measure that you use; it will be measured back to you."

Luke 6:38

Canals and Kisses

One day ,we woke up and Giorgio, our tour guide, told us that we were going to Venice, the centuries old city of canals. We could hardly wait! There was so much that we wanted to see there. Could we do it in the few hours that we had? God knows what is on your heart before you even ask Him for it.

"It shall come to pass that before they call, I will answer; and while they are still speaking, I will hear."

Isaiah 65:24

We were staying at Hotel Miami in a place called Jesolo (yayzolo) on the mainland of Italy and would be taking a water taxi to the heart of Venice. We had a fabulous tour guide called Carlo and thoroughly enjoyed the history of the great city and even saw where famed explorer, Marco Polo, lived.

Later, Cinzia and I decided that we wanted to take a gondola ride through the canals with four of our bus mates. That was absolutely glorious and such a wonderful way to get a feel of this magical place.

It is traditional to take a ride, while sipping Moscato, the Venetian champagne. It is very sweet, like a dessert wine. Our Gondolier was Mario Antonio, and a very proud Venetian. His tour took us through the old and new canals of Venice, or *Venezia*. *Bellissimo!*

Before we made our way back to our meeting point at Hotel Gabrielli, we decided to search for the celebrated Carnivale poster for 2008. We'd heard that each year of the festival, the city makes a different poster and we thought that would be a great souvenir if we could find one. The Lord was blessing us in so many ways on this trip and we just knew He would lead us to the right place to get a poster.

Sure enough, we walked into a shop with lots of masquerade masks on display. Each one was so different and elegant. As we admired all of the craftsmanship, we spied a 2008 Carnivale poster at the cash register! The shopkeeper heard our accents and offered Cinzia a poster for free. She couldn't believe it. He said the fee for it was minimal. When she asked what it could be, he said she could have the poster for a kiss. She laughed and offered him her cheek, and with that, we got our posters! God's favor, along with goodness and mercy, truly was following us wherever we went!

When we got back to the bus, our fellow tourists marveled at the posters we'd found, and even more when they heard how we got the posters! I don't believe that we paid full price for hardly anything on the entire trip.

I love the use of other languages. Early on in this trip, I had learned the two most important words in Italian that any foreigner should know when shopping: *piccolo sconto*. In English, this means *a little* discount, please. Every trip to Italy, I have used this phrase and the Lord has blessed me with favor from every shop where it has been said. It really was a blessing!

"For surely, O Lord, you bless the righteous; You surround them with Your favor as with a shield."

Psalm 5:12

Timely Truths In Tirol

When we left the Italian state of Emilia Romagna, where we'd toured Venice, we drove north through a very mountainous region called the Tirol. We were going toward Austria and would be staying in a place called Hoptgarten. It really reminded me of the Rocky Mountain West in the States. There was even snow on the peaks to add to that train of thought. Our hotel was a proper ski lodge and offered us very beautiful views wherever we looked. It was all so breathtaking! How anyone can believe there is no God is beyond me. All of creation shouts the reality of Who He is!

"The heavens declare the glory of God; the skies proclaim the work of His hands. Day after day they pour forth speech; night after night they display knowledge. There is no speech or language where their voice is not heard. Their voice goes out into all the earth, their words to the ends of the world."

Psalm 19:1-4

When it was time for us to have dinner in our mountain retreat, a couple named Ken and Karen asked if they could eat with us. This was really something. We knew that God was at work here. Ken was a very gregarious person and larger than life. He dressed as a biker, and even wore a pointy dog collar around his neck for the full effect. In her non-biker outfit, his wife looked the polar opposite of him. During our tour all over Italy and through several different countries, it was Ken who rallied the troops to move in unity when necessary. He was an interesting character to watch in action, this large, tough man. Now we were sitting with just him and his wife. Cinzia and I were all ears.

Ken began by saying that he'd heard from some of the others that I was a minister and that both of us were Christians. He wanted us to know right away that he was an agnostic and that he used to be a Baptist! I knew that I needed to share the Gospel message of the true Jesus with him, letting him know that the Lord's arms were outstretched even now to see him return to His loving arms. As I spoke, Ken's eyes began to get teary and he quickly excused himself to go to the men's room.

While Ken was gone, his wife, Karen, told us that he was sharing things with us that she had never heard in all of the years that they were married! She was truly gob-smacked by what he was telling me. Clearly, God was ploughing some ground with Ken during that dinner. When he returned, he told me and Cinzia how encouraged he was to hear that the Lord was still loving, saving, and healing people.

Before we left dinner, we prayed with Ken and Karen that all that we'd shared would create in them a fire for the true Jesus that they'd heard about over dinner. They both gave us hugs.

Once we got back to our room, we prayed together for Ken and Karen and thanked the Lord for the opportunity to plant some more seed for Him on our Italian adventure. Cinzia asked me, with a huge grin on her face, "Could it be that the Lord just used this trip as a front for an impromptu missions trip to show forth His glory?" I told her that I thought that was exactly what the Lord had done.

God can be very sneaky sometimes. He often reveals things to us on a need-to-know basis. This is best because if we knew all of what He was up to, we might get in the way of His perfect plans and timing.

"The secret things belong to the Lord our God, but the things revealed belong to us and to our children forever, that we may follow all the words of this law."
Deuteronomy 29:29

After our time in the Tirol, we boarded our bus and made our way back to the ferry boat in Calais, France to cross the Channel to merry old England. It had been a fabulous time away, full of evangelism moments and blessings in abundance, or *abundanza*, as the Italians would say. God had been very good to us and I couldn't wait to come back to this lovely country.

Mormon Inquest

The third Italian trip itself was just as beautiful as the one before and yet it was very, very different from the 2008 adventure. This time I went with my Dad and his wife. I saw different cities and towns and really enjoyed it. One of my favorite places we stopped was a fortress city on a mountain top, called Orvieto.

We went on a gloriously sunny day and took a tram up the steep cliff to the top of the mountain. What a lovely city it was! It was an absolutely perfect day for photo snapping and walking winding cobblestoned alleyways. I could hardly wait to start exploring.

We walked into the city and made our way to the cathedral in the center of town. The piazza there was magnificent and so wide open. Everyone was stunned by the majesty of the edifice before us and began to take pictures. The youngest couple on our tour were newly married and in their late twenties. I saw a serious Canon camera on the neck of the wife and so I offered to take a photo for the two of them in front of the cathedral. They were so happy that I'd done that for them and began to chit-chat with me. We introduced ourselves officially and promised to chat later on during the tour.

Once again, my ears were pierced to be alert and ready to swing into service unto the Lord. I could sense in my spirit that something was drawing this young couple to me. From there, they began to speak to me quite often at meals and elsewhere. They were very kind and sweet.

One day on the tour, they invited me back to their room to hang out and chat. The big disclosure on their part was the fact that they were Mormons, and devout Mormons at that. The wife, Kelly, brought out her blue Book of Mormon to show me, and her husband, Dirk, shared about his Mormon faith, as well. They said that they'd been drawn to the light in me and wanted to find out more. I assured them that I had a devout faith, too—in Jesus Christ and His Word. They felt that that gave them an opening to do their best to convert me!

I had had several Mormon friends over the years and two of them came to the Lord in my Mom's home group. They had been elders in the Mormon Tabernacle, and we even had a Mormon who came to the Lord in our college and career singles group back home. Again, my Mom had been very instrumental in his conversion process, so I knew all about the Mormon religion and had also learned the details of it from the class on cults that my high school taught each year. Needless to say, I was more than up to speed on that cult, yet, I still had the love of the Lord for this young, sweet, and very deceived couple.

We chatted for about three hours and even exchanged mailing addresses. Though they were not able to convert me, Kelly asked if they could stay in touch with me. I said that I'd be delighted to correspond with them. They had moved to the UK from the States to open a very special car plant—one that makes armored cars for the leaders of nations and celebrities. In fact, it was their family business.

They asked to hear my testimony, and when I shared that I'd done assignments for three US presidents, this caused them to open up about their reason for being in the UK. When I found out what they did for a living, I asked if they were the company that made the Pope's bullet-proof car, and they gave a resounding, 'Yes!'. Wonders never cease.

When I asked them how they were getting on in the UK, Kelly said she couldn't believe how hard it was to convert people there. They had not been able to convert anyone to the Mormon faith in their time in the UK. They were astounded to hear all the different sorts of people I had seen come to the Lord in the 20+ years that I'd been sharing about Jesus in the UK. Amazing.

We gave each other hugs and I returned to my room to earnestly pray that the truth that had been spoken to Kelly and Dirk would be received, sprout, and be rooted in them so that they could turn their hearts from the deception that had ensnared them their whole lives. These truths and so many others came to mind as my eyes found sleep:

"Surely You desire truth in the inner parts, You teach me wisdom in the inmost place."

Psalm 51:6

"God is spirit, and His worshipers must worship in spirit and in truth."

John 4:24

"If you hold to My teaching, you are really My disciples. Then you will know the truth, and the truth will set you free."

John 8:32

"But when He, the Spirit of Truth, comes, He will guide you into all truth. He will not speak on His own; He will speak only what He hears, and He will tell you what is yet to come."

John 16:13

Oh, that the eyes and ears of mankind would be open to the perfect, infallible truths of the Living God! I have a hearty disliking for deception and all of its many faces. With every letter I wrote to that couple, I prayed that the eyes and ears of their spiritual understanding would be open to God's pure truth and nothing but His truth.

That trip in Italy was equally as wonderful as the one before, just different. Dad and Tina had a blast and made many friends. Dad got hundreds of his own pictures that looked like postcards, too. Even as I write this, I am wondering when the Lord will allow me to go back to Italy. I am always ready and willing.

Travel Thoughts

1. Do you speak any foreign languages? If so, which ones?

    _____

    _____

    _____

2. When something interrupts your travel plans, how do you respond to the situation?

    _____

    _____

    _____

3. Do you have a favorite travel companion? Who is it and why do you enjoy traveling with them?

    _____

    _____

    _____

Charlynne M. Boddie

6

INVITATION TO ISRAEL

"Hope works in these ways: it looks for the good in people instead of harping on the worst; it discovers what can be done instead of grumbling about what cannot; it regards problems, large or small, as opportunities; it pushes ahead when it would be easy to quit; it 'lights the candle' instead of 'cursing the darkness.'"
Anonymous

"Chance favors those in motion."
James H. Austin

"There's no thrill in easy sailing when the skies are clear and blue, there's no joy in merely doing things which any one can do. But there is some satisfaction that is mighty sweet to take, when you reach a destination that you thought you'd never make."
Spirella

"Trust yourself. Create the kind of self that you will be happy to live with all of your life. Make the most of yourself by fanning the tiny, inner sparks of possibility into flames of achievement."
Golda Meir, Fourth Prime Minister of Israel

"When written in Chinese, the word 'crisis' is composed of two characters--- one represents danger and the other represents opportunity."
John F. Kennedy

"Luck is what happens when preparation meets opportunity."
Darrell Royal

"Attitude is the librarian of our past, the speaker of our present and the prophet of our future."
John Maxwell

The Birthing of An Adventure

Before I begin to share about my first trip to Israel, I feel I need to give some background on why and how I believe the Lord stirred me to go there. It all began with the supernatural events that started in December 2007. That was the month that God made it very clear to me that He wanted me to leave the UK and go for a sabbatical in Florida, alone with Him—no one else—just Him.

This was the trip where I befriended an orthodox Jewish rabbi and met two angels named Gabriel and Daniel. Because of all that happened in Florida, it was probably one of the most amazing, 30-day slots of time in my life! On that supernatural adventure, I knew, without a shadow of a doubt, that I must set my sights on Israel. I had a sense in my spirit that God was brewing an assignment for me in that holy place.

Soon after that sabbatical, I got a call from a pastor in Hastings, East Sussex, England. He was hosting a conference where each part of the event was set aside for praying for different parts of the world. Day 1 was for the UK; Day 2 was for Europe, and Day 3 was for Israel. All I heard in my spirit was a bell ringing: *Ding! Ding! Ding! Ding!* Something leapt inside of me! Yes, those of us in the world of the Holy Spirit would call it a quickening--exactly what Elizabeth, John the Baptist's mother, felt in her womb when her pregnant cousin, Mary, came to share the news that she was carrying the Messiah.

"When Elizabeth heard Mary's greeting, the baby (the unborn fetus of John the Baptist) leaped in her womb, and Elizabeth was filled with the Holy Spirit."

Luke 1:41

The pastor wanted me to come to the conference and do some prophetic workshops. He also told me that a Jewish lady, Candace, was coming who was a journalist in Israel! That did it for me. I had a total peace about agreeing to go to this event.

As it turned out, Candace and I instantly hit it off. Both of us were media professionals and lovers of Israel. Later, the prophetic teammates from our ministry team who had come with me to the conference were able to minister personally to the journalist and her husband, Mark. The personal prophetic ministry toward them at that time really blessed that couple. They were Americans who had chosen to make *aliyah*, or return to live in Israel.

After the conference, Candace and I stayed in touch via phone and email. As it turns out, she has a famous cousin in the food industry in Denver, Colorado where I am from. During those conversations, Candace decided to put my name in for consideration to be a delegate for a first-time ever program being run by the Israeli government and Yad Vashem, Israel's National Holocaust Museum.

Unbeknownst to me, hundreds of Christian leaders from around the world had applied. Only 20 would be chosen as guests of Yad Vashem. When Candace shared what she'd done on my behalf, I asked myself: *'Is this my time to go, Lord? Was this what the conference in Hastings was all about? Could I really be chosen out of hundreds of people who had submitted an application to participate in this special program that had been invented to attack anti-Semitic thought?'* God's answer to me was a resounding *yes*!

The deadline for all applications was January 15, 2010 and the program was to be run April 9-18, 2010. The Israeli government and one big corporate sponsor would cover all costs except the flight to and from Israel. I filled out my application, praying over every bit of it for God's wisdom in how I answered each question, laid hands on it when it was complete and mailed it to Israel. Waiting for the results was hard, but I did.

On January 20th, Yad Vashem contacted me, by acceptance letter, to say that I'd been accepted into the program. I was elated! I did one big 'happy dance' in my office on that special day! That was one miracle, but then the next one was that my godson's father wanted to cover my flight to Tel Aviv. The next praise report was that Candace and her husband wanted to host me at their house before the program began. Needless to say, this was a moment that I had waited for my whole life. I'd always wanted to go to Israel, and now I was literally going as an 'official guest of State' to the place where God lives! Once again, the Lord was showing me that with men, things are impossible, but with Him, *all things are possible!* This trip was special to me because *I knew that for God and His children, Israel is the center of the universe.*

"Jesus looked at them and said, 'With man this is impossible, but not with God; all things are possible with God."

Mark 10:27

Let the supernatural Israeli adventure begin!

Elvis Lives: Part 2

My arrival into Tel Aviv went very smoothly and I followed all the instructions Candace gave me to get a shuttle. In no time at all, I was driving down a highway toward Mevaseret Zion where she lives. The shuttle brought me to her complex and she and her husband met me.

The first thing that I did was take a little catnap because I hadn't slept on the flight. When I woke up, Candace and Mark took me to a nearby village where they said they had a special treat for me. I couldn't guess what that was.

We got into the car and drove out into the countryside. Imagine my surprise when my eyes looked up and beheld two large, tall statues of Elvis Presley towering over the desert!! It was like being in Scotland all over again! It made me laugh out loud. Candace and Mark were grinning from ear to ear, like two cats with a canary. They had brought me to Israel's famous Elvis Diner!

Of course, we got ice-cream, and I knew I had to get some postcards for my buddy at the Savoy Hotel in London who had been so inspired by Elvis. He wouldn't believe it when I told him where I was!

The diner itself was really cute inside, and so retro. There were tons and tons of memorabilia and incredible posters from the 1950's. Candace and Mark insisted on taking pictures of me standing next to the Elvis statues. I knew that my friend in London would have been in hog heaven!

Our Lord sure does have a huge sense of humor! If you had told me that I would have seen Elvis on my very first day in Israel, I wouldn't have believed it! Anyone but Elvis! God is such a God of joy and mirth!

> *"You have made known to me the path of life; You will fill me with joy in Your presence, with eternal pleasures at your right hand."*
>
> Psalms 16:11

Moroccan Mamunna

After we left the diner in the desert, Candace and Mark took me to a lovely village called Ein Karem. This is the hometown of John the Baptist and also where Mary, the mother of Jesus, came to visit her cousin, Elizabeth.

We parked the car and walked to the part of the village where there is a pool of water called 'Mary's Spring'. There we saw a group of performers who were led by a Moroccan Messianic Jewess named Rachel. They were doing street dramas from the life of Jesus and were very good.

When they took a break, Candace and Mark introduced me to Rachel. Rachel invited all of us to her home later that night for a celebration called Mamunna. It is the Moroccan celebration for the end of Passover, or Pesach in Hebrew. I had actually flown into Tel Aviv on the last day of this prominent Jewish feast day. What a fabulous time to be in Israel!

We thanked her for her kind invitation to her home for the celebration and promised to meet her there later. (This was the beginning of several divine appointments that the Lord had stored up for me in His precious Holy Land.)

Next, Candace and Mark took me to meet the leaders of the End-time Handmaidens in Israel. They were American and were very much interested in my returning to Israel to do some teaching for them on the prophetic. They have a large house that is near the American Embassy building that had not been used. Candace had really thought out whom she introduced me to. It was remarkable to be with her and see her scope of influence in Israel.

After that meeting, Candace took me to meet with the parents of the USA director of Jews for Jesus. This couple were a part of the first ever Messianic congregation in America! They've been married for 62 years and were highly respected elders in the Israeli Messianic community. It was a real privilege to meet them on my first day! God gave me much favor with them and for that I am grateful. They too were interested in my coming back to teach on the gifts of the Holy Spirit the next time I came to Israel. I told them that nothing would make me happier than to be able to come back to Israel and serve His people there in that way. Though they are Jewish and I am a Gentile, we are one in Jesus! I was so very excited in my spirit that several verses came to mind as we drove away from their home:

"Therefore, remember that formerly you who are Gentiles by birth and called 'uncircumcised' by those who call themselves 'the circumcision' (that done in the body by the hands of men)---remember that at that time you were separate from Christ, excluded from citizenship in Israel and foreigners to the covenants of the promise, without hope and without God in the world. But now in Christ Jesus you who once were far away have been brought near through the blood of Christ. For He Himself is our peace, who has made the two one and has destroyed the barrier, the dividing wall of hostility, by abolishing in His flesh the law with its commandments and regulations. His purpose was to create in Himself **one new man out of the two**, *thus making peace, and in this one body to reconcile both of them to God through the cross, by which He put to death their hostility. He came and preached peace to you who were far away and peace to those who were near. For through Him we both have access to the Father by one Spirit. Consequently, you are no longer foreigners and aliens, but fellow citizens with God's people and members of God's household, built on the foundation of the apostles and the prophets, with Christ Jesus Himself as the Chief Cornerstone. In Him the whole building is joined together and rises to become a holy temple in the Lord. And in Him you too are being built together to become a dwelling in which God lives by His Spirit."*

Ephesians 2:11-22

When we got home, we rested for a bit and then changed clothes to go to Rachel's house for the Mamunna celebration. This was a real first for me! I'd never even heard of that in any of the Jewish circles I was connected to. I was thrilled to go.

Back in Ein Karem, we walked up an unlit path to this hidden patio and garden that was attached to a home and seemed to be made out of a cave! It was like something right out of the book *Arabian Nights*! There were candles all over the patio and inside the house/cave. The ceilings were arched and there were tons of silk embroidered pillows everywhere on low couches.

Rachel had prepared food and drink for all of her guests, too. I ate 3 *muffalettas*, flat pancakes with butter and honey on them, right out of a hot griddle. Yum!

What was unique about this experience was all the single ladies I met there. There were so many of them! All of them wanted to be married. They told me that there was a real shortage of believing men there and my heart ached for them all. I so wanted to do a retreat day or weekend for them and mentioned that desire to Candace later. Apparently, there was a trend for some Messianic men to announce their desire to be celibate! This astounded me because all of these ladies were so beautiful and intelligent. How could all of them be single?! They all gravitated towards me because they felt a kinship in our singleness and longing to be joined to the man of God that He had for us.

We left around 11pm and Candace said that she would happily host a special single ladies' day at her house if I ever came back to Israel. Praise God! What a gracious offer. I told the Lord that I would hold her to that, if He ever permitted me to return to this precious place. As I closed my eyes, this verse came to mind:

"Hope deferred makes the heart sick, but a longing fulfilled is a tree of life."
Proverbs 13:12

We single women in the Lord can never lose our hope and must also remember that the Lord is our Husband, no matter what. He has chosen us and will never leave or forsake us! In these truths, we can all rejoice.

"For the Maker is your Husband--the Lord Almighty is His name--the Holy One of Israel is your Redeemer; He is called the God of all the earth."
Isaiah 54:5

"You did not choose me, but I chose you and appointed you to go and bear fruit--fruit that will last."
John 15:16

Power In The Tower

The next day, we walked around the corner from the souk (marketplace) and into a high-rise mall that houses King of Kings Church, the church that Candace and Mark belonged to. The same building was also the location of the International Prayer Tower. What was once a decrepit old movie theater was now a beautiful venue used by many for lots of events.

The Tower had the most perfect 360 degree view of the City of Jerusalem. Folks from all over the world would come there to pray and on the day that Candace took me, she and Mark were leading a governmental prayer watch. The nations represented that day were Australia, Dubai, Korea, Germany, America, the United Kingdom, and of course, Israel.

What I also loved about that moment in the tower was the fact that it seemed that there was a gathering of media folks, too, from around the world. One of the people I met was the only Christian anchor person in the Middle East. We were instant friends. I also met the Middle East Bureau Chief for the famous American Christian TV Network, CBN. Yes, these were all divine appointments that the Lord had pre-ordained for this trip, time, and place. He was at work in all of these things. I felt so blessed! The ironic thing is that the governmental side of the trip had not even happened yet. Wonder of wonders.

Yad Vashem Unwrapped

Our first day of classes at Yad Vashem was incredible, as were all the others that followed. The campus was really quite special and complete with memorial gardens for the victims and heroes of the Holocaust, the Holocaust Museum, the Children's Holocaust Memorial, the Administration building, the gift shop, and all the many classrooms where military personnel and civilians alike were trained. It was situated in the hills just outside of Jerusalem and I knew from day one that we were in for the ride of our lives! We were the first Christian leaders to ever be invited to undertake such a program in Israel. Hallelujah!

We left Yad Vashem by bus and toured the City of David with my favorite guide of the three we had—a man by the last name of Rabinovich. The City of David was a terraced place that had survived centuries of conquest. It was wonderful to see and walk. We even got the chance to go through the tunnels of the waterways built by King Hezekiah. From there, we were taken to a newly excavated Pool of Siloam. We also drove past the Ben-Hinnom Valley that was known as the Valley of the Shadow of Death because it was a place where pagans sacrificed their children in times past. The Bible was coming to life right before my very eyes!

Back at our hotel, we changed into formal evening attire to go and attend the Yom HaShoah Ceremony at Yad Vashem. This day was the national memorial day of the Holocaust and the 65th anniversary of that tragic happening. We didn't know it until we got there, but we would go through the strictest security check ever. It was the first time that my hands had ever been tested for C-4 or explosives residue. This was a mind-blowing experience and totally cool all at once. This level of security was necessary because of the event itself, but also because the president and prime minister of Israel would be there as well as a host of notable dignitaries from around the world.

Once all of those in my group passed the security checks, we took pictures with each other and were ushered to our VIP seating with all of the other dignitaries. Each seat had our individual names on them in English and we each were given VIP lanyards for our necks. There was lots of media there, too. Later, I heard from Candace and Mark that they saw me with my colleagues on national Israeli TV as they watched from their home. I wore a purple sequined Indian suit, and because it was cool, I was happy for the purple cape that someone in my home church had made especially for me. Apparently, the tickets to that event were in great demand and only a certain number of people had clearance to attend. We all felt very blessed and special.

Because Israel has an incredible army and intelligence agencies that keep that great nation safe, it was incredible to see where they placed their snipers for the event. Some of my colleagues in the group thought that the sniper's nests were for TV cameras! When I told them that they were not for TV cameras but snipers, they couldn't believe it. I turned around to show them the media's camera cranes and told them that when the ceremony was about to start, we'd see snipers take their place. They looked at me in disbelief until the ceremony started and the snipers did take their places. Those were the military personnel that we could see and I knew that there was a host of others that we couldn't see. I felt very safe. It was then that I was able to better understand exactly why the Israeli government and Yad Vashem had invited us westerners. We really did need to be brought up to speed on the great need to protect Israel. It has never been more necessary than right now!

The entire event was done with such excellence and it was so moving! There were six Holocaust survivors there to light six eternal flames that marked the end of the Holocaust. The speeches were great and so were the music and the video interviews we watched of all six survivors. I knew that God had made a way for me to witness a piece of important supernatural history. I savored every single moment of that precious night!

Afterwards, we were escorted to the VIP Reception following the ceremony in the Yad Vashem Visitors' Center to enjoy lots of delicious food and drink. I sat with the three other ladies in our group. Together, we laughed and discussed how wonderfully stirring the entire evening had been for all of us. As I sat there, I pondered the fact that each of us had a huge responsibility to take everything we learned on this magnificent trip back to where we came from. We must stand for Israel! We, as believing Christians, must get the word out to others in our midst!

From that trip onwards, I decided in my heart that I would endeavor to begin to study Hebrew, too. So that night, my new friend, Irit, taught me a new Hebrew word, *chibuki*. In Hebrew, it means to hug or cuddle. Languages are such fun for me and I just wanted to be a big human sponge the whole time that I was in Israel.

The Fiddler's Son

Soon, it was time for the drivers for each group of VIP's to take us all back to our respective hotels. I felt like Cinderella when the clock struck midnight. I was having a marvelous time chatting with folks from all over the world and drinking it all in. When someone called out the coach for our group, I grabbed my wrap, and the ladies with me all rose to leave.

While we waited to go up the staircase to the right level, I noticed that a very tall Jewish man was standing next to me in a formal, dark suit, with a kippah on his head. One of the men in our group from America was asking me why we had to be checked for C-4. I told him why it was necessary and that I applauded Israel's efforts because that was one of many reasons why the nation was still afloat.

Immediately, the tall Jewish man in the dark suit who was standing next to me stopped his phone call. He looked right at me and said, 'Who is this girl that she understands all of this?' He told me that his name was Jared. He was very handsome and worked as a realtor. He had a very Hebrew sounding last name and when I asked him what it meant, he told me that it means 'fiddler'. I couldn't resist asking him if he was a fiddler. With a grin on his face, he told me that he wasn't but his father was a famous fiddler who preferred to be known as a cellist. I thought that was wonderful.

Jared wanted to know everything about me—especially why I was in Israel. When I told him about the special first-ever program we were all participating in, he was extremely intrigued.

When the line moved and we were finally outside near the VIP coaches, I saw my colleagues boarding the one headed for our hotel. Jared asked for my card and promised to write to me. Before I got on the bus, he stood there and asked me if I'd go to *Shabbat* (Jewish Service) with him. I told him that the Israeli government and Yad Vashem had a very full schedule for all of us. He told me that he knew I was *supposed* to go to *Shabbat* with him. I told him that I'd be delighted to do it, if God made a way for that to happen, but at the moment, I was obligated to go where I was told and do what I was told via the program. He took my card and said I should expect an email from him later that night.

As soon as I got in my seat on the bus, the two older women in our group, who were old enough to be my mother, asked all sorts of questions about the handsome Jewish guy that had walked me all the way back to my coach. I was the second youngest person in our group and one of two single women, so the two older ladies were wondering if I was going to see Jared again during the trip 'because he seemed like such a nice young man.' They saw me give him my card and were all ears as I told them about that 'nice young man.'

Woe to single women out there who have ever been ambushed by kindhearted Christian ladies with matchmaking on their minds! I was now one of them. They wouldn't let it rest and asked how I'd left things. I told them that Jared had promised to email me later that night. They said that sounded promising. I told them that I thought it highly unlikely that a guy like that would email a total stranger in the wee hours of the morning. Besides that, I had no way to access my email while in Israel unless I borrowed someone's computer in the hotel office. (Now it is common for people, even children, to have tablets but back then I was not one of them.)

One of those nice older ladies, Delia, had just gotten a new tablet and she begged me to check my email in her room back at the hotel. To ease her mind, and mine, as it turned out, I checked my email and I was pleasantly surprised to find that Jared was a man of his word. He emailed to say that he really enjoyed talking to me and wanted to come visit me at my hotel and, yes, he still wanted me to come to Shabbat with him before I left Israel. This astounded me because I was not Jewish. I was a Gentile. He was a very devout, practicing Jew. How God was gonna handle this, I surely didn't know. I politely responded to Jared and kept that door of possibility open for the time being.

In his email back to me, Jared had kindly given me two websites for learning Hebrew and he even suggested that I come back to Israel to learn there! Delia was squealing with laughter and joy over this bit of news. You could tell she was a real mom. She encouraged me to just enjoy the moment and told me that I could use her tablet anytime on the trip. As we sat in her room chatting in our PJ's, I felt like I was at a slumber party or something. How funny! Strange as it may seem, I knew that we'd be friends even after the trip was over. I finally said good night to her and went back to my room to get ready for bed.

Wow! What a night. My mind was reeling with all that I'd seen, heard, experienced, and been asked. Yes, I couldn't help but wonder if the Lord was going to make a way for this Jewish guy to take me to Shabbat before I left the country. Again, I said, 'Your will; not mine be done, Lord.'

The Siren of Yom HaShoah

"Blow the trumpet in Zion; sound the alarm on My holy hill. Let all who live in the land tremble, for the day of the Lord is coming. It is close at hand---a day of darkness and gloom, a day of clouds and blackness, like dawn spreading across the mountains a large and mighty army comes, such as never was of old nor ever will be in ages to come."

Joel 2:1-2

Each day that I was in Israel was completely different from the one before. We woke up each day and left the hotel to go to Yad Vashem for classes that were created to grow us up into the knowledge of all things Israeli. They were superb and so were our professors. Each one held a body of knowledge inside of them that would stretch us and make us wiser in the things of Israel.

The day after the big ceremony, we assembled for class and after one session, we left our classroom and gathered outside for the sounding of the Yom HaShoah siren. The entire nation of Israel stops for the sounding of this siren. If you are in a car, you stop. If you are on a bus, you stop. If you are in a taxi, you stop. Everyone must get out of whatever vehicle they are in. Whatever you are doing when it sounds, you must stop until it concludes. It was moving and chilling, too. It reminded me of what I have heard in old World War II movies. There was yet another ceremony for that at Yad Vashem for government officials.

After lunch, my group met to go through the New Holocaust History Museum at Yad Vashem. I must say that words seem so inadequate when trying to express something so historically and spiritually important. Although it is smaller in size than the Holocaust Museum in Washington, DC, the message it gives is as strong. I felt that the message of the Yad Vashem museum sought to bring hope at the very end. You are forced to look upon the land (*eretz* in Hebrew) of Israel and consider the future of it.

There are many things on display there that I will never forget. Perhaps what stood out most in my memory after the tour was hearing the singing of the Israeli national anthem, *Hatikvah*, by children who were later killed during the Holocaust. Even now as I write this book, I can hear their sweet, innocent voices in my mind.

After our tour was completed, we went back to our classroom to debrief on our experience with Ephraim, one of our professors. I remember that moment because Delia was crying and I felt led to exhort my colleagues to use what they'd experienced during the tour to not just feel something because of what we'd seen in the museum, but to do something within our individual spheres of influence in our respective countries. Three of the men thanked me for that admonition.

Now, someone I have not mentioned yet is the mystery man who seemed to follow us wherever we went at Yad Vashem. All I knew about him was that he was an elderly American man. He went on our tours and sat very quietly in our classes at Yad Vashem, but his identity had not been revealed to any of us.

At that debrief, the moment of truth had arrived. Ephraim surprised us all by telling us that the man was called 'Al' and that he was the man who dropped the bomb on the town of Auschwitz! We were all astounded. So many of these heroes of yesteryear are no longer with us, but here was Al, alive and kicking. It was a real honor to meet him and thank him for his service during the war.

Our debrief was very solemn and rich at the same time. Soon, it was time for us to leave to go back to our hotel and have dinner. It had been a very gripping day. For those of us who were energetic, the day was far from over. We had been promised an adventure under the cover of night...

Under the Holy of Holies

At 8:30 pm, those of us who were not ready to turn in for the night hopped on a bus to go with Alan Rabinovich—the wonder tour guide-- to tour the Western Wall Tunnels. This man was definitely the crème de la crème of tour guides. Another fun thing about Alan was that he lived for a time in Boulder, Colorado, not far from where I grew up. Because of that connection, Alan gave me an eternal invite to come and visit with him and his family the next time that I am in Israel—and I intend on taking him up on that offer!

While I believe wholeheartedly that the entire nation of Israel is holy ground, I had no idea that we were actually going to see what is undoubtedly *the most holy place on earth!* Alan was taking us to the part of Jerusalem that was there when Jesus was alive. He showed us how to identify buildings in Israel that had been built by Herod. We walked on stones that Jesus walked on. That they were still there at all was truly mind-blowing.

As we walked along, we suddenly came to a place where there were several young Jewish men and women who, with covered heads, late at night, were lying down prostrate at the place that is directly beneath where the *Holy of Holies* is on the Temple Mount. Alan told us that we were standing directly under the Holy of Holies! One young man had his face pressed against the wall as close as he could get, so great was his devotion to God. It was truly a sight to behold! Several verses from the Old Testament were written on the blackboard of my mind at that moment:

"Hang the curtain from the clasps and place the ark of the Testimony behind the curtain. The curtain will separate the Holy Place from the Most Holy Place. Put the atonement cover on the ark of the Testimony in the Most Holy Place."

Exodus 26:33-34

"Exalt the Lord our God and worship at His holy mountain, for the Lord our God is holy."

Psalm 99:9

"I will bow down toward Your holy temple and will praise Your name for Your love and Your faithfulness, for You have exalted above all things Your name and Your Word."

Psalm 138:2

May we always know how holy our God is and ever seek to worship toward His holy temple. While it was the latest night out that we'd had on the program, it was so worth it! I knew that I could sleep anytime, but this was something that was priceless. As I closed my eyes that night back at the hotel, I retraced my steps in the tunnels, under the Temple.

Iberleben

Our next day of classes at Yad Vashem included a walk with Ephraim through the Valley of the Communities. It was a very long walk and we really got a chance to see the rest of the Yad Vashem estate. All of it was gorgeously laid out and quite thoughtful.

At one of the places along the way to the Valley, Ephraim made us stop at a train track going nowhere. This wasn't just any train track. This piece of track actually had one of the infamous Auschwitz cattle cars resting on it! Yad Vashem really had to think hard about where to put it because it was extremely offensive for the Holocaust survivors who lived near Yad Vashem. They put it on a lonely piece of track in a pine tree wood, on the back side of the estate. It was sort of hidden in the trees there and the location was very peaceful, but the memories surrounding it were not.

I found it hard to believe that the Nazis and their cohorts could even imagine putting 100 Jewish people into each of these small cars! Only evil and unspeakable horror could use something like that to transport millions of human beings! That was a memory I will never forget.

Our walk continued. Ephraim and his lovely wife, Stephanie, continued to be full of surprises for me and my colleagues. Within the Valley was a series of conference rooms. We took a much needed restroom break and were then ushered into a room that had a semi-circle of chairs and one lone chair in the middle. On that lone chair sat one, Hannah Pick.

Hannah was the best friend of the famous Anne Frank! When Ephraim revealed her identity, I was gob-smacked with the reality of how much trouble Yad Vashem had gone to in bringing us the most famous, living survivors of the Holocaust. Each person they brought to us was a treasure and a gift.

Hannah was such a treat! She was spunky and sat before us, holding her handbag and wearing a hat. What stood out to me was her incredible inability to be angry or hate—even now in the aftermath of death and destruction that she was left with. Hannah chose life!

She just kept on saying she couldn't understand *why* the Germans did what they did. She said none of the Jews could understand it. They had all been like lost sheep led to a slaughter they knew nothing about. Hannah told us about her friendship with Anne Frank and that she held her hand for a brief moment at Auschwitz. In the end, Hannah believed that the best way for her to defeat Nazi Germany was to survive, marry, have children and grandchildren. The Jews call this *iberleben*, surviving or outliving the Nazis. And that she has. That she has.

We spent a good two hours with Hannah and then were taken back to our hotel. It was the only night in our program that we had a free night. Hannah's inspiring life left me with much to ponder that evening as I sat with several of my friends, enjoying cheesecakes and cappuccino.

> "*This day I call heaven and earth as witnesses against you that I have set before you life and death, blessings and curses. Now choose life, so that you and your children may live and that you may love the Lord your God, listen to His voice, and hold fast to Him. For the Lord is your life, and He will give you many years in the land He swore to give to your fathers, Abraham, Isaac and Jacob.*"
>
> Deuteronomy 30:19-20

Media Moment

The next day, two colleagues and I were chosen to do an interview about the program we were on with CBN TV network. The CBN Middle East bureau chief did the interviews with the head of Yad Vashem media relations listening in. Because CBN broadcasts via satellite worldwide, I knew that the folks there would not be the only ones to witness what we said.

When the time came for my interview, I was asked to leave class and go to the area that had been set up on the estate for the taping. The CBN host wanted to know what I had learned in the training program at Yad Vashem. As I walked to the designated location, I said a prayer to myself and asked the Lord to do for me what He promised to do for a nervous young nervous prophet named Jeremiah, thousands of years ago:

> "*But the Lord said to me,' Do not say, 'I am only a child.' You must go to everyone I send you to and say whatever I command you. Do not be afraid of them, for I am with you and will rescue you,' declares the Lord.*"
>
> Jeremiah 1:7-8

This trip was one huge spiritual adventure full of twists and turns every day. I never knew what the Lord had for me to do each day until I was knee deep in that day's events. I love surprises, and this was nothing but pure fun for me!

Schindler's Friends

On this day, I woke up wondering if Ephraim and the staff at Yad Vashem could possibly surprise us more than they already had. This day turned out to be no different than all the other days before it. They raised the bar again with great excellence in the program for this particular day.

After all of our class sessions were completed, we were trundled off to visit the grave of Oscar Schindler. Yes, this is the same man that is known from Steven Spielberg's Oscar-winning film, *Schindler's List*.

Everything about our program was being filmed by the government because it was so historical and the first of its kind. The film crew went with us to the grave, too. All throughout the Bible, we see that stones represent a memorial of some sort. Seeing the huge pile of stones all around the perimeter of Oscar Schindler's gravestone was incredible! He was so dearly loved by Jews all over the world and was one of the most famous people to receive the great Jewish honor of being called a *'Righteous Among The Nations'*.

Seeing his grave put a whole new twist on the film. It was a hot sunny day and the grave sat on the back side of a hill, not far from the Mount of Olives. Apparently, Schindler came there often in the years after the war because he wanted to be close to the friends he'd come to love so well.

Two of those friends, Nachum and Genya Manor, were two more survivors that Ephraim and Stephanie brought to us. The Manors fell in love as young teens working in Schindler's factory and met us at the gravesite. Nachum and Genya were actually in Spielberg's famous film at the end.

When we all got pictures with them and the film crew got what they wanted at the grave, we went back to the hotel for a private session with them and some cool drinks. We discovered that they had been married for 60 years at that point in time and were still very much in love!

Someone in our group asked Nachum and Genya where they'd gone for their favorite date and she simply replied, 'The bedroom!' Everyone in the room roared with laughter.

Genya kept a scrapbook of Oscar Schindler and all the times he visited them in Israel, after the war. It was wonderful to see it with her. She had been told that I was a part of the film industry and asked for me to come and sit with her to see all of her 'making of the film' photos. She was especially proud of her pictures of a much younger Steven Spielberg.

As it turns out, Genya was an artist and what she showed us and gave us copies of is quite haunting, to say the least. Her depictions of the Holocaust were incredible and horrific. One of her prints she gave us is of her images of Auschwitz being a factory of death. She also gave us a print of an olive tree with new sprouts of growth appearing all over it. It left us with a final note of hope. Before I left the room, Genya asked me if I'd like her to sign my prints of her art. I gladly accepted and again, will *never* forget my afternoon with her and her husband. Such a precious couple!

In the film, there is a scene where her character is beaten by the Nazis over a ring on her finger that they wanted her to give up. The ring had been made for her from nickel by Nachum, but the Nazis thought it was silver. She wouldn't part with it and so they beat her. I asked her if she still had it and she grinned at me and showed it to me on her finger!! The ring has never left her hand and she told me I could take a photo of it. Amazing! What a picture of true love! I was so moved by their story and that of Oscar Schindler.

The icing on the cake for me about the day with the Manors was the fact that each of us were given an entire copy of the real 'Schindler's List'! Not a copy of the movie by the same title, but the actual list of the names of all of the 1,100 men and women that Oscar Schindler saved during the Holocaust. It is not enough to say how precious a gift this is. We each received a copy of the original, life-saving list that was written in German. Because I graduated from a German high school and speak German, I understood everything on that list. It was another matchless day in Israel!

Stranded By Volcanic Eruption

The program that had brought us all to Israel from all over the world was officially over and I had not watched any news of any kind since I'd come to Israel. It was Sunday, the 18th of April, and I was supposed to fly back to the UK via British Airways on the following day. When I woke up, my phone had a new message saying that my flight had been cancelled! It was then that I heard the Holy Spirit tell me to turn on the TV. I couldn't believe my eyes and ears.

There had been a volcanic eruption in Iceland earlier that week, and because of the enormous ash cloud that had resulted and was now hovering over Europe, six million air travelers were now stranded wherever they were worldwide. I was now one of the stranded travelers and so were my remaining colleagues. British Airways said that they would alert me by text as to when I might be able to get a flight out of Tel Aviv. What an incredible turn of events!

The first thing I did was pray and ask for the Lord's wisdom on what I should do, as I'd been told I may need to stay for an entire week extra in The Holy Land. Mmmmm...I have a background in natural disasters and this was the only type of disaster that I'd never been a part of. I guess I could change that now. So many things were rumbling in my spirit at that moment. The Lord was speaking to me about so many things. I needed a moment to quiet myself and hear with clarity what He wanted me to do and/or say.

The first thing the Lord asked me to do was sit down on my bed in the hotel and listen to the newscasts that were playing on this growing international travel crisis over and over again. The Spirit asked, 'What do you hear?' I said, 'Six million people worldwide are stranded because of the ash cloud. If planes fly into the ash cloud, it will cause the engines to fail and planes will crash.' Next, I heard the Spirit of the Lord ask, 'What does this particular crisis bring to mind?' Immediately, I responded with, 'The six million Jews who were murdered during the Holocaust and the ash cloud that was created over Europe back then because of the smoking ovens that Hitler's regime created to murder them.' I heard the Spirit say, 'Yes, this is true, and now you must get a message to Giselle so that she can get this message out through her network of influence around the world.'

So I immediately got a message to Giselle, an influential person in the European Coalition for Israel. She, being a journalist herself, was only too happy to put out the word I received through the various channels she had in her sphere of influence. Her first response to this message was, 'Charlynne, this is *so* profound! I had not heard that that was the exact amount of travelers affected by this eruption!' What happened next was wild--Jewish people and others who received the message from all over the world sent me notes of thanks for sharing such a message. The timing and the message itself are something that only the Lord God above could have orchestrated. I knew that my being stranded in the holiest place on earth was just the tip of a ginormous spiritual iceberg! There was a growing excitement in my spirit, although I had no idea where I was going to stay during this crisis. God was clearly speaking to me, so once my first assignment was done, I had a peace and heard the Lord prompt me to go on with the rest of that day's events that had been planned. These words of Jesus came to mind:

"There will be great earthquakes, famines and pestilences in various places, and fearful events and great signs from heaven. Even so, when you see these things happening, you know that the Kingdom of God is near."

Luke 21:11,31

Next, I heard the Lord ask me to go and wait on the sidewalk in front of the hotel. As I did, a pastor from Finland came by, singing. He had been on the course with me. He was a very jolly fellow named Rami. Now, this is where my story gets fun-- He had been offered a room during the crisis at the home of one of our tour guides—none other than Dr. Halvor Ronning! Apparently, Dr. Ronning had a guest house with two available rooms: one for Rami and one for me! Our God proved once again that He was more than faithful. He is *Adonai Jireh* (The Lord Who is our Provider/Sees to our needs in Hebrew). Amazing!

Later, I thought to myself: What would have happened if I had not obeyed that still, small, first voice of the Lord at that moment? It is unthinkable. I would have missed the incredible miracle of meeting up with Pastor Rami and getting the last available en-suite room at the Finnish guest house near Jerusalem! Another great thing about where the guest house was located is that it was in the same town as my friend, Candace! It was literally within walking distance of her house.

Pastor Rami had even arranged a ride for us both from the hotel at our checkout time. Wonders never ceased. God had the whole thing sown up for us!

"Know therefore that the Lord your God is God; He is the faithful God, keeping His covenant of love to a thousand generations of those who love Hm and keep His commands."

Deuteronomy 7:9

So I went back upstairs to my room to pack my things to be ready when the van from the guest house came. It was not time to go yet, so I knew that I had time to meet with the Jared, the Jewish man that I'd met at the Holocaust memorial night. He had stayed in touch with me by email and insisted on coming to visit me before I left Israel. He was coming at 10 a.m. to meet me in the hotel lobby.

Delia was going to stay with my friend, Candace, and her husband and really wanted to meet Jared, so I introduced her to him before Candace came to pick her up. She just grinned at me.

In the almost two hours that I had left to spend with Jared, we chatted about all sorts of things, especially my meeting with the Jewish rabbi I had befriended in Miami during my sabbatical two years prior. He loved hearing about this story because he and the rabbi were from the same sect of Judaism! This was definitely not a coincidence! Again, only the Lord could orchestrate something like this down to the fine details.

Jared seemed almost glad that I was stranded! He insisted that I come for *Shabbat* because he knew I was truly captive in Israel by the ash cloud. I promised him that if I was still in Israel, with no way out, by the next Sabbath, I'd come to his house to walk to his synagogue with him and have the *Shabbat* meal at his house afterwards.

Jared also found my work in the UK intriguing. He was fascinated by my love for languages and the fact that I can speak some German and Russian, two languages that huge amounts of Jewish people speak around the world. Because I had to leave before checkout time, I parted ways with Jared at 11:30 a.m., promising to stay in touch that week. Ihad just enough time to grab my bags and stand ready on the curb in front of the hotel, waiting for Dr. Ronning's van.

Rami had decided to invite one of the other stranded men in our group to stay with him at the guest house and share a room. Rami and I decided to make the most of our extended time in Israel. The van came and Dr. Ronning decided to give us a bonus guided tour of other places we hadn't seen on the way back to Mevaseret Zion. He was a very kind man.

As a disaster professional from the US government, I have always found it interesting to observe how people respond to stressful situations, especially natural disasters. I was so grateful for my US training *and* for the many hours of Biblical training I had via my parents and many others in the Word of God. The Word of God is a real life buoy in such times! I will never tire of being a perpetual student of the Word. I cannot live without it. During my extended time in Israel, I watched men fall apart and panic because of the crisis. Many tried to change things in their own strength, refusing to believe that there was absolutely no way to get back to wherever they were from by air. The Word tells us that Jesus is the Living Word and that He is our Peace. These are eternal truths that will never fail us! Anxiety doesn't help at all.

"In the beginning was the Word, and the Word was with God, and the Word was God. He was with God in the beginning."

John 1:1-2

"For He Himself is our Peace, Who has made the two one and has destroyed the barrier, the dividing wall of hostility, by abolishing in His flesh the law with its commandments and regulations."

Ephesians 2:14

"Do not be anxious about anything, but in everything, by prayer and petition, with thanksgiving, present your requests to God. And the peace of God, which transcends all understanding, will guard your hearts and your minds in Christ Jesus."

Philippians 4:6-7

By that evening, British Airways officially told me by text that my flight was absolutely canceled. I needed to book a new flight back to the UK the next day. In the meantime, I was at peace in my spirit and praising God that the guest house had not one but four computer terminals, with printing capability. I was so grateful that I could be reconnected to the outside world from where I was staying.

Adventures With God's Men

I couldn't have planned a better day! When I got up on this particular day, my other two colleagues were already gone so I was truly on my own. At 11am, I got a call from the CBN TV Network chief in Jerusalem. He was at the airport and wanted to know if I felt like doing a TV segment on Israeli immigration with him in their studios. That idea was the best idea I'd heard all week! I jumped at the chance and knew I had to get hopping to be ready to do a TV taping.

The phone kept ringing. The next call came from a headmaster from London that I knew who was also stranded in Israel. He was in Tel Aviv but wondered if he might be able to come to Jerusalem and take me out for dinner that night. I said that would be lovely, then kept getting ready for the TV show.

But the phone rang again. This time, it was a friend of Giselle's ringing to see if I was bored and might want to see how Israel creates their famous pop-up hospitals for countries in need during disasters. His name was Barry, and he and his wife Batya were the ones behind the famous Joseph's Storehouse ministry. Again, my cup was running over with incredible offers of adventure that day. Only the Lord knew that I had always wanted to meet these particular Messianic leaders. Getting a private tour of their headquarters was so much more than I had bargained for!

To top this all off, I later found out that in Giselle's concern for me, she had kindly asked several men of influence all over the nation of Israel to look out for me while I was stranded. Wonders never cease in God's universe! But there was more—she also took it upon herself to put some dosh into my account to cover me for the extra week in Israel! When God has your back, He covers you like no one else can!

"So do not worry, saying, 'What shall we eat?' or 'What shall we drink?' or 'What shall we wear?' For the pagans run after all these things, and your heavenly Father knows that you need them. But seek ye first His Kingdom and His righteousness, and all these things will be given to you as well.

Therefore do not worry about tomorrow, for tomorrow will worry about itself. Each day has enough trouble of its own."

Matthew 6:31-34

My whole day was all sorted out for me by the Great Appointment Maker in the Sky. Chris from CBN picked me up to go directly to CBN Studios, which sat right on top of Mount Zion itself. Wow. The studios were lovely and the view they had of the Old City of Jerusalem was tremendous!

The folks at CBN gave me a quick tour of their facility, then we took some pictures together and began to prep for the TV taping that I was there to do. Chris was happy with the interview we did and asked me to give some background information to his cameraman on their next assignment in San Remo, Italy. I knew that Giselle was going to be there, so I told him that he might want to interview her there as a part of the event that the European Coalition for Israel (ECI) was doing there to commemorate the signing of the San Remo Resolution in 1920-the event that was the pre-cursor to what allowed Israel to become a Jewish State.

I had invited my friend, the headmaster, to join us for the tour of Joseph's Storehouse with Barry. Chris was happy to get my friend from his hotel and then drive us to the storehouse for our tour.

As soon as we arrived, Barry's wife, Batya, graciously served us tea and biscuits as we waited for Barry to arrive. When Barry came, he gave us an incredible tour of his disaster relief operation. It was so efficient and helped so many in need from around the world. In fact, it was Barry's operation that was used at the first operational hospital after the Haitian earthquake. Someone from Israel opened the first hospital. I was very impressed by all that I saw that day. Barry and Batya had many talents and were worship leaders as well. Barry had also served in the Israeli military and they had a son in the forces,, too.

After our tour, Barry took us back into Jerusalem. Now it was time for me to catch up with my friend, the headmaster, and chat with him over dinner at a delicious spot Chris had recommended to me called Olive and Fish.

During my cab ride back to Mevaseret Zion, I agreed wholeheartedly that the land of Israel was *'a land flowing with milk and honey'*(Exodus 3:8). I believe it is impossible to starve in Israel. The food on offer there is so good, fresh and in such abundance. *In Israel, one can actually taste and see that the Lord is very good, indeed.*

Shabbat In the German Colony

The next day, I woke up early and got ready to trek into Jerusalem by bus, having no idea just how many, many people God was going to bring across my path that day. And so it began...

At the bus stop, I met a Jewish guy named David from Philadelphia, Pennsylvania who was married to an Ethiopian Jewish girl. He said that he'd noticed me, earlier that week, in the nearby mall. This was amazing to me because I learned very quickly that no one misses anything in Israel. They are some of the most observant people that you will ever meet. It is one of many reasons I believe Israel is still afloat. As it turned out, the guest house was very close to the Ethiopian Jewish neighborhood. David told me that he and his wife were expecting twins. He was so excited about becoming a father. He wondered if I was an Ethiopian Jew. I told him that I wasn't, but that I would call myself a closet Jew. He smiled at that and chatted with me all the way to the Central Bus Station in Jerusalem. We parted ways and I caught a cab to the Jaffa Gate entrance to the Old City and asked the driver if he could possibly come and get me at 6:30 pm to take me to Jared's house in the German Colony. Yes, Jared was finally going to get his wish of taking me to *Shabbat* and introducing me to his family and friends there.

The day was young, so I decided to buy some gifts for folks back home in the Christian Quarter. This was an adventure in itself. It was there that I met two men named Michele and Nasser. I was immediately sat down in a plush chair by Nasser who promptly served me an ice cold Coke and began pulling out all kinds of things to tempt me with in his store. I really wanted to spend all I could to bless the folks there, yet I had no idea that when it was finally time to ring up all of my purchases, Michele and Nasser would turn around and bless me with an entire set of Roman glass jewelry. They refused to charge me for it. I couldn't believe it, for Roman glass is made from real Roman antique glass and is quite costly. Again, I was reminded that you just can't out-give our God! It was a humbling experience, to say the least. That cup of mine was just running over and over again, by now.

After shopping, I walked to the Jewish Quarter and sat down in the square by the old synagogue to journal in my travel diary for a couple of hours. From there I walked to Mamilla, the newest mall in Jerusalem to stroll around for a bit and write some more.

While writing at the mall, I met an Arab guy named Hami who was divorced and wondered if I might go out with him. I kindly refused his offer and told him that I would shortly be going to *Shabbat*.

I began to write again and then someone called Amir offered to take me for a ride, but I said that I had a cab coming to take me to the German Colony. Next was Iyad, an Armenian Christian who was concerned that I might get ripped off by the cabbie taking me to the German Colony. He didn't think that the Arab driver taking me could be trusted. I assured him that God was looking out for me and that I was not afraid.

At 6:30pm sharp, my cabbie, Veerka, came to get me at the Jaffa Gate. I told him that I needed to go to Hamagid Street in the German Colony. He took me there and I got out of the cab in a lovely area that reminded me of where my Jewish friends in America live in Beverly Hills, California. The German Colony had that same atmosphere.

I realized right away that I couldn't read any of the street numbers because everything, of course, was in Hebrew, so I humbly asked an older Jewish gentleman for help. He took me right to the address on Hamagid Street that Jared had given me!

As soon as I was about to go through the gate of the property, a woman called Revekah came out to greet me. I was astounded that she called me by name and said that she would escort me to Jared's door. Up the stairs we went. She knocked on the door and the woman that Jared was betrothed to opened the door. Her name was Adina. She gave me a hug and asked if I'd like to sit for a few moments on the patio balcony. I said that would be nice.

As I sat there listening to the birds in the nearby conifers, I couldn't believe that I was really there! One night at a state affair had brought me to the home of a Jewish businessman! What was God going to do next, I wondered.

Before I knew it, Jared appeared behind me and gave me a big hug. Soon Jared, his betrothed, and myself left to walk to Shul (shool), or the *Shabbat* service. Everyone walks there because no work of any kind is to be done once the sun goes down. It is the Sabbath, and according to God's Law in the Old Testament, it is a holy day of rest for all. By now, everyone in the German Colony was walking with their entire families to Shul. What a sight! I was reminded of the American neighborhoods I'd lived in where Jews did the same thing every Friday night.

The building of Jared's temple was very modern, for this was a very affluent neighborhood. It was full of young people. I'd say that the average age of folks in that congregation was 35-40. I enjoyed what I was reading in the prayer book that was handed to me. I also enjoyed watching all of the absolutely beautiful Jewish babies with their mothers all around me. The women were seated in an upper gallery and the men were all together below us.

Soon it was over and we were walking back to Jared's place. Adina had grown up in Moscow until age 10 and had been told by Jared that I spoke some Russian, so she grilled me! Thankfully, I got it all right. She wanted to know why I spoke a little Russian. I told her that the first house I bought in America was in a Russian Jewish neighborhood. She beamed at me when I said that. Her parents lived in Germany, so she was fluent in not just Russian but German, Hebrew and English. I knew that she was one smart cookie.

By the time we got to Jared's, it was completely dark. We three and several of Jared's neighbors went into his house and it was time for all the children to go to bed and for the adults to do the traditional *Shabbat* prayers and meal. It was so comforting to hear Jared pray. We then ate a four-course meal prepared by Adina. I just love Jewish food.

Over the absolutely delicious meal, Adina asked me a zillion questions about my work. She herself was a PR executive, but she was fascinated by all that Jared had told her about me. I was hardly prepared for what happened next.

The miracle of the night occurred when Adina asked me to explain to her all the ways God speaks to us! You could have knocked me over with a feather! She said that she wouldn't rest until I told them all nine ways. It was then that I sensed the Holy Spirit, or *Ruach HaKodesh,* leading me to speak from Old Testament scriptures only. I realized it was all that they knew. I quickly shot an arrow prayer from my spirit up to heaven, asking the Spirit to guide me through this impromptu teaching I'd been asked to give to a great gathering of practicing Jews who had not yet accepted Jesus as their Messiah, or *HaMashiach*.

So I began—I heard the Spirit tell me to refer to the triune God as *Elohim*. The first and best way that God speaks to us is through His Word. When I quoted from Joshua 1 about that, they all smiled knowingly around the long table at each other. Jared and Adina were hanging on my every word. Adina and the other ladies present kept the food coming and I kept on teaching. Only the Lord, or *Adonai*, could have created such an opportunity!

Next, I told them the second way that God speaks to us is through creation and nature. I quoted from Psalms 19. At this point, one of the men in the room went to get the Torah and Tanakh to cross-check all the scripture verses I was quoting. I wanted to pinch myself because it so reminded me of what Paul experienced when he was teaching amongst the Berean believers in their synagogue.

"Now the Bereans were of more noble character than the Thessalonians, for they received the message with great eagerness and examined the Scriptures every day to see if what Paul said was true."

Acts 17:11

Then I got questions from Revekah who had escorted me to Jared's house earlier that day. She was married to Michael, who also had questions for me. They were eager for me to share all the ways that God speaks and they also wanted to hear about my Yad Vashem experiences. I continued to share on all the ways that God speaks to us and didn't miss one of the nine ways. They marveled that I was not a Jew but seemed to know more of their Testament than they did. They were all so hungry!

At the prompting of the Lord, I had brought my copy of Schindler's List to show them and the art of Genya Manor. They were astounded by those items and everyone passed around the list of Jews rescued by Schindler. I am sure that some of their family members were listed on that list.

When it was nearly 1:30am in the morning, they tried to get me to spend the night with them in the German Colony. I would have if I hadn't promised Giselle that I would minister to a friend of hers the next morning, which was to be my last day in Israel. Jared and his friends all hugged me over and over again. Revekah begged me to never forget them. Her plea brought tears to my eyes. How in the world could I ever forget such a rich experience in Israel? I felt that this was perhaps one of the biggest reasons that I had been chosen for that special program. God knew all along that this night was going to come. The irony of that moment was that they seemed so jealous of what I had in the Lord! They were Israeli Jews and yet they so wanted what I had. Paul talked of moments like these:

"Again I ask: Did they stumble as to fall beyond recovery? Not at all! Rather, because of their transgression, salvation has come to the Gentiles to make Israel envious. But if their transgression means riches for the world, and their loss means riches for the Gentiles, how much greater riches will their fullness bring! I am talking to you Gentiles. Inasmuch as I am the apostle to the Gentiles, I make much of my ministry in the hope that I may somehow arouse my own people to envy and save some of them. For if their rejection is the reconciliation of the world, what will their acceptance be but life from the dead?"

Romans 11:11-15

Jared walked me back down Hamagid Street one last time to catch a cab. My spirit was so jazzed by all that had been seen and heard that special night! I was tingling all over and knew that I would hardly sleep that night, but like I'd been telling myself the whole trip, 'You can sleep some other time.' I didn't want to miss one single thing that God wanted me to catch in Israel. I wanted to make each moment count. At about 3am, I finally got a few hours of sleep. I closed my eyes, thanking God over and over again for trusting me with this particular assignment.

Later, when I shared about the night's events with my Messianic Jewish friends, they couldn't believe their ears. One friend was so worried for me—she said that for a Gentile to have shared all that I shared was so unlikely there, and possibly a very dangerous thing to do. I told her that clearly it was something the Lord had prepared my way to do. He had gone before me and laid it all out for me to walk in. Others told me that the Chabad sect of Judaism is like the charismatic sect of the Jews because they talk about the coming of the Messiah so much. They are coming to Jesus(*Yeshua*) all over the world now. That is such good news!

Just when I thought there were no more praise reports left for the Lord to shower upon me, the guest house mystery lodger, Bethany, opened up to me! She had spoken to no one and kept to herself all the time. Though she'd never talked to me until that very moment, she had heard every word that I'd said since I got to the guest house. She told me that my witness had encouraged her and that she believed that God had brought me to Israel! She had been a former Chabad Jew who had become a Messianic Jew and, as such, life for her in Israel had been very hard. Thank you, Lord, for closing the loop on the mysterious person in our midst! It had been a treat to hear her testimony, another precious person in the ever-growing family of God.

Once I got to Ben Gurion Airport in Tel Aviv, I had a moment or two of interrogation. One of the things I was asked was why I was wearing a *Magen David*, or shield of David. I told the officer that I was wearing the star of David pendant because I love the nation of Israel. I had no sooner given my answer to the officer when I saw a high-ranking airport security person come over to me in a suit and tie. He then took me out of line to give me a personal escort to my gate! I asked him why I was being given such special treatment and he said that it was warranted because I was a special guest of the nation of Israel. I grinned as he shook my hand and turned to go. Once again I saw that membership in the Lamb's Book of Life had many untold perks! There truly is nothing like the favor of the Lord.

"For whoever finds me finds life and receives favor from the Lord."
Proverbs 8:35

"For surely, O Lord, you bless the righteous; you surround them with Your favor as with a shield."
Psalms 5:12

This was an adventure that I would always remember! I have a burning desire to return to Israel and will continue to pray for the Lord to use me there again. So watch this space...

Travel Thoughts

1. Are you interested in the history of the places you travel to? What country has intrigued you the most and why?

   _____

   _____

   _____

2. Have you ever had a pen pal? If so, how and where did you meet them? How long have you been writing to each other?

   _____

   _____

   _____

3. Have you ever been in a natural disaster while traveling? If so, what happened?

   _____

   _____

   _____

7

GRACE IN GERMANY

"Skill to do comes of doing."
Ralph Waldo Emerson

"Destiny is not a matter of chance, it's a matter of choice; it is not a thing to be waited for, it is a thing to be achieved."
William Jennings Bryan

"Don't be afraid to go out on a limb...that's where the fruit is."
Harry S. Truman

"When patterns are broken, new worlds emerge."
Tuli Kupferberg

"Do not wait for leaders; do it alone, person to person."
Mother Teresa

The last country I want to take you to is Germany. The opportunity for me to go there came about because I taught a class in the UK where one of my students was a German woman who had married an Englishman. One night after class, my student, Helga, asked if I'd like to come with her and her husband, Alan, to visit her family in Germany. I told her that if ever there was a time that seemed right for me to join them, I'd happily go with them. I said that it would give me a proper chance to work on my German language skills. It seemed like a really wonderful idea! At that moment in time, I had no idea that I'd end up going on two separate trips with Helga and Alan to Germany's Black Forest Region.

Helga came from a family that was full of believing Christians. She had three sisters and one brother. Most of them lived near each other and Helga told me that one sister lived in the farmhouse that had once been owned by her parents, while her brother lived in a converted barn with his wife and six children. Everyone loved Jesus. I was excited and looking forward to meeting all of them.

Before we traveled to Germany, I received some emails from Helga's sister-in-law, Angi, and her baby sister, Gisela. I would be speaking at the home group led by Angi and Helga's brother, but I was going to be staying with Gisela and her husband, Michael, and their three children. Angi and her husband attended a Vineyard Church near Stuttgart. They had heard from Helga about our prophetic school and asked me to come and do a weekend workshop on hearing God's still, small voice. I knew I could do it with the Lord's help and Angi's, too, as she had graciously offered to translate for me where needed. All the details were sorted out and I was ready for my adventure in Deutschland.

Stenken des Denken or Stinking Thinking

Soon it was time for me to pack a bag and make my way to Helga and Alan's house with Lesley. We four had a delicious meal together and then Lesley went back to Sussex. Helga and Alan are great chefs together and possess a beautiful gift of hospitality.

We knew that we needed to go to sleep fairly early because we were going to put Helga and Alan's Jeep Cherokee on a ferry boat to Calais from Dover, England, and then drive the rest of the way to Weissach, Germany where Helga's sister Gisela lived.

The ferries that leave Dover are like miniature ocean liners. They have restaurants on board, stores to shop in and all sorts of other amusements on multiple decks. Once we got the Jeep safely parked on deck, we three made our way into the ship to find a place to settle ourselves for the duration of our crossing. We looked around in the shops for a bit because everything in them is duty-free. Then we found a spot to view the sea and decided to get something to eat. I find that crossing the English Channel by this mode of transport is always quite enjoyable.

Soon, it was time for us to make our way down to the deck that Helga and Alan's Jeep was parked on. We climbed into the car and waited for the signal to leave the ferry in Calais, France. Once we pulled away from the Port of Calais, we settled ourselves for the drive through France, Belgium, and on into Germany.

We got to Weissach where Gisela and Gunther lived with their three children: Ammiel, Yael, and Adina. I was delighted to hear these names because all of them are in the Bible, but are not the most popular names most people choose. They had two boys and one daughter and lived in a lovely home situated near the factory famous for the manufacture of Porsche cars.

When I met Gisela and her family, I knew that we'd be fast friends. For starters, she and her husband spoke impeccable English! They were as incredible as hosts as Helga and Alan were. The other thing that struck me about Gisela and Gunther was the way that each of them spent time with the Lord before they went to work and school each day! I had grown up the same way with my single-parent mother and it blessed me so much to see a couple raising their three kids in the same way, with that same love for the infallible Word of God.

Once we got settled in our bedrooms at Gisela's place, we got into the Jeep and took off down the country lanes to go to see Hans and Angi's place. Gisela and Gunther came along in their van with their kids. The drive there was lovely—we were in the area of Vaihingen and Der Anz. Helga's family farm was in a lush valley that held acres and acres of vineyards. I thought to myself, how fitting it was that they were actually members of the local Vineyard Church! I discovered that Germany is a very beautiful country. The area I now found myself in was clearly their wine country and it was glorious to look upon.

When we got to the farm, there was Hans near the most beautiful vegetable garden ever! Every row was straight and full of pretty vegetables. Hans had some deep, orange, just-picked carrots in his hands. He was washing them off under the garden hose and offered me one. I took a bite and, oh, how sweet it was! There is nothing like good, organic, farm-fresh food.

Angi came out with a beautiful baby boy named Levi on her hip and five other children who came out to say hello. They had one daughter and five sons who spilled out onto the driveway, one by one. Each of them was so precious.

Hans and Angi had lived in Africa with their kids and had decided to come back to Germany and work as part of the family farm. In Africa, Hans had worked to share his gift for farming techniques with the Africans who needed assistance in farming. Angi was a scientist and a nutritionist. Both of them had gifts and talents that were well-suited for the African continent and its multitude of needy populations. Here was another couple in Helga's family who loved Jesus and were raising their brood of kids to love Him, too.

Angi and I had been writing back and forth about what message to bring to the folks in her Vineyard Church, but now I could put the writer with the face. All of us were in the same age group--our mid 40's—andgot on rather well. Once again, I felt that Angi and Hans would be good friends of mine.

Angi spoke to me in English, as Gisela did, and her English was just as good as her sister-in-law's. Hans, Angi's husband, had been told that I spoke some German, so he decided that he would only speak to me 'auf Deutsch' or in German only. This was both great and scary all at once. But, like the quote at the beginning of this German section says:

"*Don't be afraid to go out on a limb...that's where the fruit is.*"

Harry S. Truman

That is what I had to keep telling myself every time Hans spoke to me. For instance, the next day, Hans asked me what I had for breakfast. He spoke in German and he patiently waited for me to answer him in straight German. I shot an arrow prayer up to the Lord in that moment and asked Him to help me. When I opened my mouth to respond to the question Hans asked, I gave him the right answer, all in German. Hans gave me a resounding: "*Sehr gut*, Charlynne!"

I had apparently passed my first real German test with flying colors. In my heart all I could say was *Thank You, Jesus!* I wanted to do my very best to use what the Lord had given me via my good German education in the States. I had graduated from a German-Lutheran High School in Denver and had continued to study the German language all during my university years at Oral Roberts

University, where all of my professors were either German or Austrian. In both school experiences, I was also a member of the German Clubs students were encouraged to join. Now, all of that training was coming to bear and I had to chuckle to myself. The God we serve does not waste one thing or any experience that we may encounter in our lives. Never. He is so practical in His ways. It was time for what had been planted in me by many teachers to bear fruit. I was reminded of this passage in the Bible:

> *"I am the true Vine, and My Father is the Gardener. He cuts off every branch in me that bears no fruit, while every branch that does bear fruit He prunes so that it will be even more fruitful. You are already clean because of the word I have spoken to you. Remain in Me, and I will remain in you. No branch can bear fruit by itself; it must remain in the Vine. Neither can you bear fruit unless you remain in Me."*
>
> John 15:1-4

I knew that the words of this passage were true in every way. Not only was it time for me to bear fruit in this foreign country, but it could only happen if my full dependence was in the Lord, or the One True Vine. Again, these words kept tumbling over and over in my mind because of where I was standing at the farm. I was surrounded by vines! Those rivers of God's Living Water (His Word) kept washing over me that day as I pondered the meaning of these things in my heart about this trip and what the Lord wanted to do in our midst.

> *"...Christ loved the church and gave Himself up for her to make her holy, cleansing her by the washing with water through the Word..."*
>
> Ephesians 5:25-26

> *"...the water I give Him will become in him a spring of water welling up to eternal life."*
>
> John 4:14

The sisters had put their heads together and decided that everyone would meet up at the farm for dessert and coffee. It was really great to sit in that huge barn that Hans and Angi had converted. It had a wonderful open plan and an enormous, long farm table that held all three families that were present that day. It was great to hear lots of German speaking all at once, so good to get back into the habit of deciphering what I was hearing and stepping out on that limb to try to respond in the language of the country we were in.

Finally, it was time to go to the Vineyard to begin the workshop with the folks in the congregation who were interested. It was a good-sized group and I had all the materials that they'd need to follow along with me. Angi was excellent and so patient in translating for me, and so was the Vineyard pastor, Stephan. Where necessary, I only had to look at him to ask what the appropriate word was in what I'd call *German Christianese*. I realized that, although I had done courses in school for German, the one thing those courses didn't teach me was how to say charismatic Christian words in German. There wasn't a book on the planet where those words could be found. It was something that you just learned. I learned that the word for anointing in German is *die Salbung*. Helga had also taught me some good, low German slang which was very useful.

One of the phrases we use in our school is 'stinking thinking' to explain how our brain operates when we are not being led by the Holy Spirit. The phrase for this in German is *stenken des denken*. When I said this to the class at the Vineyard, everyone just laughed. At first, I wondered if I'd gotten it wrong. On the contrary. I'd said it correctly. They were just amazed that I'd gotten it. It made it easier for them to remember why we must be led by the Spirit as a lifestyle and not just at church or when we are with other Christians but in our thinking and doing, with or without people.

"So I say, live by the Spirit, and you will not gratify the desires of the sinful nature. For the sinful nature desires what is contrary to the Spirit, and the Spirit what is contrary to the sinful nature. They are in conflict with each other, so that you do not do what you want. But if you are led by the Spirit, you are not under law."

Galatians 5:16-18

Throughout that whole weekend, I discovered that even though my German was not fluent, these precious men and women of God in Vaihingen had the grace and mercy to accept what I had to offer. They were ready to receive what the Holy Spirit had on tap for them and everyone was blessed. Once again, I saw that there is really no language barrier at all in the Spirit. There is *freedom* and plenty of it!

"Now the Lord is the Spirit, and where the Spirit of the Lord is, there is freedom."

2 Corinthians 3:17

Everyone in the workshop had really enjoyed learning about the Holy Spirit and walked away knowing that they could hear His still, small, first voice for themselves. To God be the glory, honor, and praise for all of it. I knew that He had done it all because I was so keenly aware of all of my inefficiencies there. How wonderful to be able to rest in the knowledge that where I am weakest; He is stronger still! I was reminded of a song that I used to sing as a little girl:

"I will sing unto the Lord, for He is highly exalted. The horse and its rider He has hurled into the sea. The Lord is my Strength and my Song; He has become my salvation. He is my God, and I will praise Him, my father's God, and I will exalt Him."

Exodus 15:1-2

Signs And Wonders Shall Follow...

It had been decided before I came to Germany that I would also speak at the Sunday service on the weekend of the workshop. Angi, me and the Holy Spirit were a team once again to get a message across to the precious people who gathered there on that Sunday morning in Vaihingen.

Everything went very well during the service. I ended it by giving a call to anyone who wanted prayer to come forward. Everyone came forward and I prayed for them to have increased spiritual hearing and sight, just like Paul prayed for the Ephesians in Ephesians 1.

All was quiet and peaceful, when all of a sudden, a woman came forward crying loudly. She told me that she knew she was harboring a Jezebel spirit and that she wanted to be free of it once and for all.

I love to pray for people to be set free and here was an opportunity to see the Holy Spirit free someone of a huge controlling spirit. It is important to say here that you cannot have a Jezebel spirit in operation without the assistance of the enabling Ahab spirit that lays down and allows Jezebel to manifest in the life of a believer. I got the sense that it was definitely her time to be free. I knew as a minister that deliverance only comes to those who really want to be set free.

I looked at Pastor Stephan and asked his permission to pray a prayer of deliverance for this woman. He told me to go ahead and do whatever the Spirit of the Lord said. I asked if the woman had any family with her. She said that the whole family was there. I asked if they would come forward. She had her husband and all of their grown children with their spouses there that day. It was marvelous! All of them were weeping in acknowledgment of their wife and mother's need to be set free.

I opened in prayer, then asked her and her family to repeat after me a prayer to renounce the operation of the Jezebel and Ahab spirits that had controlled their family and marriages for too long. Everyone was very glad to do that.

That was their day of deliverance! Hallelujah! I knew that the cloud of witnesses in Heaven and on earth were all singing songs of deliverance that day! In one Sunday morning service, an entire family had been released from the grip of the enemy that had been operating for generations in their family. A major generational curse had been broken!

"You are my Hiding Place; You will protect me from trouble and surround me with songs of deliverance. Rejoice in the Lord and be glad, you righteous; sing, all you who are upright in heart!"

Psalms 32:7,11

Later, when I returned to Germany, I heard that the family truly was free indeed! Just when I thought my cup for the weekend was full to overflowing, the Lord dropped something else on me.

Pastor Stephan came up to me after the prayer and told me that the entire time that I was ministering to people that morning, each time he looked at me, he saw these letters in the air, above my head: A-P-O-S-T-L-E. He then asked me if that word meant anything to me. I told him that when I was in my 20's, it had been prophesied in America that I would have an apostolic ministry one day.

At the time that that first word was spoken over me in Denver, Colorado, the Lord told me that word was indeed from Him, but to put it on the shelf and wait for Him to make it manifest at a later date. Words like that require extra training and waiting on the Lord to place the mantle on the person to whom the word is given. I knew I needed to mature in authority and responsibility before the Lord would change the mantle He had me working under at that time.

When Pastor Stephan asked if anyone else had seen or spoken anything like that to me in Europe, I told him that since I had moved to the UK, two British prophets had also prophesied that I would do the work of an apostle in that season. Pastor Stephan grinned at me and said he confirmed that those words were now manifesting. When he spoke to me, these words came to mind:

"The apostles performed many miraculous signs and wonders among the people..."

Acts 5:12

"The things that mark an apostle—signs, wonders and miracles—were done among you with great perseverance."

2 Corinthians 12:12

The Lord always confirms everything with His Word. He cannot lie and never will. His word is perfect and infallible. That is our firm foundation and it is rock solid and incapable of crumbling—ever!

Pen Pals

My whole life has been about learning how to communicate with others with excellence. For most of my life, that is how I made my living. There are so many forms of communicating in today's world, yet I must admit that my absolute favorite way of communicating with others is through the pen, using old-fashioned paper and writing instruments and even sometimes sealing a letter with wax, just like they did in Biblical times. In too many instances to count here, the person receiving what I have written on paper became saved and found faith in Jesus Christ through something that the Lord led me to write to them. The Apostle Paul did likewise through ink and parchment in the times that he lived, so I guess I am in good company.

I have many, many 'pen pals' all over the world as a result of years of writing. My love affair with pen and paper began as a little girl and really took on an international spin with a supposed accident with the US State Department. When I was in high school at my German-Lutheran school in Denver, my German professor was contacted and asked if he would consider matching his German students with German students in Germany. Well, it seemed a wonderful idea, but when we got the package of students we were to write in Germany, it turned out that they gave us Italian students instead of German students! The situation was never corrected, but I decided to write to a friend in Italy instead and that friendship lasted well into our adult years.

Having said that, I always wanted a German pen pal. That first trip to Germany righted the wrong that happened all those years ago in high school. Gisela, Helga's baby sister, decided that we should become pen pals! Hooray! This was perfect for me because I really wanted to grow in my German Christianese and this was a perfect way to do just that. As you can imagine, Gisela and I have been writing each other back and forth via email and pen and paper for five years now. I have been to visit her house twice and they have come to visit me at my house on the South Coast of England. What a joy that has been to me! She is my newest pen pal.

When we travel, we often meet people with whom we find a 'kindred spirit' sort of connection. One of the best ways to keep the memory of what was shared alive is to agree to become pen pals with someone. It is a great way to build relationship with someone who lives far away. In this technology-driven age, where there are so many different ways to email, I am a firm believer that every human being out there still likes to receive what I call good, old-fashioned 'snail mail'. It is a sure way to put a smile on someone's face in a world without Jesus that gives us so many reasons not to smile.

Every time I open the pages of the Bible, I am truly amazed at the fact that what I am holding in my hands is thousands of years old and yet so active and alive!

"For the Word of God is living and active. Sharper than any double-edged sword, it penetrates even to dividing soul and spirit, joints and marrow; it judges the thoughts and attitudes of the heart."

Hebrews 4:12

As I end this chapter on Germany, may the Lord God be able to say this about you and me at the end of our days:

"You yourselves, are our letter, written on our hearts, known and read by everybody. You show that you are a letter from Christ, the result of our ministry, written not with ink but with the Spirit of the Living God, not on tablets of stone but on tablets of human hearts."

2 Corinthians 3:2-3

Travel Thoughts

1. Have you ever hosted someone you met in a foreign country in your house? If so, where did your guests come from?

   _____

   _____

   _____

2. Have you ever eaten something in a foreign land that you liked so much you brought it home with you? If so, what was it?

   _____

   _____

   _____

3. What's the next place or country you'd like to visit and why?

   _____

   _____

   _____

4. After reading this book, what might you consider changing about the way that you usually go about traveling?

   _____

   _____

   _____

5. If you have never kept a travel journal, might you consider taking one along for your next trip?

   _____

   _____

   _____

EPILOGUE

"I like living. I have sometimes been wildly, despairingly, acutely miserable, racked with sorrow, but through it all, I still know quite certainly that just to be alive is a grand thing."
Agatha Christie

"Let us be grateful to people who make us happy; they are the charming gardeners who make our souls blossom."
Marcel Proust

"We are not here to merely make a living. We are here to enrich the world, and we impoverish ourselves if we forget this errand."
Woodrow Wilson

"The only things that stand between a person and what they want in life are the will to try it and the faith to believe it's possible."
Rich DeVos

"Slow down and enjoy life. It's not only the scenery you miss by going too fast-- -you also miss the sense of where you are going and why."
Eddie Cantor

"Life is either a daring adventure or nothing."
Helen Keller

"The great use of life is to spend it for something that will outlast it."
William James

"The quieter you become, the more you hear."
Unknown

It has been my sincere pleasure to share with you some of the most meaningful memories from the travelogue of my life as a missionary based in the UK but sent to the world as an ambassador of Jesus Christ. I hope that you were encouraged by what you read here and have a greater sense of how the Living God moves in and out of our lives wherever we are in this life.

The testimonies I have shared here are not just for someone called to be a missionary, but give us a glimpse of life in the Spirit. Whenever you and I choose as an act of our will to not just hear but obey God's ever-present, still, small, first voice, we can rest assured that something supernatural is about to happen. Adventures await every time that you and I choose to obey that inner leading of the Holy Spirit that resides in us.

We have an eternal transmitter on the inside of us that allows us to connect with God any time of day or night. He may speak to us Himself or choose to send a heavenly messenger that stands in His presence to give us His desires or a special assignment of some sort. We must remember that we are not human beings having a spiritual experience. We are spirits having a human experience. The realization of this gives us a thrill and a joy in our salvation that nothing can compete with in this life.

In all that I have shared here, I hope that you have also seen the importance of being still at some point in your day. If you make it a habit, your spirit will begin to crave these moments set aside for just you and the Lord. If this is a new thing for you to try, you will soon wonder why you never did it before. If this is something you used to do, remember that the Lord's arms are always stretched out wide to receive you back to that place that is just for you and Him to explore together. Stillness allows the Holy Spirit to refresh you from the inside out. It is a free spa treatment for your whole being—body, soul, and spirit.

Prophetic psalmist Don Potter said it best in his song 'In The Spirit':

"In the Spirit He is real.
In the Spirit I can feel.
In the Spirit I am healed.
By the power of His love.
In the Spirit I'm alive.
In the Spirit I can fly.
In the Spirit of the Living God."

Everything that I have shared here is only possible through the Holy Spirit. He is the Source of all of these tales. I believe He wants to create new adventures in the Spirit for everyone who longs to be connected to Him and experience what life in the Spirit is all about. Be still, knowing that He is God, and expect Him to move in your life. He most certainly will!

Finally, if you have a zeal for travel with the Lord and would like to share some of your adventures with me from your latest adventure in a foreign place, please feel free to drop me an email or even some snail mail by way of a postcard. I'd love to hear from you!

Charlynne Boddie Ministries
142 Gainsborough Drive
Selsey, Chichester
West Sussex PO20 0HH
Website: www.charlynne.com
Email: charlynne@charlynne.com
and charlynneboddie@icloud.com

Made in the USA
Columbia, SC
21 July 2019